' "But, surely," I said, "in twenty years in China you must have had many strange experiences?"

"Oh yes," said Gladys, "but I'm sure people wouldn't be interested in them. Nothing very exciting happened."

It was at least fifteen minutes more before she confessed that she had "once taken some children across the mountains".

The rest of the conversation went in this manner, a verbatim memory which I have never forgotten:

"Across the mountains? Where was this?"

"In Shansi in north China; we travelled from Yangcheng across the mountains to Sian."

"I see. How long did it take you?"

"Oh, about a month."

"Did you have any money?"

"Oh no, we didn't have any money."

"I see. What about food? How did you get that?"

"The Mandarin gave us two basketfuls of grain, but we soon ate that up."

"I see. How many children did you say there were?"

"Nearly a hundred."

I became conscious that I was saying, 'I see', rather often, and actually I was not 'seeing' anything at all, except that I was on the brink of a most tremendous story.'

ALAN BURGESS

'The humour as well as the courage in her formidable narrowness of purpose is beautifully brought out' – *Daily Telegraph*

'Well worth reading' – *Observer*

'A most inspiring book' – *Books and Bookmen*

THE
SMALL WOMAN

ALAN BURGESS

UNABRIDGED

PAN BOOKS LTD : LONDON

First published 1957 by Evans Brothers Ltd.
This edition published 1959 by Pan Books Ltd.,
33 Tothill Street, London, S.W.1

330 10196 X

2nd Printing 1961
3rd Printing 1961
4th Printing 1963
5th Printing 1963
6th Printing 1965
7th Printing 1966
8th Printing 1966
9th Printing 1969
10th Printing 1969

Printed in Great Britain by
Cox & Wyman Ltd., London, Reading and Fakenham

ILLUSTRATIONS
IN PHOTOGRAVURE

(between pages 96 and 97)

Gladys Aylward, London parlourmaid

Gladys Aylward, China missionary for 20 years

With some of her converts at prayer over Mrs Lawson's coffin. In the back row, muleteers who visited the Inn of Eight Happinesses

With some of the children before they crossed the mountains to Sian

One of the 'children', Lian Ai, sent Gladys Aylward this picture, taken on her wedding day

Bandaged feet. One of Gladys Aylward's first duties as Foot Inspector was to break down the centuries-old custom

(between pages 160 and 161)

Local Chinese farmer with grandson

Town crier calling villagers to the west gate of Yangcheng

The village fruit market

Gladys Aylward tells a Bible story to the convicts at Chengtu

Happy ending in Shanghai for 'Ninepence' and her small son

Photostat of part of a letter received by Miss Aylward's parents in Edmonton

The 'Small Woman's' certificate of Chinese naturalisation

With the Bible which accompanied her on her travels, Miss Aylward today preaches the Gospel all over England

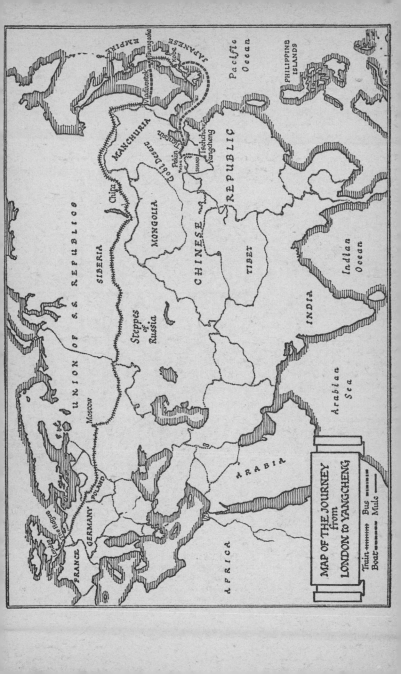

MAP OF THE JOURNEY
from
LONDON to YANGCHENG

Train ++++++++   Bus ========
Boat =======   Mule ─────

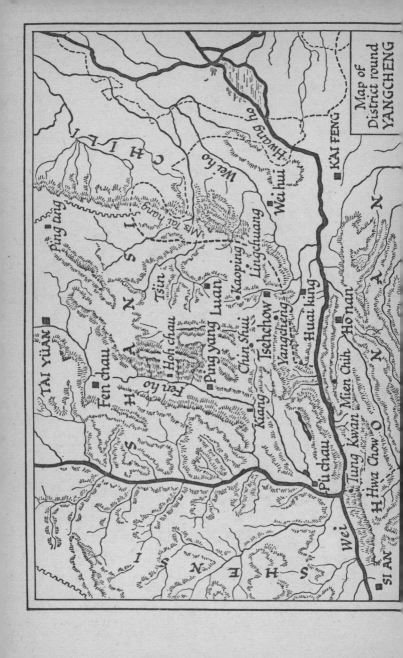

Map of
District round
YANGCHENG

CHAPTER ONE

THE WHOLE affair of the small woman both intrigued and concerned the senior physician. Her nearness to death; the fact that out of one quarter of the human race inhabiting the enormous Chinese continent, the tiny, dried-up husk of a woman with an ebbing pulse of a heartbeat should wash up against his door, and depart beyond his help, as great an enigma as when she arrived, aroused in him an interest beyond his professional concern.

That she was dying he did not doubt. Who she was, no one knew, but in China in those autumn days of 1941, with the Japanese invader pressing in on many fronts and one half of the world trying hard to destroy the other in a furious holocaust of tanks and planes, guns and ships, violent death was such a near neighbour that the departure from this life of one small, unknown woman was of little concern to anyone.

The few English-speaking staff at the Scandinavian-American Mission at Hsing P'ing, far off in North-west China, knew neither her name nor where she came from. Two Chinese peasants had delivered her to the front gate, heaving her out from the back of an ox-cart as unceremoniously as if she had been a rag doll. With a fatalistic lift of their shoulders, they had admitted to the gateman that had she been Chinese they would have left her to die. They knew she was a foreigner, even though she was dressed in Chinese clothes and carried a Chinese Bible; therefore they thought it more seemly that she should die close to her friends, her soul consigned to her own gods. The gateman was not interested in either their philosophy or their corpse—the body looked close enough to death to be mistaken for a cadaver—and he did not inquire where they had found it, or even where they themselves came from; so the peasants retreated into the unknown, and the gateman went to tell his masters that they had a body on their hands.

The Scandinavian-American Mission sent a wire at once to the Baptist Mission Hospital at Sian, asking if a doctor could come; and with a generous humanity which in the next few weeks was to be so freely given by all at that hospital, the senior physician caught the next train. He arrived late in the afternoon, and examined the patient. Her body was thin and undernourished; crow's feet of intense weariness and suffering pencilled dark lines from the corners of her eyes; she bore the scar of a fairly recent bullet-wound across her back; and although it was not apparent, she was also suffering from internal injuries caused by a brutal beating up which had taken place some months earlier.

Her temperature was in the region of 105 degrees; she was in a raving delirium, and she was quite certain that the senior physician was a Japanese officer!

His experience told him that she was probably suffering from relapsing fever. He took an immediate blood-slide, and sent it back by special messenger to the Baptist Hospital. A second messenger returned next day with news that the blood-film confirmed that he had diagnosed correctly. At once he gave her an intravenous injection, which he knew would lessen the fever; as by this time a Swedish-American nurse named Miss Nelson had also arrived, he felt that he could now leave the patient in her hands, for the fever would abate within forty-eight hours, and only time and good nursing could effect a cure. He returned to Sian, content that he had done all he could.

Five days later a letter arrived at the Baptist Hospital informing the senior physician that the unknown woman was again in a raving delirium; that although her temperature had indeed dropped to near normal, it had suddenly shot up again to 105 degrees, and she was most dangerously ill.

He caught the next train, and found his patient just breaking out in the rash of that most dreadfully perilous disease, typhus, which she must have been incubating while suffering from relapsing fever! As three doctors at the Baptist Hospital had died of typhus during the past few years, and as the resistance of this woman, due to malnutrition, shock and fatigue, was negligible, in his own mind the senior physician held out no hope for her at all. Especially when further examination revealed that a patch of pneumonia had developed on one lung!

By a God-given coincidence, however, one of the Swedish-American missionaries who had just returned from furlough in the USA had about twenty tablets of the new drug sulphapyridine in his personal kit; he gladly offered them to the senior physician as treatment for the woman's illness. Using the tablets he managed to curb the pneumonia; but it was quite clear to him that, if the small woman was to have the slightest chance of survival, she would have to be moved at once to the hospital at Sian.

The senior physician had been in China for nearly twenty years; he had survived the siege of Sian, when the armies of two local warlords had fought for the city and 20,000 people had died of starvation; he had many contacts and some influence in the district, and for this small, unknown woman he did not hesitate to use both. He rang up a friend of his who controlled that section of the railway and, addressing him by his nickname, said:

"Rails? Tomorrow I want a special carriage attached to the first train that leaves. We've a patient we shall carry to the train on a camp bed, and we shall have four helpers to hold it steady during the journey. Will you do this for me? It's urgent!"

'Rails' said he would. Had the small woman, in her delirium, known that a special carriage was being arranged for her benefit *alone*, she would certainly have laughed until she cried.

At Sian the train was met by bearers, and the unconscious woman was taken to hospital. One of the lady doctors had willingly moved out of her own room so that the desperately sick woman could have the benefit of a large and airy chamber. Miss Nelson and the hospital matron, Miss Major, continued to nurse her.

11

It was fifteen days later, when the small woman was still mentally deranged, although the typhus fever was beginning to abate, that the Japanese, after several weeks of inactivity, decided that they would bomb Sian. The senior physician sat with his patient as the bombs began to fall. Her thin, wasted form jerked and twitched in agony as each bomb whistled down and the rumble and crash shook the room. Her whole body ran with a cold sweat, and the doctor, who in all his experience had never seen such an agony of delayed shock, held her wrists and tried to comfort her.

Having taken all the trouble to get her into the hospital at Sian, he realized that he would now have to take a lot more trouble to get her out again to some quieter place, for the raids, now that they had started, would most certainly continue, and the small woman would most certainly die. Already it seemed she was only lingering in the corridor of death waiting for the last door to open.

She was still almost a complete enigma. As a nurse stood by her next day a spasm of pain crossed her face, and a whisper came from her lips. "My children?" she said. "Where are my children? The Japanese are all round us. They'll kill us. I know they'll kill us."

The whisper mounted to a scream, and then abruptly she was raving in an uncouth Chinese dialect which no one could understand, but which later someone recognized as coming from a wild mountain region far to the north. The spasm of delirium passed. A faint smile formed on her face. There was such nostalgic reminiscence in the painfully articulated words: "Remember that first night of *Lilac Time*? That little tune that went, pom-pom-pom tiddley-om-pom-pom . . ."

From the constricted throat, slowly into the hot room of the hospital, where the flies buzzed lazily against the white-washed ceiling, dropped the short, uncertain notes of the tune which had generated a hundred errand-boys into whistling activity a decade, or was it a lifetime, ago? With equal slowness the disordered mind of the sick woman grasped or was eluded by the images around her. Flies?

12

There were flies on the faces of the dead at Yangcheng. And this clinically-smelling gentleman who bent over her and with such gentle insistence, day after day, week after week, probed into her past. It was not unpleasant to lie there in a world of darkness and colour and delirium and let one's mind drift back down the years.

They had been good years. No one could take them away from her. Her name? they asked. What was her name? But everyone knew her name. In a province as big as the whole of England everyone knew her name. Ai-weh-deh, the virtuous one! They did not want her Chinese name, but her English name, her European name? She did not tell them that straight away. . . . You did not reveal such secrets in wartime. . . . You never told who you were nor where you came from.

That night when she met General Ley in the mountain village, for example. She remembered him going away into the darkness, his black robe flapping about his legs, going back to his rifle and to join his band of armed guerillas. He was a Roman Catholic priest, but she never knew his real name; she only guessed that he was Dutch. He had sat across the table from her, the yellow light from the flickering castor-oil lamp stencilling black shadows into his face; they had talked hour after hour of the immense dilemma in their hearts; then he'd gone away over the mountains to . . . to kill . . .?

And the Mandarin, that splendid person in his gown of scarlet sculptured silk, living far off in his mountain *yamen* among the wild peaks of Shansi; he had never wanted to know her Christian name; and Sualan, the pretty one, she with the pale skin and hands as restless and delicate as butterflies, dedicated from birth to be a smiling slave-girl to all the Mandarin's retainers; or Feng, the Buddhist priest, shaven-headed, condemned to years in the filthy gaol; or the muleteer whose wife and children they had burnt to death; or even Linnan—Linnan the man she loved? Not even he had used the name she had brought from her own country.

The gentle voice in her ear was insistent: "Tell us your

name," it said. "Don't be frightened. There's no need to be frightened now."

Frightened! She could tell them that being frightened did not concern her any more. She had been frightened sleeping in the snow among those dark Russian pines; frightened of the man who had trapped her in that hotel bedroom in Vladivostok; frightened in that dreadful Chinese prison when the maniac with the blood-stained axe turned towards her; frightened in the mountain cave when the wolves howled and the brilliant green flints of their eyes were tiny reflected lights in the darkness; frightened when the Japanese cried "Halt", and the bullets ricocheted from the tombstones all around her. . . .

"Your name," said the small, insistent voice in her ear. "What is your name? Where do you come from?"

It seemed such a silly question to ask. Surely they knew her name was Gladys Aylward. That she had been born in Edmonton. Surely they had heard of Edmonton, in North London? In those days the fields had flowed right up to its boundaries; but that was before the grey stone, the red brick and the grime of London City had imprisoned it. They had moved to Cheddington Road when she was very small. A row of red-brick houses, lace curtains, privet hedges. Aspidistras in the windows. Grey pavements. Each morning an unending procession of cheerful milkmen, greengrocers, bakers and their horse-drawn carts down the streets. A happy childhood. She remembered her father coming home, clumping up the road in his heavy postman's boots, wearing his dark uniform with the red piping. Mum would be in the kitchen getting the tea, and she and Violet, her sister, would be screaming around the house or running wild with the other children in the street.

When the Zeppelins came over to bomb London in the First World War, she remembered how she'd first discovered the antidote to being 'frightened'. She would bring all the children in the street into the front parlour and sit them down against the inside wall. Then she would sit at the tiny old foot-operated organ, pedal furiously and scream out a hymn at a decibel scale calculated to reach almost as high as those ominous silver cocoons droning through the sky. Her belief in the morale-raising qualities of a good lusty hymn sung at four-engined jet acoustic never deserted her.

In all the years in China she had discovered how it could lift their hearts, no matter how depressing the circumstances. Hadn't they sung as they marched over the mountains, all those tired and footsore children, marching not on Jordan or on Georgia, but down to the immense, untamed, ancient configurations of the Yellow River? And the disappointment there. Was there ever a disappointment to equal it? Maybe that time in London at the China Inland Mission? Maybe that disappointment would equal it.

She remembered the black winter branches swaying against the pale London sky outside the study window. The Principal, a tall, thin, scholarly man with a domed forehead, had faced her across the table. The edges of his kindly blue eyes were arrival points for a network of deep, inter-communicating lines; looming above were buttresses of bushy grey eyebrows. She remembered how he'd looked at her, oh! so seriously. Twenty-six years old, very small and slender, a neat figure, dark brown eyes, an oval face, dark hair parted in the middle, and gathered uncompromisingly into a bun at the back. Perhaps he discerned some of the inherent stubbornness and inner strength in the tightening of her lips. But also he would see the tension in her face; tension that would soon be replaced by disappointment, for he had known that she was unwilling to relinquish all hope until he deliberately and finally destroyed it.

He had spread the reports in front of him and pursed his lips.

"You've been with us now for three months, I see, Miss Aylward?" he said.

"Yes, sir."

"Theology, now——?"

"I wasn't very good at theology, was I?" she had said quietly.

He had looked up under his eyebrows. "No, you weren't. Not good at all."

15

She remembered how she sat with her fingers tightly clenched in her lap. She hardly heard the voice which reiterated her list of failures. She knew she could never make him understand. She knew she lacked the persuasiveness to argue with him or the education to pass his examinations; she knew she hadn't the 'background'; she knew she had no chance. But she knew also, with a single-minded, agonizing clearness, that she *must* go to China!

"You see, Miss Aylward, all these scholastic shortcomings are important," he said sympathetically, "but most important of all is your age. If you stayed at the China Inland Mission Centre for another three years and then we sent you out, you would be about thirty by the time you arrived." He had shaken his head doubtfully. "Our experience tells us that after the age of thirty, unless pupils are quite exceptional, they find it extremely difficult to learn the Chinese language.

"In view of all this, you will understand, I'm sure," he had continued, "that there seems to be little point in your continuing with your studies here. We accepted you to be trained in good faith, on trial. If you went on, it would be a waste of everyone's time and money . . ." He left the rest of the sentence unfinished.

"I understand," she said quietly. "Thank you for letting me come. It's not your fault that I couldn't do all these things."

The Principal had tried to soften the disappointment. "You mustn't be too distressed at this . . . er . . . setback. There is so much other useful work to be done in Britain by people like yourself." He had paused. "Have you any idea what you will do now?"

"No," she said.

He glanced at her papers. "I see you were in . . . er . . . service before you . . ."

Her eyes lifted abruptly to meet his. "I don't want to go back to being a parlourmaid unless I have to," she said quickly.

"No, I understand that." He paused. "There is one other way you could help us, Miss Aylward."

"Yes? How?"

"Two missionaries have just returned from China. An old married couple who need someone to look after them. They have borrowed a house in Bristol. Would you be prepared to consider the job?"

She remembered how that offer had chilled her. She had unlocked her fingers and examined the palms of her hands. Such a sad humiliation! Housekeeper to two retired missionaries too old to care for themselves! If that was the closest she was ever going to get to China, then perhaps it was better if she did go back to her job as a parlourmaid. But she had to consider the harsh economic facts of life. She was a woman, and it was mainly a man's world. She was a spinster of twenty-six, and the society into which she had been born expected her to work towards some first-floor lodging of security. It was usual in those days between the two world wars that a young woman who craved God, sublimated that urge into Sunday attendances at church: a sort of genteel insurance policy that could be reclaimed at the gates of the heavenly kingdom. But she also knew with certitude that the God to whom she owed allegiance wanted more from her than this milk-and-water reaction. In those grim slump days, if you had a job you stuck to it. But she was determined to make something of her life. She had gone straight from school into service. She had moved from one parlourmaid job to another, and unemployment was still something to be feared.

How the desire to go to China first arose she hardly knew herself. It could have originated from that evening when, rather bored, and with nothing else to do, she had seen a banner proclaiming a religious revival displayed outside a local church. Inside, a dynamic young clergyman had exhorted his small audience to serve God. All the other girls, seeing which way her inclinations were turning, declared quite bluntly that she was 'barmy'. "Don't be silly, Glad," they protested. "Come with us to the pictures, or to a dance, or to the theatre, or let's go and see those nice chaps we met in the park, who want to take us for a row on the Serpentine." Suddenly, however, Gladys wanted more

17

from life than that. She had joined a local evangelical society, and gradually the urge to go to China had eased into her mind. Eventually she had been accepted as a probationer at the China Inland Mission Centre.

Although she tried to hide it, what a disappointment her failure had been! At the memory of that day all those years ago, the tears began to roll down her cheeks. The young Chinese nurse at her bedside tried to comfort her as she wept. Then, almost as quickly as the tears came, so laughter returned. It really was very, very funny. Only a few months later and there she was, twenty-six years old, a 'Rescue Sister' on the Swansea Docks in South Wales. Her laughter echoed through the ward, and the small Chinese nurse looked at her in perplexity. She'd got the job shortly after she went to help the old missionaries in Bristol. A rescuer of fallen women, and at twenty-six she hardly knew how they 'fell' or what she was supposed to be rescuing them from. Night after night she patrolled the dock area, seeking to dissuade young women from the fate which Victorian tradition insisted was worse than death, but about which there seemed to be a general disagreement among the girls. That she was only five feet tall and weighed about eight stone, and that drunken sailors under the blotchy yellow street lamps—the beer and the songs and the relief from the sea singing in their heads—were just as likely to mistake her for a prostitute, and act accordingly, did not really worry her.

The younger girls, who had come by train down from their dark valley villages for a gay night out in the big city of Swansea, were usually grateful. Outside the pub they were sick down her frock and bleated incoherent intimacies about their sailor boy friends or 'being afraid to go home to Mam'; but they were grateful to be suddenly befriended when Gladys put her thin arm around them and guided them off to a bed at the mission hostel. Next morning they whispered their white-lipped thanks as she gave them a few coppers and put them on the train, to go home to face biblical parental wrath in small cottages back in the Welsh mountains. The older prostitutes, time-hardened by the economic pressures of the slump, were quite different. They came to regard the young welfare worker, so eager and so full of the Lord, with tolerant amusement. Occasionally they even capitulated to her appeals, and several times on Sunday evenings she was able, triumphantly, to lead a party of them to Snellings Gospel Mission. Here, if not reformed, at least, for a transient moment, they were transfigured by the thunder and rattle of the full-throated Welsh hymns against the tin roof of the chapel, and lifted gloriously away from the harsh physical world of beery breaths, clutching hands and the urgent passions of Argentines, Greeks, Lascars, West Indians, sailors, stewards and stokers, and all who ply in ships to the port of Swansea.

She knew, however, that although these experiences strengthened her spirit, they added nothing to her corporeal bank balance. It was becoming increasingly obvious that if she was ever going to get to China—and she was determined to get there in some capacity or other, no matter what anyone might think—she would have to pay her own fare.

The only way she knew of earning money was to go back into service again. She was reluctant to do this, but as a 'Rescue Sister' she spent or gave away the little she earned. She said goodbye to her friends and returned to London.

An employment agency found her a post in the London household of Sir Francis Younghusband, the eminent soldier, author and explorer. It was ironical perhaps that, as she dusted the books in the library of his stately Belgravia residence, the man who first crossed the heart of Central Asia by traversing the Muztagh—the great mountain barrier between Kashmir and China—was not even conscious of her presence. Yet she was to cross human and geographical terrain as formidable as any he ever faced.

She remembered vividly her entry into the household. Dispirited after the long journey from the suburbs of Edmonton, she knocked at the front door, and was shown to her bedroom by the butler. It was small and neat and comfortable, but still a servant's bedroom. It was not China. She sat on the bed and looked at the suitcases she had lugged up the stairs. She took out the black, well-thumbed Bible and put it on the dressing table. She turned out her purse, which contained all the money she possessed. There were two pennies and one ha'penny. She placed the coins on top of the Bible. She felt like weeping. She was back where she had started—in service—and China seemed so far away. And, suddenly conscious of her deep need, she cried out, "Oh God, here's my Bible! Here's my money! Here's me! Use me, God!"

The door opened. A rather puzzled fellow-housemaid who had been approaching and heard the appeal, poked her head in.

"You Gladys?" she said. "Missus wants to see you in the drawing room. Always wants to see all the new staff as soon as they arrive."

"Thank you," said Gladys.

She walked slowly down the stairs. Her mistress regarded the small, dejected figure with curiosity.

"Miss Aylward . . . isn't it? I hope you'll be happy with me. Now, tell me, how much was your fare from home?"

"Two and ninepence," said Gladys. She did not understand the point of the question.

Her mistress reached for her purse.

"I always pay the fares of my maids when I engage them," she said. "Here's three shillings. The housekeeper will explain your duties later. . . ."

Tiny spurts of jet-propulsion lifted Gladys's heels as she soared back up the stairs. Exultantly, she spread out the three coins on her Bible. The bright silver shone against the black leather cover. Three shillings and twopence ha'penny! All to be hoarded against her fare to China. In spirit she was half way there!

She chuckled again as she remembered her first encounter with the ticket people. The elderly booking-clerk at Mullers, the travel agency in the Haymarket, was quite certain she was mad. It seemed that in all his years of advising upon the pleasures of foreign travel he had never heard such an outrageous demand. Had he not just finished patiently explaining that the cheapest boat fare to any portion of China was ninety pounds? Had he not pointed out, in passing, that *although* the cheapest and quickest route was overland through Europe, Russia and Siberia to Tientsin via the Trans-Siberian railway—the fare for this journey being only forty-seven pounds ten shillings—it was quite impossible to travel by that route? Yet this young person facing him across the counter had chosen deliberately to misunderstand his words. She thrust three pound notes across at him, said she'd have a ticket on the railway, and would he please accept this on account? He had tapped his slender fingers on the counter and adjusted his pince-nez to regard her more closely. A journey round the globe, a safari in Africa, a discreet weekend in Le Touquet; they could all be managed, but this . . . this!

"As I was going to say, madam," he had said severely, "the journey by Trans-Siberian railway is quite impossible because a conflict between Russia and China is raging at the eastern end."

"I couldn't really care about a silly old war," she had said. "It's the cheapest way, isn't it? That's what I want. Now, if you'll book me a passage, you can have this three pounds on account, and I'll pay you as much as I can every week."

"We do not," the clerk had replied, choosing his words with the pedantic care of the extremely irritated, "like to deliver our customers—dead!"

She had stared up at him. His acidulousness had no effect whatsoever. She was quite logically feminine about it all.

"Oh, they won't hurt me," she said. "I'm a woman. They won't bother about me."

It was three o'clock in the afternoon. Mullers was almost empty. He had time therefore to explain gently and dispassionately how important a communication link the China Eastern Railway was to both the forces of Russia

21

and China. He explained that the Chinese, spurred on by a young warlord named Chang-Hsüeh-liang, were trying to force the Russians to abandon all claims to the link-line which crossed Manchuria and connected with the Trans-Siberian Railway. An undeclared war was in progress. No guarantee would be possible for the safety of one young woman, even armed with that magical document, a British passport.

At the end of his speech her dark brown eyes still regarded him steadily; the small hand in the worn glove still pushed the three pound notes in his direction.

"It'll be all over by the time I get the rest of the money, I'm sure," she said. "If you'll order me a ticket, I'll bring in my money every week until I've paid the balance. Is that all right?"

The elderly clerk looked at her carefully. Then he sighed, picked up the three pounds and, defeated, reached for his receipt book.

"Very well, madam," he said. "I don't know what the management would think about this, but I expect it will be all right."

Exactly what she thought she would be able to do when she arrived in China without a penny in her pocket, understanding not one word of the language, she hardly knew herself; but she was determined that, even if she could not pass through the scholastic eye of the China Inland Missionary needle, she could at least equip herself as an evangelist and know the Bible intimately. "I must learn to preach," she said to herself. "I must learn to talk to the people."

With the essential simplicity which characterized her, in every moment of spare time she went to Hyde Park, or to any street corner, where she mounted, literally, a soap box, and preached mainly to an iconoclastic, and often a jeering audience. Tired Londoners, bearing the tribal insignia of bowler hat, folded newspaper and rolled umbrella, moving Tubewards in the evenings, were startled on street corners to find themselves exhorted by a small girl in a black dress to turn, not homewards, but to God. Against the clamour of London's traffic, her thin starling treble argued and pleaded, and although not much more notice was taken of her than of the small black birds which festooned Nelson's Column, she was not disheartened.

Then she had her first piece of luck. From a friend she heard of Mrs Lawson. "A dear old soul, my dear. Seventy-three years old this year, and still working away as a missionary in China. She came back to England last year to retire, but she just couldn't stand it. So she returned to China; she said she'd sooner end her days out there. She wrote only a few days ago saying she wished she could find some younger woman who could carry on with her work."

Gladys Aylward remembered how her mouth dropped open in astonishment, how all she could do was whisper weakly, "That's me! That's me!"

She wrote off at once. Could she help her? Could she join her? Could she come to China?

Now it became imperative that she save the money for the train ticket. In the Belgrave Square household she was willing to do anything. No chore was too long or arduous. She besieged other employment agencies offering her services to work on her day off, to work weekends, to serve at banquets, to carry trays at society parties, to work all day and all night if necessary. By now the clerk at Mullers was an old friend, accustomed to the enthusiastic young woman who appeared at his desk every Friday, bearing sums which would be counted out in pennies and shillings and entered against that magical total—forty-seven pounds ten shillings.

Then came that wonderful morning when the letter bearing the bizarre and brightly-coloured Chinese stamps dropped with a plop on the hall floor. It told her that if she could manage to get to Tientsin by herself, a messenger would meet her there and guide her to wherever Mrs Lawson was working.

The excitement! She had to get a passport at once! She had to finish paying for the ticket! She had to plan what she was going to take! "I'm going to China," she said to all her friends. "I'm going to China!" Oh, the thrill of that

23

moment! She laughed aloud at the memory; excitedly she tried to lift herself up in the hospital bed.

The young Chinese nurse turned to an orderly who had just come in. "She is mad in the head," she said quietly. "She is mad in the head, this dying one!"

CHAPTER TWO

EXPEDITION 'GLADYS AYLWARD' assembled on the platform at Liverpool Street Station on Saturday, 18th October, 1930. It must be numbered amongst the most ill-equipped expeditions ever to leave the shores of England, possessing in currency exactly ninepence in coin and one two-pound Cook's travellers' cheque. The cheque was sewn carefully into an old corset given to the expedition by its mother, in the severe belief that even horrible foreigners would not dare to pry too closely into such an intimate, and intimidating, feminine accessory. The corset, in fact, was a treasure house. It contained, besides the travellers' cheque, her Bible, her fountain pen, her tickets and her passport.

She kissed her mother, and father, and sister, goodbye, and settled herself into the corner seat of her third-class compartment. The whistle blew, the train hissed and puffed; she waved through the window until her family were out of sight. She dried her eyes, sat back and spread out on the seat beside her the old fur coat which a friend had given her and which her mother had cut up and made into a rug. Her two suitcases were on the rack. One contained her clothes, the other an odd assortment of tins of corned beef, fish and baked beans, biscuits, soda cakes, meat cubes, coffee essence, tea and hard-boiled eggs. She also had a saucepan, a kettle and a spirit stove. The kettle and the saucepan, with a sort of gay insouciance, were tied to the handle of the suitcase with a piece of string.

Soon they were out of the city, past the suburbs. She looked at the identifying symbols of the English landscape with a perception she had never felt before. The square-towered church behind its screen of autumn trees; the black-and-white timbered cottages; the fawn-coloured fields ploughed into rolling arabesques and sown with winter wheat; the browsing cattle in the pale green fields; the thin drift of blue smoke from the leaf fires burning at the hedge-sides; the black crows circling above the high, bare elms against the pale blue sky. She wondered if she would ever see her native countryside again? She pressed her face against the cold, misted window and whispered, "God bless you, England". She did not know—she would not have wished to know—that it would be twenty long years before she saw that landscape again.

She disembarked at The Hague, tipped the porter who carried her bags the ninepence in coppers and secured a corner seat. From Holland the train rattled across Germany, Poland and into the great steppes of Russia. She sat 'facing the engine', cocooned in her fur rug and watched the Continent slide past. In Russia she was shocked by what she saw: the crowds of apathetic people waiting on the bare, cheerless stations, surrounded by their bundles; women working in gangs; poverty and peasantry on a scale she had never imagined.

The main station at Moscow was full of soldiers. They carried their bread ration under their arms, broke off a piece to munch when they felt hungry. To the meticulous Miss Aylward cooking herself an egg with a Ryvita biscuit spread with a little butter for breakfast, and having 'elevenses' of an Oxo cube in the hot water she boiled in her kettle, the rough-looking, bearded men who spat on the ground and blew their noses on their fingers were alien and a little horrible. She wrote in letters which reached her mother that she could not believe that Russia was happy—she believed the people to be downtrodden and wretched, and the sight of small children working on the roads both saddened and sickened her. Once or twice a day she took gentle exercise along the corridor of the train, and occasionally, when the engine stopped to take on wood, all the passengers disembarked to stretch their legs and replenish their water supply.

Ten days after leaving England the train crossed into Siberia, and she was at once enchanted by the grandeur of the scenery: the towering mountains, the great belts of dark pines, the endlessly stretching snow, the bright sunshine and the immense loneliness. At one halt a man came

26

into her compartment who could speak a little English, and through him the other people, who had long ago tired of trying to ask her questions in sign language, now began to satiate their curiosity. He was a kindly man, and he conveyed to Gladys that the conductor of the train who had examined her tickets wished to tell her that no trains were running to Harbin, and that she would probably be held up at the Siberian-Manchurian border. If this were true— and she concentrated on trying hard not to believe it—then her chances were remote of proceeding onwards through Harbin to Dairen, and so by steamer to Tientsin.

To increase her fears, at each station halt more and more soldiers crowded on to the train. Two officers shared her compartment now, and although they could not talk to her except by gesticulation, they were quite pleasant. At Chita the train emptied of all civilians, except Gladys. The conductor came along and with fantastic signs tried to entice her out on to the platform. Gladys, however, now firmly rooted in the compartment, was having none of it; she believed that every mile forward was a mile towards China. She stayed put.

The train filled up with soldiers and rumbled onwards. A few hours later in the darkness it halted again at a tiny station and the soldiers got out, formed up on the platform and marched off up the line into the darkness. The train lights went out. She took a short walk up the corridor and satisfied herself that she was the only person left aboard. Then, borne on the thin, freezing wind, came a noise which, even although she had never heard it before, she recognized immediately. The sound of gunfire! Rumbling, ominous, terrifying! She poked her head out of the carriage window and saw the distant flashes light the sky. She scrambled her belongings together. She realized a little shamefacedly that the elderly clerk at Mullers had been right after all. There *was* a war on! She had a quick mental picture of him shaking his head at her across the counter and saying reprovingly, "But I did tell you, madam, that we do *not* like to deliver our customers, dead!"

Laden down by bags and rug, she wandered along the

platform and, in a small hut by the track, found four men clustered round a stove: the engine driver, stoker, the stationmaster and the conductor who had unsuccessfully urged her to get off the train at Chita. They made her a cup of strong coffee and with a running commentary amplified by gymnastic gesticulations reiterated the fact that she had, indeed, reached the end of the line. Beyond was the battlefield.

This brief undeclared war between China and Russia over possession of the China Eastern Railway received little publicity in the Western Press. It lasted a few months, resulted in many casualties and the Chinese eventually withdrew their forces. The train, they said, would remain at this halt for days, perhaps weeks, until such time as it was needed, then it would take wounded back to hospitals behind the line. They pointed down the track the way they had come. "Go back," they said.

The line wound drearily through snow-covered pines. It ducked through dark tunnels; it was hemmed in by high mountains; the snow in between the sleepers was thick and soft; icicles hung from the pine cones. But to walk back to Chita, they said, was her only hope.

She set off. Not many miles from the Manchurian border, the Siberian wind gusting the powdered snow around her heels, a suitcase in either hand, one still decorated ludicrously with kettle and saucepan, fur rug over her shoulders, she crunched off into the night, a slight, Chaplinesque figure, dwarfed by the tall, sombre trees, the towering mountains, and the black sky, diamond bright with stars. God obviously did not mean her to be eaten by the wolves, for there were plenty about. Occasionally in the forest a handful of snow would slither to the ground with a sudden noise or a branch would crack under the weight of snow, and she would pause and peer uncertainly in that direction. But nothing moved. There was light, no warmth—nothing but endless loneliness.

Four hours later, when the cold and exhaustion became too much for her, she sat down on the icy rail, lit her spirit stove and boiled some water for her coffee essence. She ate two soda cakes, and felt miserable. She decided she must sleep, at least for an hour or two. She arranged her suitcases into a windbreak, scooped up snow to fill the cracks, wrapped herself firmly into her old fur rug and lay down. Drowsily, she listened to the noise of far-off howling, and with the childlike innocence attributed as a rule only to young babies with large blue eyes, said to herself, "Now I wonder who let all those big dogs out at this time of night? Noisy lot!" Not until a couple of years later in China did she realize that she had heard a hunting wolf pack.

A pale dawn was lighting the mountains when she woke up, stiff but refreshed. She made herself more coffee, ate another soda cake, gathered up her luggage and set off again along the interminable railway track. She decided that it was going to be a long walk to China. Late that night, staggering along, almost unconscious with cold and weariness, she saw the lights of Chita gleaming far down the track. It gave her new strength. She struggled onwards, lifted herself wearily on to the platform, dropped her suitcases into a heap and draped herself on top of them. There seemed to be nothing else to do. Several other groups of Russians were doing the same thing. It seemed to be an occupational disease in the USSR.

During the night no one came near her, and Gladys dozed intermittently under her fur rug. Next morning a succession of station officials came to look at her, nod their heads and depart.

Anything they said made no sense to her. She continued to camp out on the platform in the bitter cold. No one seemed to care. She dozed occasionally, but now she was getting colder and stiffer. As it seemed quite absurd to freeze to death on a Russian railway platform after braving the terrors of the Siberian forest, in the forenoon she decided to do something about it. Obviously, the only way to get anything done at all was to start a riot.

She eyed an official in a red cap coming along the platform towards her and wondering whether to kick him on the shin or knock off his imposing hat. Then she perceived that violence was unnecessary, for the official was accompanied by three soldiers, and his objective was obviously Aylward. In mime, he conveyed to her that she was under arrest and must come with him. She had never been more happy to be arrested in her life. Gathering up her baggage, she followed him along the platform and into a side room. It was so filthy and stank so abominably that she was almost sick. The door was locked and there she was left. She preferred the Siberian cold of the platform. Later that day the door was opened and she was led into another room. An interrogator managed to make her understand that he spoke English. Gladys was pleased to understand this, but it didn't seem to get them any farther. He talked for a long time. She could make out almost nothing of what he was trying to say. Eventually he left her. Gladys got out her bedroll—this room didn't smell so much—and under the incurious eye of the soldier who had been left to guard her, she went fast asleep.

Next day the interrogation continued. They examined her shiny new passport and spent an interminable time discussing the entry that read: *Profession—Missionary*. This they seemed to be suggesting had something to do with 'machinery'. They also seemed to be hinting that she might like to stay in Russia; they had need of people like her.

It is well known that during these years many young Communists from all over the world were flocking to Soviet Russia anxious to play their part in building a proletarian Utopia. That Gladys Aylward was mistaken for one of them is not unusual, but the mistake terrified her. Frantically, she thumbed through her Bible, which had a coloured picture text inside it, and showed them scenes of biblical times. It seemed to do some good, for after some more discussion they handed her a piece of paper with official stamps on it which appeared to be a new visa; also, what looked like tickets for another journey.

That afternoon they escorted her to a train and managed to convey to her that she must change at a place called

Nikolshissur Junction, and then catch a connection to Pogranilchnai, and so continue to Harbin.

A few hours later she disembarked at Nikolshissur. The connection to Pogranilchnai? No one spoke English; no one understood a word of her request. She tried the station officials, she tried the man in the red hat. No one understood. It was now late. Surrounded by her baggage, she settled down to spend another night on the station platform. It was so bitterly cold she thought she would freeze to death. Next morning she brewed her morning coffee on her spirit stove, ate two of the inevitable soda cakes, parked her luggage at the station cloakroom and went off in search of some sort of Government office. She felt certain that once there, at least she would find someone who spoke a word or two of English. She found the Government offices, but nobody spoke English. She was shown eventually into an office, and a man interviewed her. Gladys, by now, was used to exhibiting her Bible and drawing pictures, but on this occasion in a moment of inspiration, she pulled out a picture of her brother, Laurie. It showed him in the full dress of a drummer in the British Army. By Russian standards of army uniform, he looked like a major-general. Whether or not they thought she had high Army connections, she never found out, but the picture produced instantaneous and electrifying results. With a sudden spurt of understanding they seemed to know exactly what was wanted. She was whisked off first to the station cloakroom to collect her baggage, and then to a hotel, where she spent the night. The next day she was escorted to a train, her tickets were altered and she was re-routed to Vladivostok. As she jolted through the interminable Siberian landscape she offered up a little prayer of gratefulness to brother Laurie.

On the platform at Vladivostok no one took much notice of her. The collector examined her ticket and let her out through the barrier. On the station wall she saw a poster advertising 'Intourist Hotel', and decided to go there. By trying various phonetical intonations on passers-by she eventually reached its doors; it was not far from the station. The hotel clerk signed her in. A thick-set man with a pale Mongolian face, a creased suit and no collar examined her passport and pocketed it. As far as Gladys could understand he was something to do with the police. The letters OGPU meant nothing to her.

From then onwards he attached himself to her with a fondness that Gladys found rather embarrassing. He insisted upon showing her the sights of Vladivostok, and what she saw horrified her: the filthy, unpaved roads full of water-filled potholes, the long food queues; the women in kimonos, eyes dark with hunger and weariness, babies on their backs; the shabby, unpainted buildings; the clattering trams packed with unwashed, ragged passengers. That afternoon she stood with him at a corner and watched one of these trams draw to a standstill. A thin, half-starved-looking woman ran to get on. The reason for the altercation Gladys never understood, but she saw the packed crowd of men threatening the new passenger; then she saw them, just as the car was moving off, pick up the woman bodily and throw her into the roadway.

The woman fell with a thud and rolled over in the mud. The men screamed and jeered at her. Slowly the woman got up. She was weeping in such silent and bitter distress that Gladys's heart moved out to her. She took a step in her direction, but the man's hand on her arm restrained her. Her head bowed low, the woman trudged up the windy street after the tram. The impression of her body still remained in the mud; the rain would wash it away.

The cicatrix of the memory incised on Gladys Aylward's mind was there for ever. For her the cold wind which sifted through the streets carrying on its breath the desolation of Siberia epitomized Russia. She felt in her bones the bewilderment and hopelessness of so many of its people. She could not canalize her feelings into a coherent, critical appraisal; she only knew how desperately she wanted to leave this country.

The next morning the pale-faced interpreter was waiting outside her bedroom door. She sensed somehow that his unctuous attitude had changed. As they went down the stairs, she said, "Shall I soon be able to get my connection to Harbin?" He looked at her sideways, "Why do you wish to go to the barbaric land of China? In this country of immense revolution you have a future. You are young, you could work here. We need people with skill like you." She looked straight ahead, tried to make each movement of her limbs a normal, ordinary reaction. She tried to conceal the sudden quickening fear his words had started in her. "But I have no skill. I only want to be a missionary." She added with the frankness she could not alter, "Besides, I don't like Russia; all this poverty, the poor, thin, underfed women, the dirt."

His dark eyes turned towards her. "How can you get to China, anyway? You have no money to buy tickets."

Gladys was angry. "I paid my fare from London to Tientsin. If your railway people were honest they would see that I got there," she said indignantly.

"But what is the point of proceeding farther? You can work here just as well as China. We need people like you who can handle machines. . . ."

"Machines! I've never worked a machine in my life."

"You should stay here," he said. "China is a long way off. We will see that you are taken care of."

Gladys saw very little as she walked through the streets of Vladivostok that morning. She was now more worried than she had been since the journey started. It seemed plain that this man had received instructions from someone to delay her. But why? There were millions of people in Russia. They did not need her.

As she entered the hotel foyer on her return, she was conscious that someone was walking close behind her. The OGPU man had gone back to his post at the desk. She glanced over her shoulder. She saw a girl, dark, plainly dressed, but attractive. The girl drew level with her. Without turning her head she whispered in good, if strongly accented English, "I must speak to you now. It is important. Follow me!"

In mesmerized fashion Gladys allowed the girl to precede her, and followed her into the corridor. The girl took her arm and steered her into a dark corner. "I waited until I was sure the OGPU man had left you," she said.

"But I don't understand. Who are you?"

"It doesn't matter now. What matters is that you are in danger."

The little black raven of fear sitting on Gladys's shoulder flapped its wings.

"But what can I do?" she said anxiously.

The girl's voice was quick with urgency. "You want to get out, don't you? If you don't get out *now*, you never will."

Gladys's tightly compressed lips seemed to stick together. Again she felt the quick shock of fright.

"I'm a British subject. I've got a passport."

"Where is it?"

"Here in my bag."

"Take it out . . . open it."

Gladys fumbled in her bag, and suddenly remembered. The man at the desk; he had put it in his pocket and not returned it.

The girl's eyes were fixed on her, reading her thoughts. "They still have it. You must get it back! They need skilled factory workers desperately. If they decide to, they can send you off somewhere in the middle of Russia and you'll never be heard of again. Examine your passport when they return it."

There was utter horror in Gladys's voice now. "But what am I to do?"

"I can help you."

"Help me? How can you help me?"

"Listen. Tonight after midnight be dressed and have your baggage ready. A knock will come on your door. Open it and follow the man outside. Do not speak to him. Simply follow him. You understand? And ask them for your passport back."

Gladys nodded her head weakly. No word could pass her lips. She stood in the dim corridor for a few moments after the girl had gone trying to formulate a plan of action. She *had* to get the passport back. That was essential. She walked to the desk in the foyer. The OGPU man was sitting on a tilted chair smoking a cigarette. He looked contemptuously up at her.

"My passport?" said Gladys. "I would like my passport back."

He rocked his chair back to floor level, took the cigarette out of his mouth, and blew out smoke. "It is still being examined. I will bring it back to you—this evening."

"Thank you," said Gladys. She walked away quickly, not knowing what her next action should be. She must pull herself together. Could that girl possibly be right? The idea seemed absurd, an episode out of a not-very-well-written thriller.

That night she sat in the cold bedroom after eating her supper. She hadn't enjoyed the biscuits and the tinned fish very much. A knock came on the door. She walked across and opened it. It was the OGPU man, grinning, waving the passport tantalizingly in one hand. He put his foot in the door. Instinctively warned, with a quick movement Gladys reached up and snatched the passport from his hand, and flicked it over her head into the bedroom. The bitter, sardonic grin on his face frightened her. He forced the door wide open and stepped inside.

"Don't you dare come in here," said Gladys simply. "Get out! Get out!"

"I am coming in, and you won't stop me," he said gutturally. His slitted eyes flicked across to the bed and back to her.

With eyes dilated, she stared at him. Her vicarious experience warned her that here was the absolute, the fundamental horror: a beast of a man forcing his way into her bedroom at dead of night aflame with lust and desire! She had read about such things in women's magazines all her life. Every second movie she had ever seen featured the exploits of Pearl White or Lilian Gish escaping from express trains, ice-floes and foul gentlemen with twirly dark moustaches. A whole Victorian folk-lore had been fashioned around the fiend and the female, and Gladys had imbibed enough of it to know that the next reel, or the next chapter, always showed the heroine weeping in a corner, or thrown out into the snow carrying a small yowling bundle.

Now it was happening to her. It was unbelievable. She was so petrified with astonishment that she allowed him to take three steps towards her, before she leapt backwards like a small scalded cat. With inspired rhetoric, she declaimed wildly:

"God will protect me! God will protect me!"

The man stopped. He looked puzzled. He stared at the small embodiment of virtue, rooted dramatically in front of him and started to grin. The grin turned into a laugh, then into a roar of laughter. Astonished, but implacable, Gladys glared at him. Abruptly his mood changed. He swore at her savagely, cursed her in Russian and English. He lifted his hand threateningly, thought better of it and took a few steps backwards out of the door. He slammed it behind him. Gladys dived at the bolt and thrust it home. She could hardly breathe, so intense was her shock. She leant back against the door, pressing her palms against it in an agony of relief. She had to get out of the hotel that very night. At once!

She raced across to pick up her passport. What had the girl said? Something about examining it? She opened it, flipped through the pages. Her finger trembled with fright as she saw what they had done. The word '*Missionary*' in the line marked '*Profession*' had been altered to '*Machinist*'. She closed it, crammed it into her bag, hauled her suitcases from under the bed and began to pile in her belongings. She had to leave that night; she must escape somehow or other. She finished her packing and sat on the bed trembling, waiting for midnight, praying that the knock on the door would ʉ ɯ ʊr ɦɛʊ. Wus the girl telling the truth, or was the story some part of an artful plan to trap her? She didn't care. She had to take a chance. She had to get away.

The knock was so gentle that she hardly heard it. She hesitated before unlocking the door, then decided she must go through with it. A strange man in a drab mackintosh and a trilby hat stood outside. It was so dark she could hardly see his face. He motioned to her to come out and held the door open while she bundled through with her suitcases. Then he went on ahead, and she followed him along the corridor, down the stairs and past the reception desk. The clerk was nodding in his chair by the stove; there was no sign of the OGPU man. The revolving door grated a little as it spun round and Gladys had more difficulty with her cases. Then they were out in the cold night air, and she walked briskly after the stranger. The streets were unlit and she stumbled continually into potholes. As they hurried through the dark side-streets she had a feeling they were approaching the sea. Against the night sky she could see the thin shape of dockside cranes. Soon they were stumbling over railway lines embedded in cobblestones. From the shadow of a pile of packing cases another figure stepped out. It was the girl, and with a sigh of thankfulness Gladys hurried towards her.

"I am glad you have come," she said.

"What do I do now?" asked Gladys anxiously.

"You see that ship." The girl pointed to the black bulk of a ship looming beyond the dark sheds and cranes.

"Yes?"

"It is a Japanese ship. It sails for Japan at dawn. You must be on it."

"But Japan! I've got no money . . ." Gladys's voice rose into a wail.

"You'll find the captain of the ship in that small wooden hut over there. You must go and see him. Plead with him, tell him you are in great trouble. You *must* leave on that ship. . . ."

"All right, I'll try." Gladys's voice was doubtful.

The girl stood there in the darkness, and Gladys did not know how to thank her.

"What about you? I haven't even thanked you for what you have done. Why have you helped me like this?"

"You needed help." The girl's voice was low and sad.

"But you . . . ?"

"I live here. I shall be all right."

"But how can I thank you? What can I give you? I have no money. . . ."

"It does not matter."

Gladys sensed the hesitation in the girl's voice.

"There is something?"

"You have perhaps . . . clothes?"

Every garment Gladys possessed she was wearing against the bitter cold. She had nothing except what she wore, but she had to show her gratitude somehow. She whipped off her gloves.

"Here, take these, please. And these stockings." She fumbled in her coat pocket and produced a pair she had thrust there in her hurry.

"They're old and darned, but please have them."

The girl took them. "Thank you," she said quietly. "Good luck!"

Their hands touched for a moment in the darkness. Then she turned on her heel and walked away, her feet echoing on the cobblestones.

Gladys picked up her cases and walked slowly towards the hut. She realized, as she picked a path across the muddy ground, that she would never find her way back to the Intourist Hotel in the dark. She pushed open the door of the little hut. A naked electric bulb hung from the roof. There was a bare wooden table piled with papers. On the other side of it sat a young Japanese in Merchant Marine uniform. He looked up gravely as she came in.

She put down her bundles and looked at him.

"Please," she said, "are you the captain of that boat? I'm English, and I must get on it. I *must* get on it!"

He looked at her impassively. Then he said in excellent English, "Good morning. Please speak slowly. What is it you wish?"

"I want to go to Japan on your ship."

"Indeed! Have you the money to pay your fare?"

"No. Nothing!"

His black eyes were unblinking and quite incurious.

"No valuables of any sort?"

"No, nothing at all. But I must leave here. I must!"

The Captain nodded his head. His face had shown not the slightest sign of emotion.

"You say you are a British subject? You have a passport?"

Gladys fished her passport out of her bag and handed it to him. He leafed through it carefully. As she watched him, Gladys had a feeling that he had done this many times.

"A British subject in trouble. We really cannot have that, can we? Yes, I will take you on my ship. There are some papers you must sign, that is all. If you will come with me, I will find you a cabin."

Six hours later, dawn was colouring the bare red hillsides along the coastline of the Golden Horn as the Japanese steamship slowly slid out towards the open ocean, with Vladivostok a smudge of smoke behind them. At the rail Gladys Aylward looked back with tired but relieved eyes. She felt as if she had spent a lifetime crossing the great continent of Russia and Siberia. Now a sense of freedom washed through her like a fresh spring of water. She wondered who the girl was who had helped her. The man who had knocked at her door? She knew she would never meet either of them again; that they would always remain eternal enigmas in her past. She was glad that there were some good people in Russia. She wished them luck. She felt that, already, she herself had received a fair allowance of that glittering, fateful currency.

CHAPTER THREE

THREE DAYS after leaving Vladivostok they steamed in towards their destination, the small port of Tsurugaoha on the east coast. Farther to the south was Kobe, and from there, the Captain explained, she would be able to catch a boat to China. He also informed her that she would have to wait on board while he got in touch with the British Consul or his representative.

Not long after they docked, therefore, a rather disconcerted but extremely pleasant young Englishman, whose importance at the Consulate Gladys never discovered, arrived to interview her. After a few questions, he conveyed both her and her baggage to a small restaurant near the dock area "where they could talk properly". He was obviously embarrassed by the encounter. He said, "It's all rather difficult. I wonder what we can do for you now?"

"I shall be quite all right when I reach Kobe," said Gladys firmly. After her adventures in the USSR she was confident of the value of repeating statements firmly. Experience told her that if you repeated your desire often enough and convincingly enough, something was bound to happen.

The young man's surprise showed in his face. "In that case I'll get you a ticket to Kobe, and put you on a train straight away," he said quickly. His gratefulness showed all the way to the station. As she leaned out of the carriage window to chat with him, Gladys could sense that his relief was so great, she was almost surprised when he didn't attempt to kiss her goodbye.

On the train, in the inevitable corner seat, she watched the countryside go by. She contrasted the beauty and delicacy of the landscape with the savage disorderliness of the continent she had just left.

The train puffed and jolted round the coastline, and she watched the vistas of shore and coastline slip behind her. On the landward side, far away, high snow-covered peaks shaded down to green hills and fertile fields. On the other, green islands toppled into a blue, sun-bright sea. Tiny lattice sail-boats poised in silhouette against the glare of sea and sky. They passed shady villages of tiled-roofed houses which were hung with banners and flags, and where the trees flamed with scarlet blossom, and shouting children frolicked in the clear shallows of the beaches. In the fields the rice was golden ripe, each stem bent with the weight of its kernels, waiting for the sickle. And at every halt chattering groups of Japanese people in clean, bright shirts and kimonos bundled on and off the train.

During her stay in Japan she never could reconcile, or equate in mind or memory, the attractive, happy people she met then, with the outrageous warriors she was to know with such horrifying intimacy in later years.

On the platform at Kobe she saw a sign in European lettering which said JAPANESE TOURIST BUREAU. She walked in and approached the counter clerk. Although she could not get much sense out of him, she did change her two-pound travellers' cheque and received a bewildering assortment of yen. She walked out into the dazzle of bright autumn sunshine. At the station entrance, before she could protest, she was seized by a rickshaw boy, piled into his flimsy two-wheeled vehicle, festooned with her luggage and then borne at speed through the traffic-filled streets of Kobe. The yen notes crackled in her pocket. She submitted to this treatment with equanimity. She felt like a new species of Western millionaire.

With intense pleasure she looked at the crowds, the open bazaars, the narrow alleyways hung with bright banners inscribed with the gold and scarlet arabesques of Japanese lettering. And suddenly into her mind sprang the conviction that while she was in London she had heard something about a Japanese Christian organization. "The Japanese Evangelistic Band! That was what it was called," she said to herself. While she was still trying to recall other aspects of the organization, she saw, hanging outside one hall, among the alien shop signs, a notice board nailed with a cross and above it the words, KOBE MISSION HALL.

It is possible that her rickshaw boy, with the instinctive knowledge of humanity shared by psychiatrists, taxi-drivers, waiters and policemen, had deliberately taken her in this direction, for at her shrill exclamation of recognition he trotted obediently over to the front door. She dismounted. A pleasant Japanese inside spoke a little English. He directed her rickshaw boy to the house of the English missionaries who he felt would be happy to receive her. Indeed, the Dyers, the English missionaries at Kobe, were delighted to meet their unexpected caller. They listened to the story of her adventures. Mr Dyer frowned as he heard of the circuitous way in which she had reached Japan.

"But if you paid for tickets to Tientsin, the travel people should get you there, no matter how you were diverted," he said seriously. "Give me all the tickets you have left, and I'll see the agency people here tomorrow."

They gave her a bath in a large wooden tub, Japanese style, which nearly boiled her to death, and then put her to bed in a pretty room lit by a lantern of red and blue. It was the first good night's sleep she had had since leaving England.

The next morning, after a session with Cook's Tourist Agency, Mr Dyer reappeared bearing an envelope containing a steamship ticket from Kobe to Tientsin, which they had agreed to exchange for Gladys's unused vouchers from Chita. She was almost sorry to leave Japan. It was so sunny and quaint, and the Dyers most friendly.

Three days later, from the deck of a neat little Japanese ship, she stared across muddy yellow sea at a dark smudge on the horizon. Behind it the sun was setting with gaudy flamboyance. The Japanese Captain had asked her up to the bridge specially to see the landfall. It was dark purple in colour. It could have been a cloud formation and held no particular beauty or interest, but Gladys stared at it until all the colour had shredded out of the sky and the dark bank of land was swallowed by the night. That was China. With such eyes Sir Galahad must have searched for the Holy Grail.

At Tientsin she found a large mission with a European staff where they trained many Chinese converts. Yes, they had heard of Mrs Lawson. As far as they knew she was in the territory of Shansi in north China at a mission station in an old walled town called Tsehchow. It was north of the Yellow River in very wild and mountainous territory. It would take many weeks to reach there. They would see if they could scout around and find a guide who could take her part of the way into the hinterland. Meanwhile they would be glad to put her up.

Seven days later, as the train drew out of Tientsin station away from the sprawl of Westernized suburbs, Gladys felt the pulse of the train wheels echo her own excitement. Ninety miles to Pekin, and then on for days and days into the wilderness! Mr Lu, a sober young man in a dark Chinese robe and a trilby hat, was to accompany her for some of the journey. He had business in Shansi; he was also a Christian. She had changed her last few yen in order to buy a Chinese pass which permitted her to go inland. It had cost twelve shillings. All the money she now possessed was six shillings. This fact did not worry her in the slightest as the train jogged, slowly at first, across the flat, uninteresting, featureless landscape. It was a bright day in late autumn and the fields, denuded of the harvest, shone with a short golden stubble. Soon along the western horizon an immense semicircle of purple mountains tumbled against the sky. The countryside lost its flat dullness, and the train chugged across fertile agricultural country, past farms and mud-walled villages backed by clumps of trees. There were cemeteries enclosed by grey stone walls and entered by magnificent ornamental gates, where lay the generations of well-loved, worshipful ancestors. Along open roads sunk in the soft, fruitful earth the blue-garmented, pigtailed peasants drove their heavy two-wheeled carts drawn by shaggy Mongolian ponies. The ponies, in their fashion, were almost as famous as the generations of well-loved and long-dead ancestors.

Mounted on these beasts, the horde of Genghis Khan's Tartars had driven south to extend their empire. It was against successive waves of similar invaders that the 1400-mile-long Great Wall of China had been built. Men might scale the wall; horses never. Mounted, the Tartars raided as swiftly and devastatingly as locusts. Deprived of horses they were small men with bandy legs, and the Chinese were a match for them.

Gladys Aylward was enchanted by the countyside. At the halts as they neared Pekin, flower-sellers thrust bunches of pink or white lotus blossoms through the windows. The feeling of immemorial continuity and dignity overwhelmed her. Yes, it was alien: that still-distant barrier of savage mountains, the occasional swaying, tan-coloured caravans of Gobi camels, and eventually the soaring, square-bastioned walls of Pekin, a city of temples and pagodas, statues and calm pools reflecting the leaves of the lotus flower. But every new scene excited her.

That night they spent at a Chinese inn in Pekin, and went on again by train the next morning. The line petered out three days later at Yutsa. From there on they made progress by means of ramshackle old buses. Each night now they stopped at a Chinese inn. Privacy had disappeared; everyone slept on the *k'ang*—the communal·brick bed under which flowed hot air from the stove. No one undressed; everyone endeavoured with philosophical calm to preserve a few inches of flesh from the foraging and hungry fleas and lice. They feasted upon Gladys as gourmets enjoy some exotic rarity from far away.

The province of Shansi is cut off in the south and west by the mighty Hwang-Ho, the Yellow River, which rises in the distant province of Kansu, and forces its colossal snake-like configuration across 3000 miles of China's soil before it spews into the ocean at Shangtung with such power that ships' crews sixty miles out notice the turgid yellow coloration. To the north and east it is protected by high masses of barren mountains. Shansi is the home of Chinese agriculture, the cradle of Chinese civilization. Here in the valley of Wei and Fen-ho the people first acquired the art of pottery, which thousands of years later was to produce the translucent porcelains, to reach an incredible magnificence in the Ming and Sung dynasties.

The Fen-ho valley has been cultivated continuously for over 4000 years, for millet, wheat and barley crops, able to live upon only a small amount of moisture, have always grown there in a wild state. Rice did not become the main food of the Chinese until they spread out into the Yangtse valley and the river-water allowed them to flood their fields. In north-west China the people eat grain to this day, as Gladys discovered at the Chinese inns, where she found that boiled dough strings formed the basis of all meals. Fleas, and unappetizing dough strings, however, did not, and could not, deter her. A month after leaving Tientsin they arrived at Tsehchow, the city where she had been told she would find Mrs Lawson.

Two old ladies, one of whom was a Mrs Smith, ran the Mission there. They were both about seventy years old. Mrs Smith's husband had been a missionary for many years; after his death she had decided to stay on, and had been joined by this friend of hers who was a teacher. They told Gladys that Mrs Lawson had stayed with them for several weeks. Then she had moved into the wild, mountainous area to the west, country into which Christianity had never penetrated. It was forbidding terrain; the villages were isolated; the small towns were walled and fortified. They had heard that Mrs Lawson was living for the time being at Yangcheng, a walled town which lay two days' journey away, along the ancient mule track from Hornan to Hopeh.

"How do I get there?" asked Gladys wearily. The long days of travelling had worn her out.

Mrs Smith was the kind of old lady one finds in teashops in Bath and Harrogate and Cheltenham, but rarely several hundred miles from anywhere in the middle of China. To some extent, in fact, her gentle good looks belied an extreme competency; she was a niece of Archbishop Lang, and a very talented woman with a great gift for the Chinese language and dialects. She peered at Gladys through her spectacles.

"My dear, the only way is by mule through the mountains," she said. "The road ends here. Only tracks lead onwards. It's very rough going and there are immense stretches of lonely country. It's a day's journey to Chowtsun, the first village, and then another day on to Yangcheng."

"I'll start tomorrow if I can," said Gladys.

Mrs Smith looked at her thoughtfully. "I wouldn't wear those European clothes either, if I were you, my dear," she suggested kindly.

Gladys looked down at her soiled red frock and coat. "But it's all I've got."

"We'll find you others," said Mrs Smith. "You see, there are bandits in the mountains. They would know you are a foreigner and might think you were rich. We can fit you out with the blue jacket and trousers that everybody wears. Where you are going, they've never seen a European woman before. They're very simple, primitive people; they think all foreigners are devils! It's better not to draw too much attention to yourself."

At first light next morning, seated uncomfortably inside a mule litter, a canopied platform secured upon the animal's back, Gladys started on the last leg of her journey. For nine miles they travelled over the plain, and then the narrow, flinty path turned up into the mountains. Before dark they had reached Chowtsun, where they were breaking their journey.

No one travelled at night. The paths were too steep and precipitous, and travellers trusted neither bandits nor wolves in the high country. Chowtsun, secure within its walls—for all the villages in the province are walled—was full of inns and shouting children and teams of mules and muleteers. There was a chill in the air that night, and the stars between the dark peaks seemed brighter and nearer.

At dawn they were off again, winding along a narrow path which had been hacked from the mountainside. As the grey light peered down into the cracks and fissures of this lunar landscape, she saw the marbled faces of the mountains, the tumbling streams racing through the rocky valleys. The *clip-clop* of the mule's hooves on the flinty track echoed in the clear air. High overhead a pair of eagles soared lazily in the first sunlight. Seven hours later, rounding a bend in the trail, the muleteer pulled his animals to a halt and pointed with a grimy forefinger: "Yangcheng".

It stood far off on its mountain peak like a castle in a fairy story. Its high walls grew from the natural rock like a tooth from a jaw. Delicate pagodas and temples, still only silhouettes, but made more mysterious by distance, rose high above the walls. Against the satin sky of late afternoon it gave her an impression of unattainable beauty. Weary as she was, she felt her spirit lifted up at the sight. As they drew nearer she saw that amongst the barren mountains, two quite close to the city were covered with trees and dense foliage. The trail passed over one, tunnelling through green shades until it came out into the hard sunlight again and the path climbed steeply to the East Gate. On all sides, from that altitude, glorious panoramas of mountain and valley rolled away into the distance. Gladys was enthralled by the natural grandeur. She had never for one moment suspected that such a place existed.

Yangcheng has sat there on its mountain saddle, a tiny crock of Confucian civilization astride the ancient track between Hornan and Horbay, longer than man can remember, or history has recorded. The mule track passes in through the East Gate and out through the West. On three sides the country falls away steeply, but there are inns and cave dwellings on the slopes. On the south side it falls sheerly, thousands of feet to the wild valley below, and standing on the city wall one can look out towards the distant mountain ranges. At nightfall all gates are locked, and mule trains arriving after that hour are refused admittance to the city. They cannot pass forward, and find shelter for the night in one of the inns in the shadow of the walls and on the slopes.

At the East Gate, Gladys's muleteer halted and questioned one of the old men sitting there in the sun. He pointed to the narrow roadway that turned down left outside the city wall. The muleteer urged the beasts towards it. A hundred yards down the track, lined on both sides by the blank courtyard walls of private houses and inns, he stopped and indicated a building. The tired mules, with the sagacity of their breed, nosed in towards the narrow entrance to the courtyard, their hooves clattering on the stones.

Out of the door to meet them came a small lady with pure white hair and the bluest eyes Gladys had ever seen. She was dressed in a plain blue robe and trousers. She looked up at Gladys and screwed up her eyes in the bright light.

"Well, and who are you?" she asked abruptly.

"I'm Gladys Aylward. You're Mrs Lawson?"

"Yes, I am. Well, come on in."

The brusque reception did not startle Gladys; she was accustomed to the extraordinary by now. The muleteer helped her off the litter and she followed Mrs Lawson into the house.

Like most Chinese dwellings, it was square, enclosed by four high walls. From a square recess in the front wall, a small door led inwards to a large courtyard. The rooms of the double-storey dwelling opened on to balconies which looked down on to the courtyard. This house was almost derelict. Practically every door was off its hinges; there were piles of rubble on the flagstones, gaping holes in the tiled roof; dirt everywhere.

"I've only just managed to rent it," said Mrs Lawson. "Got it cheap because it's haunted. Bit rough, but it'll be all right when it's cleaned up."

She hopped about like a chirpy bird, darting from room to room. Gladys followed her into what appeared to be the only habitable place. In the room stood a table and a couple of chairs. There was no other furniture except a few odd packing cases and soap boxes.

"Are you hungry?" asked Mrs Lawson.

"Famished," said Gladys weakly.

Mrs Lawson called out in Chinese, and an old man came in. He was introduced as "Yang, the cook".

Yang smiled at her, an old Chinese with a toothless smile.

Gladys warmed to him immediately. A few moments later he brought a large bowl of the inevitable boiled dough strings into which some chopped vegetable had been mixed. She ate it ravenously. After the meal she went out to get her baggage and to look at the view. As she turned through the courtyard doorway a group of Chinese infants saw her and fled, howling. Some older children appeared over a wall, surrounded her and began to jeer in sing-song voices. Two women farther down the street picked up pieces of dried mud and flung them in her direction. In consternation Gladys walked quickly back to Mrs Lawson and told her what had occurred.

"It happens to me every time I go out," said Mrs Lawson calmly. "I usually come back covered from head to foot with the filth and mud they've thrown at me. So far, it hasn't been stones, thank goodness. They hate us here. They call us *lao-yang-kwei*, foreign devils. It's something you'll have to get used to."

CHAPTER FOUR

JEANNIE LAWSON was five feet tall, seventy-four years old and in appearance rather frail. It was a deceptive appearance. Her mop of pure white hair, an odd phenomenon in China, convinced every peasant in Yangcheng that not only was she a foreign devil, but also an evil spirit. This hair terrified the life out of them wherever she went, a fact which did not trouble Jeannie Lawson in the slightest. She had arrived in China as a young girl of twenty-one, married another missionary, bore her children and saw her first-born die of the black fever; watched them all grow up and go off into the world; and she had outlived her husband by many years.

She was Scottish. Her ancestors had wielded claymore and dirk for centuries against the invading English, and spiritually she was determined to brandish the word of God in the face of all unbelievers. Like her glowering countryman, John Knox, 'able in one hour to put more life in us than five hundred trumpets continually blustering in our ears', her blood ran hot for the Lord. Not for her the tame Christianity of the plains with its Bible classes, needlework and issues of aspirin; in these mountains there were heathens to be shown the light of God, and Jeannie's self-appointed task was to seek them out and show it to them, even though it meant dragging them to the kirk by their queues. If Chinese urchins followed them in mocking groups every time they walked in the streets, and women slammed their doors and spat, and men hurled mud at them, it would all be endured in true Christian fashion; eventually she would find a way to come to grips with them. If there was ever a militant Christian abroad in the mountains of Shansi, it was Jeannie Lawson.

Poor Gladys, in those early few weeks, found life harder to bear. Possessing a personal fortune of precisely six shillings, many thousands of miles from her homeland, speaking no word of the language, spat upon and reviled every time she moved from the house, she often came home in tears to wash the mud off her clothes. She remembered with nostalgia those scores of neat little Japanese converts in Kobe; clean and smiling and virtuous, singing their psalms and hymns as prettily and confidently as if each had had a personal interview with the Almighty.

Yangcheng was not remotely like that. One day, quite early in her stay, the difference was made plain to her. She was walking through the city. Within the walls the townspeople had become more or less accustomed to the 'foreign devils' by now, and while they still moved out of their path, it was too much trouble to keep throwing mud. As Gladys walked towards the market square she saw a crowd gathering. Then she saw the Chinese woman who lived in the house next door and smiled at her occasionally. The woman beckoned her excitedly, and as Gladys, pleased by this sudden indication of friendship, came up to her, she grabbed her wrist and hurried with her through the crowd. 'Jugglers,' thought Gladys excitedly, 'or perhaps a man with a performing bear!' Jeannie Lawson had told her that it was fairly common to see such strolling players performing in the market square.

The impetus of their rush took them right through the crowd to the front rank. Gladys was puzzled by what she saw. A man, shaven-headed, his pigtail looped round his forehead, stood there. He was bent forward, his shoulders hunched in a queer, almost pathetic manner. A soldier, his back to Gladys, stood close to him. In bewilderment she stared, sensing the tragic, suddenly wide-eyed at the bright flash of steel as a curved execution sword swung high in the air. Petrified, she glimpsed the blade poised aloft, burnished by the sun; shocked beyond comprehension she watched it slash downwards. Rigid, in utter horror, she saw the blade strike home, and the jetting man-spurt of scarlet blood arch upwards and splash on the flagstones. A gusty moan of suppressed excitement came from the crowd as the head bounced and rolled. Gladys clamped her eyes shut, screwed up her face in an effort to blot out the nightmare memory. She jerked her wrist free from the hand of the Chinese woman who was completely obsessed by the scene, turned and forced her way frantically through the milling, jabbering onlookers. She broke into a trot, then into a run; she raced back through the streets, deserted now, for everyone had hurried to see the execution. With tears streaming down her face, she doubled round through the East Gate and ran down to the house.

Jeannie Lawson was sitting at the table writing in her journal when she burst in, almost incoherent with grief and shock.

"Whatever's the matter?" said Jeannie, surprised.

"I've just seen a dreadful thing, a most dreadful thing," sobbed Gladys. "They've killed a man in the market square with a sword."

With deliberation, Jeannie, veteran of over fifty years in China, placed her pencil down at the side of her notebook.

"Well?" she demanded, curtly.

Gladys's face was muddy with tears. She blinked with astonishment.

"But they cut off his head with a sword!"

Jeannie's gaze was still steady. "It is the law for certain crimes. He was probably a bandit, or a thief, or a murderer. He must have been tried before the Mandarin in the *yamen*. If they're found guilty, they chop off their heads straight away, more often than not."

"But it's horrible!"

"Did you expect things to be the same in China as in England?"

"No, but . . ."

"Listen to me, Gladys Aylward. You haven't come here to China to alter their laws. They'll throw the body down the mountainside, where it will be eaten by wolves or carrion birds. There'll be no Christian burial. Understand that," she added, sparing her nothing. "And they'll stand the head up on the city wall so that everyone can see it."

"It's awful—so feudal!"

"Yes, it's feudal. Sometimes they won't have an execution for months. Then suddenly there's a batch, and the

52

whole wall's lined with heads. You may as well get used to it. There are lots of things in China you'll have to get used to. We'll try and change these things through the love and wisdom of Jesus Christ, by making them understand truth and justice, but we won't do it by running home blubbing our eyes out."

Gladys had no reply to that, but despite Jeannie's admonition she never forgot the horror of that scene. In the future she would see worse sights, but the memory of that execution, even in the years which followed, demonstrated and dramatized for her the odd streak of cruelty which she decided lay skin against skin in even the most civilised Chinese.

It was a period of 'settling-in'. Jeannie Lawson explained her financial position. She had a small private income; the rent for the house, because it was old and derelict, and according to local legend full of ghosts and evil spirits, worked out in British currency at two shillings and fourpence a year. Millet and wheat and vegetables cost only a few *cash*. The value of cash—the small copper coins with holes in the centre which were strung in bunches on pieces of string—was 200 to the Chinese dollar, which at this time stood at about one shilling and twopence. Financially, they were reasonably secure; but what was the use of security if they could not do the job for which they were both in China? They arrived at the brilliant idea one day as they were walking back up the slope which led to the West Gate, after a short excursion into the countryside. They passed through the narrow main street and skirted the yamen or town hall where the Mandarin lived and all the official business of the city was carried out. Thin alleyways led off in all directions from the main road, and inside the strong arms of the wall the life of the city bubbled noisily.

It was a scene which never ceased to fascinate Gladys. At that moment, in the late afternoon, the city was crowded. Across the alleyways hung the scrolls, garish with scarlet, blue and gold lettering. Moving among the people were the priests: Buddhists in bright orange robes, the blue-black stubble of their shaven heads oiled to a pale golden colour: Taoists in scarlet robes; priests and acolytes inhabiting the dozen and one dark stone temples along every alleyway dedicated to Sun gods, Moon gods, Cat gods, Ancestor gods and every conceivable form of spirit-like being which had plagued or comforted the Chinese people through forty centuries. The women—you could pick out the lucky and well-loved ones by the bloom on their pale porcelain skins, and their shining blue-black hair stuck with ornamental combs—gossiped in little groups and fingered bales of silk and cotton in the bazaar. In the darker alleyways the old crones, the male grandchild cradled on their back, sucked their gums hungrily around the food stalls. The old men, the food sellers, with thin white beards, crouched like sorcerers around wide, shallow black bowls, blew charcoal embers beneath them into furious flame and mixed the oil, the chopped chicken, vegetables and maize, into the small crock dishes to be scooped by chopsticks into the champing mouths of their customers.

There were beggars everywhere; not belonging to Yangcheng, but passers-through along the ancient highway who could not afford the legal price of two cash for a place on the warm brick k'ang of any inn. Old and young, women and children, they slept by night in draughty doorways and held out pleading hands.

The early mule trains were already coming through the gates to find lodging at the inns within the city walls. The whole purpose of Yangcheng's existence through the centuries had been this: a fortified post guarding an important trading route; a stopping place for mule caravans and travellers who passed along it. So great was the traffic that other inns had grown up outside the city walls, and every night Yangcheng was packed with muleteers and carriers. The nearest village in either direction on the trade route was a day's journey away. A team usually consisted of seven animals; two muleteers travelled with it and, as often as not, up to twenty carriers, heavy bundles slung from either end of their pliable shoulder-poles, plodded behind them and completed the convoy.

As the mule trains passed by, Gladys voiced her thoughts. "If we could only talk to these men, they'd carry our message for hundreds of miles through the province."

Jeannie Lawson walked on without a word for several paces. Then suddenly she rounded on Gladys.

"You've put your finger right on it," she said. "We'll open an inn."

Gladys stared at her, thinking she had not heard correctly.

"Open an inn?" she repeated incredulously.

"Of course! Why didn't I think of it before? Our house was built as an inn in the first place, hundreds of years ago. We've plenty of rooms. There are three k'angs specially constructed to sleep large numbers, two downstairs, one in the large room upstairs. We'll have to get the roof mended. We could put up at least fifty men and their animals. We've got a cook. It's quite easy to feed them." Her voice was full of enthusiasm.

"But we didn't come here to be innkeepers," said Gladys dubiously.

"Don't you see what I'm after?" said Jeannie impatiently. "Once we've got them inside we can tell them stories of the Gospels. The Chinese love stories. All the inns offer roughly the same service—a bed and food; we can only charge the same price, two cash a night; but as an added inducement we shall tell them stories. It's a wonderful idea!" She began to walk forward again. "Now the first thing we've got to do is get that roof repaired. Then we'll have to get food in. . . ."

Gladys was carried along on the floodtide of this enthusiasm; there was no alternative. Yang, the cook, said he thought it a good idea; he was a mild old man with a wrinkled mountaineer's face and a sharp peasant intelligence, and if he said it was feasible, then it was.

The roof was mended, the large courtyard cleaned out. New doors were fixed to the rooms. The balustrade around the first-floor balcony was rebuilt. The windows were repaired; as the panes were only made of opaque paper, that wasn't too difficult. Large quantities of millet and maize and vegetables were soon stored.

"A name," said Jeannie. "We must have a signboard outside the house giving the name of the inn. They all do."

"I suppose we could call it the Red Lion or the White Hart," said Gladys flippantly, "though I think my mother would be a bit shocked if she thought I'd come all the way to China to work as a barmaid in the Red Lion."

Jeannie Lawson laughed. "I've got it," she said. "A wonderful name. . . . The Inn of Eight Happinesses. Isn't that good?"

"It sounds more oriental than the Red Lion, I must admit," said Gladys.

A sign-painter living in one of the narrow alleyways off the main street was commissioned to do the job, and although it was some time after the inn opened that it was completed, eventually the narrow yellow signboard painted with Chinese letters in black and gold hung outside their house in exactly the same way as a signboard hangs outside an English inn. The name followed the true tradition of classical Chinese nomenclature, which encourages the flowery and euphonious. No one in Yangcheng thought it whimsical. Gladys and Jeannie never consciously isolated their eight happinesses into a logical sequence. Both had different ideas of the virtues they would have chosen. Jeannie Lawson plumped for: Love, Virtue, Gentleness, Tolerance, Loyalty, Truth, Beauty and Devotion.

Gladys was quite certain that some of their customers would choose: Hard Work, Willing Mules or Full Bellies, but she agreed it was a name well suited to their Inn of Yangcheng in the wilderness of southern Shansi.

A few days later the inn was officially open. The smell of good food eddied out from Yang's kitchen, and they waited patiently for the first customers! Muleteers crowded into the inn opposite, and the ones farther down the street. Muleteers and carriers plodded past, looking up at the inviting appeal of the 'Inn of Eight Happinesses', but no one came into the hostelry of the 'foreign devils'. Obviously they were being boycotted.

Jeannie held a council of war. They decided that more seductive, or forceful, measures would have to be taken.

"You," said Jeannie, levelling a stubby finger at Gladys, "will be responsible for bringing the customers into the courtyard."

"But how?" protested Gladys. "If they don't want to come into *our* courtyard, how can I get them in?"

"It isn't a case of them '*wanting*' to come in," said Jeannie positively. "You've got to drag them in."

"*Drag* them in?" Gladys's voice was at least one octave above normal. Jeannie Lawson chattered questioningly in Chinese to Yang. He nodded his bald head in agreement. "Ai-ai," he said.

Apparently, according to him, there was a physical psychology attached to bringing a customer to bed in a Yangcheng hostelry that was unique in the accommodation business. Some of the staider muleteers made reservations at the same inn every time they passed through. You did not try to poach them—that was unethical; but there were many other casual visitors. When a muleteer came down the track looking to left and right at the inn signs, you took it that he was a casual. Legitimate prey! Then the innkeeper who stood bland and benign at his courtyard door went into action. As the lead mule passed he made a grab at the animal's head and tried to drag it in the direction of his own courtyard. The other mules were all tethered behind him with no choice but to follow. That, said Jeannie Lawson, was going to be Gladys's job.

"But what if they bite me!" she wailed.

"Now, don't be stupid," said Jeannie. "You're the youngest and most active. I'm too old. Yang will be busy with the food. You'll have to do it."

Gladys, rather than being savaged, could apparently expect to be aided and abetted by the sagacious mules. They, poor beasts, after a hard day on the mountain trails, were only too anxious to be unloaded and given food and water. A derivative intelligence, dating back roughly 4000 years, told them that once they got their heads inside a courtyard in the late afternoon or early evening, work was over. They were there to stay. No carrot, promise or enticement would lure them out again until next morning. Therefore, any tugging of the lead-rein in the direction of a courtyard doorway would be met, on their part, by complete approval. Jeannie Lawson did not think they would put up much resistance even when a 'foreign devil' grabbed their reins.

The next evening, bolstered by this knowledge, and equipped with a sales-cry which she was to call out to the passing muleteers, Gladys stood gloomily at the doorway of the Inn and waited for business. The inducement she offered, a sentence in which she had been carefully coached by Yang, announced: "*Muyo beatcha—muyo goodso; how—how—how; lai—lai—lai.*" The translation of this lugubrious refrain being: "We have no bugs, we have no fleas; good, good, good; come, come, come!"

Gladys tried it out on the first three mule trains which clopped past her. Neither animals nor muleteers took the slightest notice. It was plain that there was no magic in the words. Anxiously she realized that physical assault was also necessary.

With hands tucked into the wide sleeves of her coat, the hereditary stance adopted by all Chinese innkeepers waiting for customers since mules first crossed the mountains, Gladys stood in the shadow of the doorway. A mule train clip-clopped slowly down the street. The muleteer was obviously tired, lagging a yard or two behind his lead animal. Aylward, the five-foot tiger, waited tensed and poised in the doorway. The mule came level, and Aylward struck! So enthusiastic was her leap that its momentum carried her past the mule's head into full view of the muleteer. In the half light he recognized her at once as a 'foreign devil' and screamed in terror, but he had the lead-rein firmly tied to his wrist and could not escape. Gladys, recovering her balance, jerked at the mule's head and found herself borne into the courtyard astride the glad nose of the weary beast, the muleteer being dragged in along with his team. Hooves struck sharply on the flagstones, steam rose from their flanks; they gathered in a tired group.

Gladys looked at them in awe. She had never been so close to the front end of a mule before, not even on the journey from Tientsin. She put out her hand and patted a velvet muzzle. Brown eyes looked at her in reproach. 'Packs off,' they intimated; 'fodder, water?' Gladys had captured a mule train single-handed, but only one man. The others had all fled.

At that moment Jeannie and Yang came out of the kitchen.

"Well done!" said Jeannie, hopping with delight. "Indeed, well done!"

That did it: the muleteer had regarded Gladys with awe; the sight of the white-haired spirit advancing on him was too much. He tore the lead-rein from his wrist with a shriek, and bolted from the courtyard.

"Now look what you've done!" wailed Gladys. "At least we had one man. Now you've frightened him away, too!"

Jeannie Lawson clapped her on the back. "Don't worry, they dare not leave these mules; they're much too valuable. They'll be back; you'll see."

Yang was despatched up to the city gate to find the muleteers, reassure them and bring them to the inn.

Ten minutes later he returned, and one dubious Chinese crept fearfully into the courtyard after him. Yang had explained that the 'foreign devil' ladies offered clean accommodation, good food and, as an extra attraction, stories which were to be told free of charge, inclusive, for a cheap price of two cash a night. Where else in the whole province of Shansi could he expect such a bargain? What did he fear? Was not he, Yang, an old and respected Chinese, living with the 'foreign devils'? He had not been bewitched. Let the muleteer spend but one night at this inn of the utmost comfort and find out for himself. Yang knew, as did the muleteer, that no human agency could lure the mules out of the courtyard until the sun rose next morning, and that there was nothing else to do but make the best of it. The muleteer fetched his fellows. They unfastened the packs, watered and fed the tired animals, and went into the large downstairs room where the heated k'ang ran the entire length of one wall. Yang brought in the steaming cauldron of food and slopped it into their basins. They ate hungrily and agreed that it was good food, but when Jeannie Lawson and Gladys entered there was a perceptible movement towards the farthest corner of the room.

Jeannie was unabashed. She had her audience. "Don't be afraid," she said cheerfully. "I want to tell you a story which you will enjoy. All the stories we tell at the Inn of Eight Happinesses are free." The men looked a little more interested, and Jeannie perched herself on the stool she had brought in with her. "The story I am going to tell you tonight," she said, "concerns a man called Jesus Christ. He lived long ago in a faraway country called Palestine..."

The Inn was open. The storytelling had begun.

CHAPTER FIVE

THEIR SUCCESS as innkeepers was hard-earned. Evening after evening Gladys stood in the doorway and dragged in reluctant teams. When the reputation of the Inn was established, more often than not the courtyard was filled with six or seven teams of mules, and the upper and lower floors, which between them contained three k'angs, were packed with bodies; but in the early weeks practically all their clients were hauled bodily into the courtyard by Gladys.

Learning the Chinese language was also, she discovered, a slow business; but Yang was a willing teacher. He led her round the kitchen identifying articles by their Chinese names and making her repeat them after him. Poker—chopsticks—fire—pot—eggs. He had volunteered to become cook to Jeannie Lawson in the first place because he had heard of this Christian Gospel and wished to know more about it.

Very often, now that the local inhabitants had stopped throwing earth clods at them, they ventured outside the city boundaries, walking along the mountain tracks to the isolated villages which lay within a few miles of Yangcheng. As they entered the gates of a new village they were invariably greeted with jeers and shaken fists. Although Gladys was nervous at first, under the iron tuition of Jeannie Lawson she soon became accustomed to this reception. She also knew that, once the villagers had failed in their effort to drive away the 'foreign devils', their natural curiosity would get the better of them and they would gather round and listen while Mrs Lawson talked. Indeed, after a few minutes the women would become so intrigued that they would be asking all sorts of questions, and staring with awe at the large, unbound feet and strange skins of their visitors. Hour after hour, day after day, Gladys practised her Chinese. There was no alternative;

Mrs Lawson was the only person who spoke English, and the daily business of living had to be carried on in Yangcheng dialect. She learned some of the Bible stories in Chinese by heart, and relieved Mrs Lawson from time to time at the evening storytelling. Even Yang insisted on taking a turn, although at first he was liable to get his religious relationships confused. On two occasions they discovered him describing enthusiastically how Jesus Christ put all his animals aboard the Ark and sailed to safety across the flood-waters to Bethlehem!

Gladys was happy, even though at times Jeannie Lawson, hot-blooded, dogmatic and getting on in years, was a little difficult to live with, and inclined, in the manner of old people, to be assertive and demanding. Just to live and be able to work in Yangcheng was enough. She would run around in circles if necessary to please Jeannie Lawson, as long as she could stay. She realized now how circumscribed her life in England had been; how dull her parlourmaid's chores in Belgravia, with its vicarious routine which passed for living. In Edmonton she could see only as far as the end of the street; in Belgrave Square she was confined eternally to 'servants' quarters' in a rigid caste system. No such thing existed in China. In Britain, long ago, God had been firmly reconciled with the value of bricks and mortar; given a suitable place in the household; worshipped decently at a reasonable hour after breakfast on Sunday— an ecclesiastical appetizer before a hearty lunch, one might say—referred to again, if one felt in the mood for 'that sort of thing' for a short period before dinner.

In the immense terrain of China, solitudes which reached north, south, east and west, across thousands of miles of loneliness, the faith in which she believed seemed clearer and more forceful. Physically as well as spiritually she felt that a barren mountain top lifted her closer to God than the top of a bus. There was a clarity, a need, an urgency in this country where the spring sun flushed the snow down the rocky gullies in rushing torrents to join the deep, wide rivers; there was immense natural majesty in the rocky spurs and peaks fined down to skeleton bone by generations of wind and rain. The mountains were barren, yet in the cracks and niches in the small villages there was a fecundity of green and growing things. And where the mountains were not barren stretched the 'loess' lands—soft, pliable, rich earth, in which grew wheat, maize and millet. In the mountains the peasants terraced their plots, hoarded the precious soil, encased it between stone walls; offered up prayers to the gods of wind and rain and sun, so that in their force and frequency they would be gentle, and the crops prosper. In the spring, in these latitudes, there was an ache in the air: mountain air, clean, fresh and soft, and often redolent with the scent of flowers and wild roses.

She was up at first light, for the muleteers were always on the trail early. There was an inspiration in those early moments which she had never felt before. The clear, first light seemed to bring a fragrance and a peace. It was an opalescent beginning through which the dawn sounds— the cockcrow, the far-off bark, the children's shouts, the irregular shuffle of the hooves on the courtyard stones— penetrated into her consciousness as acutely as the opening notes of a well-loved symphony. The smoke from the fires rose slowly into the windless air, climbed upwards against the strong, sloping walls, then mounted higher still, to shred and disperse into the backdrop of brightening sky. The sun threw into silhouette new ridges and buttresses of the mountain peaks. It was cool. Mist still hung in the valleys and in thin wisps around the hills. Soon the heat and the dust would rise, and within the city walls the clamour and noise would begin; but in the early mornings there was a beauty about this high country which never failed to enchant her.

She began also to understand the muleteers, the carriers and the coolies. To her, at first, they had all looked alike: men with one face, men inseparable from the timeless, immeasurable background of ancient China.

Over the flinty, narrow trail which curved and climbed through the mountains they led their mules, laden with side-packs, carrying the coal and the cotton-wool and the pots and the iron goods. The coolies bent under shoulder-poles which supported fifty pounds dead weight in grain at either end. (Mules did not carry grain, because they made it smell.) They were human links of communication and transport with a heritage that stretched back to the beginnings of industry. They had dark, tanned faces, shocks of blue-black hair, narrow, slitted eyes; many of them tall, like most northern Chinese, and sinewy and strong. Their knowledge of mules and mountains was infinite; their knowledge of the world and its ways infinitesimal. Yet they were contented, simple people. At the end of the day a bowl of food, a place on the warm brick bed were all they desired. After six weeks' or three months' travelling they returned to a wife, children and a small home at either end of the trail. Often they stayed there for several weeks and helped with the harvest. A little like sailors was this possession of a wife at both ends of the trail; two wives, two families, two homes was the normal domestic situation of the average muleteer. Very often one wife would send a small gift with her husband along the old mule track to the other: perhaps a gift for a newly-born child. They never met. They kept house and bore children, and waited patiently for their husbands, and in the fulfilment of time grew old and were accorded the dignity that old age brings in China. But the mountains always separated them.

In Yangcheng Gladys found life an immense and endless adventure. The pastoral mountain background was so broad and vivid; she was not merely an observer, an interested traveller passing across an alien landscape: she was an integral part of the whole, and this realization was a source of endless satisfaction to her. Until Jeannie Lawson quarrelled with her, she was fully and completely absorbed in her way of living.

The quarrel was absurd, no more than a slight difference of opinion, but its results were unforeseeable. By now, after nearly eight months at the Inn of Eight Happinesses, Gladys was accustomed to Jeannie's quick outbursts of spleen. Usually she could circumvent them, keeping out of the way until they had boiled over and evaporated. Jeannie liked to go for a walk every afternoon; more often than not Gladys went with her, but she was trying desperately to become proficient in the Chinese language; she spent several hours a day swotting up sentences and words she had written phonetically in a notebook. On this occasion, when Jeannie Lawson asked her to come for a walk, Gladys begged to be excused; she wanted to go on studying Chinese. Mrs Lawson flew immediately into a rage. Gladys could not calm her. She tried to explain that all she wanted to do was to understand more Chinese; if only she could learn the language, she could be more use to Mrs Lawson, more help at the inn.

Jeannie was not listening. With uncompromising suddenness her temper lifted to boiling point. The harsh words came out in a cataract. If Gladys couldn't bother to come for a walk, then she needn't bother to stay there. As far as she was concerned, Gladys could leave, and the sooner the better. In fact she could leave right that minute. Indeed, she would help her to leave. She stormed out and returned with an armful of Gladys's possessions, which she proceeded to throw at her. Weeping, Gladys fled to Yang and hid in his kitchen. Together they crouched there and listened to the tirade, while odd garments were flung down into the courtyard. Yang was very concerned. Like all Chinese, he respected old age, and Jeannie Lawson was most certainly old enough to receive ancestral treatment.

"Perhaps it is better you do as she demands," he advised anxiously. "Leave us for a little while. Go back to Tsehchow and visit the Mission there. Those ladies will be glad to give you a little holiday. Stay there for a time and then return. She will send for you after a day or two; of that I am certain. The old one will have forgotten her rage and we shall all be happy again."

"But how can I get there?" sobbed Gladys. "It's two days' journey. I can't walk all that distance."

"I will arrange with a friend of mine to provide a mule and a man to go with you," said Yang.

"But supposing I never come back?"

At that moment one of her own battered suitcases flew over the balustrade and skidded along the courtyard.

Yang spread his hands. "We both understand the honourable old one," he said gently. "She will forget and forgive. She likes you and she needs you. Perhaps it is better you make her feel that you are necessary. . . ." His shoulders lifted and his eyes were speculative.

"All right," said Gladys, wiping her eyes. "I'll go."

The shudder of a heavily slammed door overhead meant that Jeannie Lawson had retired to her room. It was Gladys's opportunity. She rescued the suitcase and packed her few things into it. Yang carried it to the gate with her and down the street to his friend who owned a mule. For a few cash the bargain was struck. Still sniffing, Gladys hoisted herself aboard the mule. It was a sad journey. Not even old Mrs Smith at Tsehchow Mission could cheer her up.

"We all know Jeannie," she said. "She flies off the handle for a day or two, then the whole thing is forgotten. You have a nice little holiday here, my dear, and then go back, and, you mark my words, Jeannie will be overjoyed to see you."

"But what if she won't have me back?" said Gladys, voicing her deepest and most secret dread. "I've no money. I'm stuck here in the middle of China and I don't want to go home. I just can't go back to England."

"Now don't worry, dear," said Mrs Smith soothingly. "Everything will turn out all right. Just don't worry your head. We know Jeannie. She might even send a messenger for you."

Her prophecy was accurate. Three days later, in the early morning, a messenger did arrive, but from the Tsehchow yamen. He gabbled excitedly to Mrs Smith; Gladys could see her brow furrow as she listened. She looked a little agitated.

"The story seems quite silly," she said, "but it looks as if Jeannie's had an accident."

A premonition of disaster overwhelmed Gladys. "What does he say?"

"He says that Jeannie Lawson is somewhere on the road, and—and——"

66

"And what?" cried Gladys in a voice full of apprehension.

"That she's dying," concluded Mrs Smith. "Really I don't know what to make of this."

"But where?" cried Gladys, distraught. "Where is she? I must go to her."

In quick phrases Mrs Smith cross-examined the man. He shrugged his shoulders. He was simply repeating something that had been passed forward by relays of disinterested and not very accurate messengers.

Gladys was in tears. "It's my fault," she wept. "I shouldn't have left her! I must go back at once!"

"Now don't upset yourself, my dear," said Mrs Smith gently. "We'll get you a mule and someone to go with you, and you can go off and find her at once. I'm sure she'll be all right. I know from experience how distorted these messages can become."

For a second time Gladys scurried round, gathering her possessions together. Astride her mule she jogged out through the gateway and turned to wave goodbye to Mrs Smith. As she passed him, the gateman took off his straw hat and clapped it on her head.

"You will never keep hope if the sun beats on your brain," he called. "Good luck!"

More than any other thing on this journey she remembered the wild roses that covered the mountainsides and filled the air with perfume as they clopped up through the foothills. She spent that night at the village of Chowtsun. From the garbled report which had reached Tsehchow, she knew that Jeannie Lawson had left Yangcheng and gone into the mountains. It was no use therefore returning to that city, so she and the muleteer took a side trail detouring through walled villages, asking everywhere for news of the old lady. No one had any word of her. On the fourth day it was getting dark and they were approaching the small, walled town of Chin Shui. They had made a wide circle around Yangcheng and were now returning to the main mule trail farther on. They passed a man leaving the city and repeated the question they had asked a hundred times.

Yes, indeed he had heard of this old foreign one. She was lying very ill at an inn in Chin Shui. She was probably already dead, but they would still find her body if they hurried.

They went quickly on into the city. They had no trouble finding the inn where the 'foreign devil' lay. It was current gossip amongst the townspeople. They passed through the outer door, and there in the open courtyard under the balcony they found Jeannie Lawson. The sight of her horrified Gladys. She was lying near a heap of coal against a wall. She was black with blood and coal dust, and at first Gladys thought she was dead. But when she ran to her crying, "Jeannie, Jeannie!" Mrs Lawson turned her head slightly. Her lips moved.

"Is that you, Gladys?" she whispered. "Thank God you've come."

Tears streamed down the girl's face as she tried to make her more comfortable. It was almost dark. She stood up and shouted imperiously, "Bring lanterns, so I can see. Bring lanterns at once! Do you hear!"

The servants of the inn came scurrying at the scolding of this second 'foreign devil' come to plague them. The globes of lighted paper lanterns went bobbing through the darkness. They brought hot water. Gladys bathed Jeannie's open cuts and, little by little, coaxed the story from the half-delirious woman. Apparently, the day after Gladys's departure, still in her temper, she had left the Inn at Yengcheng in the charge of the cook, hired a mule and had set off westwards. She had arrived at Chin Shui and hired an upstairs room at this inn. In the darkness she had walked out on to the balcony and shouted down to the cook to make her some scrambled eggs. She had put out her hand to lean on the balustrade, which in Yangcheng fenced off the upper balcony. But there was no balustrade; it had rotted away long ago. Over-balancing, she pitched forwards and downwards, crashing heavily on to the pile of coal twenty feet below.

As Gladys bathed and bandaged her cuts with pieces torn off her underclothes, she perceived how badly she was injured. She seemed to have broken the fingers of both hands. Her face and body were badly grazed and coal-grit was embedded in all the cuts and grazes. What was far worse, however, was the fact that she appeared to have injured her spine, for the slightest movement racked her with pain. Her scream as she fell had brought the Chinese in the inn running to her assistance. They had lifted her off the heap of coal and placed her under the veranda. They did not know what else to do, and the old lady, dazed with shock and pain, could not tell them. The Chinese, too, were scared of the 'old one with the white hair'. They were quite certain she would die within a few hours, so they left her alone. From time to time they gave her water, but not food. What was the use of wasting food on a dying 'foreign devil'? Besides, she didn't want any; she was quite delirious.

That she was dying, Gladys also was prepared to believe, but she did everything she could to make her more comfortable. The nearest European doctor was six days' journey away at Luan, and in Jeannie Lawson's condition and at her age it was unthinkable that she could stand such a journey.

For six weeks Gladys stayed in the inn, and scarcely left Jeannie alone for a minute. Her condition hardly seemed to improve at all. The wounds healed, but she was still in pain, and at times she seemed mentally deranged. At the end of six weeks Gladys decided that somehow or other she *had* to get her to the hospital at Luan. Unless she managed this, Jeannie would never get well, she decided. With the help of the cook and a local merchant she hired two mules and secured a thick quilt between them. She packed it with straw, and put bedding on top. It made a comfortable litter. With an attendant muleteer—the one who had accompanied her from Tsehchow had left long ago—she said goodbye to the friends she had made at Chin Shui and set off on the long journey to Luan. They spent the next two evenings at Chinese inns on the mule trail, and at each halt Gladys supervised the removal of the sick woman. Then they came to Yangcheng, and it was not really a happy homecoming.

They found that Yang was still managing the Inn of Eight Happinesses with success. In his old age he had found a job which both comforted and amused him. Gladys listened to his evening story-telling, and discovered without much surprise that it was Noah who fed the loaves and fishes to the five thousand, as he was sailing past the coast of Galilee in his Ark. Yang had a fondness for Noah and his mercantile adventures which nothing could eradicate. He was always willing to credit a miracle or two to him; and even though he accepted Gladys's correction with good grace and a bland nod of his head, she had a feeling that he quickly restored Noah to favour as soon as her back was turned. He accepted Mrs Lawson's condition with a fatalism which was typical of the Chinese. The gods had willed it so. She would soon be at peace with her honourable ancestors. He was perfectly happy to go on running the inn until Gladys returned.

When they reached Luan, travelling in the same laborious manner, Jeannie Lawson was admitted to the hospital at once. There was an English doctor working in the wards, and two British nursing sisters. For four weeks more Gladys stayed with Jeannie, living in a room at the hospital.

The doctor was quite frank with her. "She has injured her spine, I'm afraid, and there is little we can do for her," he said. "She's seventy-four years old. The shock of the fall and the injury have unbalanced her mind. She'll have periods of coherence, but slowly she will become more and more paralysed, and then she will die. We don't quite know when. A few weeks, a couple of months? She's lived a long and useful life, and you must not grieve about it."

That afternoon Gladys sat by her friend's bedside and held her hand. It was one of Jeannie's moments of lucidity, and perhaps she divined the truth from the look of deep pity in the girl's eyes. Impulsively she whispered, "Oh, Gladys, let's go back to Yangcheng. Please take me home!"

Gladys looked down at the worn face of the woman who had befriended her, opened the gates of China to her; this woman, now old and dying, who had been seized with a spirit of service to God so long ago. She must have been very pretty when she was young, Gladys thought, as she looked into the eyes which were still a deep, clear blue. All the years of her life Jeannie had spent fighting to establish the word of her Christian God in this alien land. Her husband had died and she had been left alone, but she had still worked on. Now she was so far divided from the people and the land which bore her that she called a tiny hilltop city in southern Shansi, 'home'! Yet this was how she wished to end. Gladys knew that Jeannie Lawson would desire no one to shed tears for her. If she had willed it, she could have remained in Britain and dwindled her life away at a guest house in Bognor Regis or a private nursing-home in Dundee. She had chosen this more adventurous, this more gallant finale of her own free will.

"I'll take you home today, Jeannie," said Gladys gently. "I'll go and see about the mule litter now. We'll go off home together."

They set out three hours later.

Yang was pleased to see them back. Gladys did not realize they had so many friends, as they all came round to greet her. Jeannie was happier, but her condition grew slowly worse. The slow, paralysing decay which the doctor had predicted ran its course. Day by day she died a little.

The last night in November she raved wildly. There was a full moon, and its light poured in brightly through the open window. A little wind with a growl of winter in its throat rattled the shutters. The dipping yellow light of the lamp, fed from its castor-oil reservoir, wavered uncertainly. Gladys's shadow when she moved to tend the sick woman was a dark spider on the walls. The old woman's face was sunken, but her lips moved, endlessly repeating in disjointed phrases the great rhetoric that had guided her life from the beginning:

"*The light of the body is the eye: if therefore thine eye be single, thy whole body shall be full of light. But if thine eye be evil, thy whole body shall be full of darkness. If therefore the light that is in thee be darkness, how great is that darkness. . . .*"

Gladys went out on to the veranda and looked up at the bright, high moon sailing against the wash of clear sky.

The moonlight touched the tiles of the pagodas above the city walls with brightness. It accentuated the knife-edge ridges of the far-off peaks; it lit the gauze-like wisps of mist, wreathing them in a soft radiance. She knew now that Mrs Lawson was dying. It had been plain to Yang for several days, and through him they had ordered the plain black coffin which stood in the courtyard below. Gladys looked down upon it. How this Chinese habit of producing the coffin before life had flickered out of the corpse would have horrified her at other periods of her life. Now she accepted it as normal custom. Wryly, she reflected how much she had changed in her short year in Shansi.

Jeannie Lawson was dying. That fact she had to accept. She rested her chin on her elbow and propped her elbow on the balcony. Yet one was lucky even to be born. What enormous chances there were against it, when one considered the billions and billions of life-cells in the world: animal and vegetable structures, the vertebrates, anthozoa, coelenterata, the dead, and the non-dead existing upon the earth. In the permutations of cellular structure, the chances against ever being born at all must work out at an astronomical figure. To be born a human being with a soul, that indeed was a God-given gift. Jeannie had possessed the gift. She had savoured the golden luxury of simply being alive, enjoyed every year allotted to her. It was sad that the gift was now withdrawn; that she was sinking back into the cradle of matter beyond all practical knowledge.

Gladys mused for many minutes there in the moonlight over the perplexities of life and death, and indeed over her own situation. When Mrs Lawson died she would be alone in this wild, mountainous province of Shansi. The rent for the year had been paid, but Mrs Lawson's tiny income would stop. Gladys had no more than a few pence in all the world, yet at that moment she felt no fear, only a great calm, a new dignity. But she did not want Jeannie to die at night in the darkness; she was a little afraid of that. In the daylight it would be more bearable. Jeannie would prefer it that way; she knew that also.

She heard Mrs Lawson's voice suddenly soft and resigned inside the room:

"*Come unto me, all ye that labour and are heavy laden, and I will give you rest. Take my yoke upon you and learn of me: for I am meek and lowly of heart; and ye shall find rest unto your souls. For my yoke is easy and my burden is light.*"

Next morning, the sun rose up in the east and the day came down from over the mountain peaks; and at noon Jeannie Lawson died.

CHAPTER SIX

To GLADYS her God was a suit of chain-mail, proof against
any arrow or bullet the mortal world could fire at her.
Her faith was durable; it was like a warm blanket on a cold
night, medicine when she was sick, food on the table, a roof
over her head, a bed in which she could lie enfolded and
secure. None of the intellectual problems of the theologians
ever troubled her; the fears and dilemmas of the doubting
intellectuals blew above her head at stratospheric level.
Legs gripping an earthbound mule, she rode forward
cheerful as a London sparrow, strong as Richard Coeur de
Lion, in resolution redoubtable as the Krak des Chevaliers.
The word of God was plain for all to read. She knew her
task was to scatter that word like seed through her adopted
town and through the mountain villages. In the pages of
the faded black book she carried everywhere she had been
bequeathed all the emotions, the philosophies and glories
that her mind could encompass. And many were the
strange vicissitudes this faith was to lead her into during
those early years in Yangcheng.

The weeks following Jeannie Lawson's death were
amongst the most precarious that she ever experienced in
China. She was saved from possible disaster by two of the
unlikeliest people: a cook and a Mandarin. Yang laid
Jeannie into her coffin and sealed her down, and because it
was a solemn and reverent occasion, he induced an old
man who owned a plate camera in the city to come and take
a picture. In the courtyard, with the muleteers and neighbours and the converts and a few odd children all anxious
to have their photograph taken, they assembled decorously
around the coffin of the 'old one', and the shutter clicked.
The old man hurried away to develop the picture. That it
is reproduced in this book today is due to the fact that
Gladys sent it home to her mother in Edmonton, for, had
she kept it, it would certainly have been lost for ever.

Now she discussed their financial position with Yang. Their rent was paid for a year. The few cash they earned every night from the muleteers just about covered their overheads, but there was no margin of profit and hardly a livelihood. Still, the Mission was in being, and Gladys had no intention of abandoning the Inn until she was forced to. Her Chinese was improving daily; she was now fairly fluent in the mountain dialects of the Yangcheng district. Each province around had its own dialect; villagers twenty miles from each other in the mountains often could not understand the other's speech. They rarely moved from the place where they were born; they knew nothing but their own dialect and their own folklore. In the years that followed, Gladys found it necessary to speak five distinctive dialects from that one province.

It was several weeks after Jeannie's death that Yang evolved the idea of Gladys visiting the Mandarin of Yang-cheng to pay her respects.

"But why?" she demanded. "The Mandarin doesn't want to see me. I don't particularly want to see him. It's a waste of everybody's time."

She did not realize at that moment the complicated system of taxes, licences and residential passes upon which the economy of the province was based. Jeannie Lawson's experience had protected her from them; she had performed all official duties.

"But your time of mourning is over," insisted Yang. "You should put on your best clothes and pay your respects to him. It's necessary. It is a courtesy."

"But I've never met a Mandarin in my life," protested Gladys. "I don't know what to say to him. How many times do you bow? Who speaks first? You go and find out these things and I'll consider it; but I can't afford a new robe to go in, anyway."

Yang shuffled off into the city and returned an hour later looking very crestfallen. Nobody, apparently, knew the laws governing a 'foreign devil' woman's mode of conduct when meeting the Mandarin. Everybody else, from coolie to Government official, was covered by firm protocol;

there were so many bows, so many obeisances. But Gladys was a strange species. Dejectedly Yang sighed, and explained that obviously a special law would have to be passed for her, and until it was, she obviously could not be granted any audience with the Mandarin whatsoever. It was regrettable, but for the time being she would have to remain that unrespected and inferior being—a woman. Gladys sensed his disappointment at her lack of importance.

The Mandarin of Yangcheng was a powerful figure. In that part of mountainous southern Shansi, the chief city was Tsehchow. Several days' journey away, grouped in a rough circle around the capital, were the four smaller sister cities: Yangcheng, Chin Shui, Kaoping and Ling-chuang, tiny walled citadels nestling in the high mountains. The Mandarin of Yangcheng ruled his city and district by decree from the governor and warlord at T'ai Yuan, the capital of Shansi far to the north. The government at T'ai Yuan owed nominal allegiance to the Nationalists. Yang-cheng lay deep in the mountains. News travelled only as fast as a man could walk. The Mandarin as Magistrate commanded the power of freedom or imprisonment, life and death over all the people in his territory. In a feudal society he was an absolute lord and treated with obeisance. That he should make the first move towards the strange woman who had elected to live under his authority was, therefore, all the more surprising.

Gladys was busy in an upstairs room when she heard the commotion down in the courtyard. She looked over the balustrade to see Yang running for the outer door. At the gate he turned and shouted up at her:

"The Mandarin's coming! The Mandarin's coming!"

He sounded very frightened; she saw his pigtail swing as he disappeared through the gate, and it was the last she saw of him for three hours, for although Yang had been insistent that she should meet the Mandarin, his own courage failed him completely when it came to the fulfil-ment of the wish.

Gladys patted her bun into place at the back of her head, and quickly smoothed her rather grubby tunic into place.

It was awkward that he should catch her like this, quite unprepared, but it was his own fault if he didn't give her proper notice, she decided.

She ran down the stairs and into the courtyard just as the retinue began to troop in. It was so magnificent that she halted in mid-stride, frozen with a mixture of awe and delight. Coolies bore the sedan chair, curtained against prying eyes. Around it were grouped the Mandarin's clerks in robes of dark blue, while gathered at a respectful distance were other retainers; a backcloth of spectacular, learned-looking gentlemen with thin faces, tight skullcaps and black almond eyes.

A clerk stepped forward and carefully opened the door of the chair, his arm proffered to help the Mandarin out. Gladys's eyes were as round as brandy balls as he emerged through the curtained door. He was quite magnificent. He was tall, with black hair, a pale ivory face and a moustache which drooped at the corners. His wide-sleeved gown fell smoothly to pointed black shoes. His long, glossy, jet-black queue hung down his back.

His bright black eyes caught hers, and she closed her open mouth and gulped, bowing low. When she came up for air he was standing looking down at her with a faintly worried expression on his face, his retainers grouped like a vase of flowers behind him. As there appeared to be no possible topic of conversation between them Gladys decided the best thing to do was to make another deep bow. She hinged over at the waist, counted five, returned to the perpendicular, and decided that she had been subservient enough for even the most high-born, worshipful Mandarin.

"I come to ask your advice," he said at last.

"Oh!" said Gladys. She knew it was not a very intelligent comment, but she was so stupefied by his appearance she could think of nothing else to say. She was surprised to hear her own voice.

"You are aware that for many generations the custom of foot-binding has been practised in this province?" he went on.

"Has it?" she murmured. His Mandarin Chinese was

77

pure and beautifully evocative. She felt pleased with herself that she had no difficulty in understanding him.

"The feet of females are bound soon after they are born," he explained.

"Oh!" said Gladys again. She realized that she was not taking a very virile part in the conversation; she knew a little about the custom of foot-binding, but as she had no idea in which direction this discussion was leading, she did not know how to react.

"Now we have received a decree from the Central Government that all foot-binding must cease immediately," he said.

"Have you?"

"Every woman in this province has bound feet. There-fore, someone with big feet, unbound feet, must undertake the work of inspection."

With a sudden twinge of alarm Gladys looked down at her own size threes. In England they were reckoned small; here they were gargantuan.

"Obviously, no man can undertake this work. It must be a woman. You have friends in the outside provinces who would know of such a woman. Will you write to them and ask them if they could send such a woman for this pur-pose?"

"I will do that with pleasure," said Gladys automatically. A momentary flutter of panic gripped her as she realized that, with the exception of Mrs Smith at Tsehchow, she did not know anyone in all China, but she sternly repressed the thought, and hoped the quake of fear was not repro-duced on her face.

"It is not a well-paid position," explained the Mandarin. "The wages will be one measure of millet a day and a farthing to buy vegetables. A mule will be supplied to make the journey out to the lonely villages, and a guard of two soldiers will accompany the female. You will find such a woman for me? She is most necessary."

"I will do my utmost," repeated Gladys and, deciding that convention demanded it, she bowed again.

Everyone bowed to everyone else, or so it seemed to her.

It was all very polite. The Mandarin got back into his sedan chair, and the deputation moved out of the courtyard. Gladys felt rather breathless. She would have been even more breathless had she been aware that she had just secured for herself the job of official foot inspector of the Yangcheng province of Shansi; become in fact a humble and lowly servant of his High and Mighty Eminence, Mandarin of Yangcheng. She was unaware that she was to attain this new rank until several weeks later. In an effort to obtain a female foot inspector she wrote letters all over China: to the Mission in Tientsin, to Luan, to Hong Kong, to Shanghai, to wherever she thought there might be a Christian community. The replies were almost identical. Firstly, any suitable girl, with large feet, could not speak the dialect; secondly, she could not, or did not wish to, ride a mule; thirdly, she did not wish, or was not able, to exist on a staple diet of millet. Girls with big feet or little feet, from Hong Kong or Tientsin or other parts of China, liked rice! They could not enjoy life without rice. There was no rice in Yangcheng or its province, and Gladys did not think mules would be used to carry sacks of this special diet across the mountains for anyone as lowly as a foot inspector. The girls, it seemed, were not prepared to face a diet of grain for all the Mandarins in Shansi.

Approximately two months later, complete with his retinue, the Mandarin swept once again into the courtyard of the Inn of Eight Happinesses. He dismounted from his sedan chair, and his followers grouped in a serious semi-circle behind him.

"You have not found a woman?" he asked accusingly.

Gladys decided that this time she would omit the bowings and scrapings. "I am still trying," she said humbly.

The Mandarin's dark bird's wings of eyebrows contracted slightly.

"Why have you not found a girl?" he said coldly.

Gladys explained all the reasons put forward by the Missions. Could not ride a mule; did not want to ride a mule; could not eat grain; thought the place was too far away and too lonely.

With a contemptuous flick of his fan the Mandarin silenced her. "Then it must be *you* who becomes foot inspector," he announced.

"Me!" repeated Gladys in a strangulated voice. At moments like these her conversation seemed to fail her.

"You are the only woman in the province with big feet. You must take the job!"

Gladys's mouth opened and closed again. She searched in her mind for some conversational straw on which to cling. "But I'm a Christian . . . I'm not Chinese. I don't know anything about feet. . . ."

"It is very simple. You will travel from village to village and tell the people of the Government's decree. You will assemble the women in the centre of the village or in their houses and inspect their feet. If the feet of the infants are bound, you will unbind them. You will report any hindrance on the part of any village elder to me and I will deal with it. You will be armed with my authority and report to me personally. The Central Government is most anxious to stamp out this reprehensible habit and you must start your duties at once. Do you agree?"

As he talked, Gladys's thoughts fell into place. She wondered why she hadn't thought of it before. A mule out to the most distant villages? A guard to protect her? It was an opportunity without parallel for her to visit every part of the province, preaching wherever she went. But would he accept this? She did not know whether the protocol allowed her to suggest 'conditions' to the Mandarin; she decided to risk his displeasure.

"You must realize, Excellency," she said, "that if I accept this position I shall try and convert the people of this province to Christianity wherever I go!"

There was a short silence. The retainers in the background appeared frozen in horror. She wondered if she had committed an unpardonable error. Then he said quietly: "I care nothing for your religion or to whom you preach. This is a matter for the conscience of each individual. But it is important that you should do this work. The Central Government is impatient."

Gladys was knowledgeable enough about local conditions by that time to realize that the Central Government was probably demanding facts and figures about the incidence of foot-binding from this mountain province. She smiled inwardly. This was certainly something to write home about; a foot inspector on the payroll of the Mandarin. Her mother would never believe it.

She bowed low. "I am anxious to be of assistance," she said. "I will gladly accept the position."

As she straightened up she caught a gleam of amusement in his eye.

"Thank you," he said. "The mule and the soldiers will be ready for you tomorrow morning and whenever you need them from now onwards. I will you good fortune."

Everyone bowed and smiled. The important 'foreign devil' from across the sea had consented to act as the Mandarin's representative. A curt reply could now be dispatched to that stupid Under-Secretary back in T'ai Yuan. The crisis was averted. Everyone's 'face' was preserved. The deputation then took its leave.

Yang came out to peer with a sort of curious terror at Gladys. "You are now important," he said. "You work for the yamen, you are the Mandarin's personal servant." He bowed low and humbly. It was the first time Gladys had ever really impressed him.

"Important? On that salary?" exclaimed Gladys. "A measure of millet and a farthing a day! I shan't get rich on that, shall I?"

"It is an honour," insisted Yang, determined to squeeze every vicarious drop of civic pride out of the appointment. "You are the Mandarin's personal foot inspector."

"The Mandarin's personal foot inspector!" she echoed. The Gilbert and Sullivan flavour of the entire situation suddenly overwhelmed her and she began to quake with laughter. She hooted with mirth while Yang looked at her in horror. He shook his head and shrugged his shoulders; as he went back to his cooking pots he was still muttering to himself about the conclusive madness of all 'foreign devils', especially the female of that species.

Gladys's journeys to the distant villages did not start at once. There was a great deal of inspection to be done within Yangcheng itself and in the houses and cave dwellings outside the city walls. What Yang had implied was true. The official blessing of the yamen plus the physical presence of two rather grubby soldiers gave her an importance she had never experienced or expected. People stood up when she spoke to them. Babies' feet were unwrapped at record speed when she demanded it.

She never forgot the first village at which she arrived as official foot inspector. It stood near a fast-running river pounding through a narrow gorge; the houses were single storey, built of rock and mud and with green tiles. Dusty little tracks connected them, and in the dark rooms the floors were of beaten earth with only the brick communal bed raised from the ground. On the rough tables stood blue-patterned chinaware and the inevitable chopsticks of wood. Children were everywhere: small, grimy, noisy, quilt-padded infants, brown-faced and clamorous, some still at their mother's breast; others seething like human foam around the flanks of her mule. It was an isolated, pleasant village. The mountains rose steeply all round, but in the settlement the prune and peach trees were in blossom and little fields of yellow mustard seed, dark green cotton and bright green millet stalks terraced one face of the mountainside.

The villagers began to assemble as soon as they passed through the gate. The soldiers inquired after the Village Elder. When he appeared they told him of the Mandarin's decree. He was an old, shrivelled man with a thin goatee beard; a peasant whose experience and age had elevated him to the post which made him responsible to the Mandarin. He nodded his head seriously as he listened. The village 'crier' was dispatched to tell the villagers to assemble in the square. There was a little difficulty about it; peasants had to be fetched from the fields, from their houses, from tending their animals. With everyone present, the Elder informed them in a high, cracked voice that foot binding would cease from now on; that the feet of children still able to recover would be unbound. The Mandarin had given these orders. The soldiers, who thoroughly enjoyed their small authority, then reiterated the proclamation, and made it quite clear that anyone who disobeyed the order would at once be thrown into prison, which would be very uncomfortable indeed for them.

They then turned to tell Gladys that it was time for the inspection. She did not know quite what to do, but, to make some sort of move, walked across the square towards the first small house she could see. A crowd gathered behind her. Reassured by the raucous presence of her two soldiers, she went in through the open door. The soldiers waited outside. The house was clean and neat, but there was no furniture, only a few cooking pots and utensils; the quilted bedding was piled on the brick k'ang where the family slept. A small dark-eyed girl, aged about three, clung to her mother's trousers and looked nervously up at Gladys. A single glance was sufficient to tell that her feet were bound.

"That one," said Gladys, trying to insert a note of authority into her voice. "Unbind her feet!"

Two women neighbours and a grandmother had now appeared in the room. The mother took the child on her lap and all four women began to undo the bandages.

To cover her own nervousness, Gladys maintained a running commentary, which she improvised as each fold of cloth fell away.

"That's it. Come on now. Hurry up! If God intended little girls to have horrible stubby little feet, He'd have made them like that in the first place, wouldn't He? Feet are to walk with, not to shuffle up and down with, aren't they? I don't care if the husbands say you should do it or not. They should try it sometime, and see if they like hobbling about on little club feet. Any other man who tells you to do it goes to prison at once; that's the law now. . . ."

The last bandages dropped, revealing tiny white feet with toes bent downwards and up into the soles.

"Look at those feet!" exclaimed Gladys. "Disgraceful,

absolutely disgraceful! How d'you expect the poor child to walk properly with those feet?"

She almost pushed the women away, and, kneeling down, gently prised the toes up and away from the sole. The child regarded her with wide, timid eyes.

"There," said Gladys softly. "Five little piggies all ready to go to market."

She massaged the foot tenderly. Suddenly there was a quick liquid giggle of sound from the child, who wriggled with delight.

The spell was broken. The women came closer, chattering happily. In the years that followed Gladys was to realize what an independent, courageous group these mountain women were. Even now they were friendly. "Yes, it is a good law," they said. Everyone now wanted to help in the foot massage; everyone wanted to tell of the pain and the trouble their own feet had given them for the past ten years. One of the neighbours rushed off to the next house to explain what had to be done, and the news went round the village before Gladys had finished her first examination. As she proceeded she soon found housewives dutifully exhibiting all their little girls with unbound feet. What part the soldiers' cheerfully repeated order "Unbind feet or go to prison!" played in this social reform it is difficult to know, but everyone was very amiable.

Gladys stayed that night at the house of the Elder, and the rest of her journey through the villages saw this scene repeated many times.

Many of the villages in the remote valleys were isolated from the outside world. The earth was carefully harboured in terraces; they possessed cattle and pigs and chickens; they wove their own cotton and woollen cloth. They were self sufficient, growing their own food, making their own clothes, retaining a folklore handed down to them through a thousand generations. They were simple, kindly people, possessing a cheerfulness, fortitude and calm which Gladys had never encountered before, and which she came to understand and admire.

Her visits became events of considerable excitement; she

brought news of the outside world, such as it was; and as a storyteller she commanded their devotion and admiration. The children clamoured behind her old grey mule as she jogged in through the gateway, and the soldiers shouted and waved to old friends as they made for the inn or the Elder's house where they were staying. In the evenings the villagers crowded in to learn the new songs which jostled along with a lilt and intonation quite different from their own, and to listen to the stories she told of a man called Jesus Christ whose honourable ancestor was the great God who lived in the clouds, high above. It appeared to them that this man Jesus had lived in a simple society closely akin to their own. He had encountered much the same problems as they did. He had obeyed roughly the same rules of civilized conduct as they did. He was indeed an enthralling person, and the official foot inspector's supply of stories seemed inexhaustible.

These, for Gladys, were the years of endless content. With the Inn of Eight Happinesses as a base, and a small Christian community growing up around it, her wanderings through the mountains were always adventures. The weeks passed into months and the months into years, and there was a harvest of happiness to be gathered from each day. Rumours of other happenings occasionally came over the mountains, brought by the muleteers, but it was news of a different world, a world too far away to matter, a world beyond the broad barrier of the Yellow River, a world almost as far away as the moon. Living was conditioned and divided by the seasons. In winter the frost would rime on the tilted roofs of the pagodas. the mule teams would steam as they clopped up the street; breath was a gusty white mist blown on the air; there was ice on the pails, long dripping icicles hanging from gargoyles' noses on the temple roofs, and one never took off trousers and coat, padded warmly with cotton wool, from December to March. When the snow came howling over the mountains from the north, it packed down in drifts into the valleys and gorges, filled the streets of the city three and four feet deep, built itself into fantastic, wind-sculptured cornices in the walls. Sound was deadened; echo departed from the valleys, and nowhere in all the hundreds of miles of the mountain country did anything move except the crashing avalanches and the snow-laden wind. Life came to a standstill.

You hibernated under a thick cocoon of snow. You sat round your k'ang—fed by coal carried in from seams to be found everywhere on the mountainsides—mended your clothes, darned and sewed and made new shoes and thought of what the spring might bring. The mules in the stables swished their tails, looked out at the blinding white world with liquid brown eyes, neighed gratefully when you heaped more fodder into their bin. Children were conceived. Old men dreamed by the warm stove. Toothless grandmothers grew impatient for hot food, and gathered the children round to tell them stories invented by other grandmothers a thousand years before. You visited no one, talked little; you sat secure in your winter world with enough grain to last you out, and waited patiently for the snows to pass.

And then the spring came, putting the new-old ache into bone and blood, fusing such an awareness of beauty on the retina of the eyeballs, and the cells of the mind, that the finite world with its carapace of sky, its jagged spurs of rock, its rushing, gorge-choked waters, its flowers along the river banks, its helpless baby mules and clucking golden balls of newborn chicks, and almond-eyed mites that bawled and gurgled; its maidens suddenly aware of men, and young men suddenly aware of mystery—this world became such a place of shining glory that Gladys Aylward knew instinctively that only a God of infinite pity, love and gentle humour could have conceived it so.

In this wide terrain of high mountains and deep valleys, where the material way of living was meagre and hard, she grew to maturity. All that had gone before was a preparation for this and this only a preparation for what was to come. She understood that here was the stable platform upon which forty centuries of human peasantry and pomp, exigent passion and lunatic aspiration had been acted out; that any religion which attempted to act as a chastity belt, or which was thin, humourless and arid, would be rejected by these simple mountain folk as they had rejected every other form of invasion. The religion she preached was a simple one. It told of strength through humility, wisdom through love, and life everlasting through faith.

•   •   •   •   •

There arrived during her second year at Yangcheng a pleasant young man called Lu-Yung-Cheng. He was a convert sent from Tsehchow by Mrs Smith, who said she would pay his salary, which worked out at ninepence a month. He was useful if only because he could keep an ear to Yang's romantic interpretation of the Scriptures. It was about two weeks after he arrived, that he and Gladys were standing in the courtyard when the messenger from the yamen rushed in waving a piece of scarlet paper. He gabbled at such a rate that Gladys found it difficult to understand him.

"What's the paper for, anyway?" she asked Lu-Yung-Cheng.

"It's an official summons from the yamen," said Lu-Yung-Cheng nervously. "A riot has broken out in the men's prison."

Gladys was really not very interested. "Oh, has it?" she said.

"You must come at once," said the messenger urgently. "It is most important!"

Gladys stared at him. "But what's the riot in the prison got to do with us? It can't have anything to do with my foot inspection."

"You must come at once!" reiterated the messenger loudly. "It is an official order." He hopped from one foot to the other in impatience.

Lu-Yung-Cheng looked at her doubtfully. "When that piece of red paper arrives from the yamen, you must go." There was a nervous tremor in his voice.

"All right, *you* go and see what it's all about," said Gladys. "It's obviously a man's job. I know nothing about prisons. I've never been in one in my life. Though I really don't see what you're supposed to do."

87

She could see from Lu-Yung-Cheng's face that the prospect did not appeal to him.

"Hurry, please hurry!" cried the messenger.

Reluctantly, Lu-Yung-Cheng trailed after him to the door. Gladys watched him reach the opening, take a quick look behind at her, then dodge swiftly to the left as the messenger turned to the right. She could hear the sound of his running feet as he tore down the road.

Within two seconds the messenger discovered his loss. He stormed back through the doorway crying "Ai-ee-ee!" and shaking his fist in rage. He raced across the courtyard towards Gladys, a little fat man without dignity.

"Now *you* must come," he shouted. "This is an official paper. You are ordered to come. You *must* come. Now! With me! If you refuse you will get into trouble!"

"All right," she said mildly. "I'll come. I really don't know what's the matter with Lu-Yung-Cheng. He must feel ill or something. But I certainly don't see what a riot in the prison has to do with me. . . ."

They hurried up the road and in through the East Gate. A few yards inside the gate the blank outside wall of the prison flanked the main street. From the other side came an unholy cacophony: screams, shouts, yells, the most horrible noises.

"My goodness!" said Gladys, "it certainly is a riot, isn't it?"

The Governor of the prison, small, pale-faced, his mouth set into a worried line, met her at the entrance. Behind were grouped half a dozen of his staff.

"We are glad you have come," he said quickly. "There is a riot in the prison; the convicts are killing each other."

"So I can hear," she said. "But what am I here for? I'm only the missionary woman. Why don't you send the soldiers in to stop it?"

"The convicts are murderers, bandits, thieves," said the Governor, his voice trembling. "The soldiers are frightened. There are not enough of them."

"I'm sorry to hear that," said Gladys. "But what do you

expect me to do about it? I don't even know why you asked me to come. . . ."

The Governor took one step forward. "You must go in and stop the fighting!"

"I must go in . . . !" Gladys's mouth dropped open; her eyes rounded in utter amazement. "Me! Me go in there! Are you mad! If I went in they'd kill me!"

The Governor's eyes were fixed on her with hypnotic intensity. "But how can they kill you? You tell everybody that you have come here because you have the living God inside you. . . ."

The words bubbled out of the Governor's mouth, his lips twisted in the acuteness of distress. Gladys felt a small, cold shiver down her back. When she swallowed, her throat seemed to have a gritty texture.

"The—living God?" she stammered.

"You preach it everywhere—in the streets and villages. If you preach the truth, if your God protects you from harm, then you can stop this riot."

Gladys stared at him. Her mind raced round in bewilderment, searching for some fact that would explain her beliefs to this simple, deluded man. A little cell in her mind kept blinking on and off with an urgent semaphore message: 'It's true! You have been preaching that your Christian God protects you from harm. Fail now, and you are finished in Yangcheng. Discard your faith now, and you discard it for ever!' It was a desperate challenge. Somehow, she had to maintain face. Oh, these stupidly simple people! But how could she go into the prison? Those men— murderers, thieves, bandits, rioting and killing each other inside those walls! By the sounds, louder now, a small human hell had broken loose. How could she . . . ? "I must try," she said to herself. "I must try. O God, give me strength."

She looked up at the Governor's pale face, knowing that now hers was the same colour. "All right," she said. "Open the door. I'll go in to them." She did not trust her voice to say any more.

"The key!" snapped the Governor. "The key, quickly."

One of his orderlies came forward with a huge iron key. It looked designed to unlock the deepest, darkest dungeon in the world. In the keyhole the giant wards grated loudly; the immense iron-barred door swung open. Literally she was pushed inside. It was dark. The door closed behind her. She heard the great key turn. She was locked in the prison with a horde of raving criminals who by their din sounded as if they had all gone completely insane. A dark tunnel, twenty yards long, stretched before her. At the far end it appeared to open out into a courtyard. She could see figures racing across the entrance. With faltering footsteps, she walked through it and came to an abrupt standstill, rooted in horror.

The courtyard was about sixty feet square, with queer cage-like structures round all four sides. Within its confines a writhing, fiendish battle was going on. Several bodies were stretched out on the flagstones. One man, obviously dead, lay only a few feet away from her, blood still pouring from a great wound in his scalp. There was blood everywhere. Inside the cage-like structures small private battles were being fought. The main group of men, however, were watching one convict who brandished a large, bloodstained chopper. As she stared, he suddenly rushed at them and they scattered wildly to every part of the square. Gladys stood there, aghast at this macabre form of 'tag'. The man on the ground with the gash in his skull had obviously been well and truly 'tagged'. No one took any notice whatsoever of Gladys. For fully half a minute she stood motionless with not one single cell of her mind operating to solve her dilemma. The man rushed again; the group parted; he singled one man out and chased him. The man ran towards Gladys, then ducked away. The madman with the axe halted only a few feet from her. Without any instinctive plan, hardly realizing what she was doing, she took two angry steps towards him.

"Give me that chopper," she said furiously. "Give it to me at once!"

The man turned to look at her. For three long seconds the wild dark pupils staring from bloodshot eyes glared at her.

He took two paces forward. Suddenly, meekly, he held out the axe. Gladys snatched the weapon from his hand and held it rigidly down by her side. She was conscious that there was blood on the blade and that it would stain her trousers. The other convicts—there must have been fifty or sixty men cowering there—stared from every corner of the courtyard. All action was frozen in that one moment of intense drama. Gladys knew that she must clinch her psychological advantage.

"All of you!" she shouted. "Come over here. Come on, form into a line!" She knew vaguely that the voice belonged to her, but she had never heard it so shrill. She screamed at them, gabbled at them like an undersized infuriated sergeant-major, like a schoolmarm with a class of naughty children. "Get into line at once. You, over there! Come on, form up in front of me!"

Obediently the convicts shambled across, forming into a ragged group before her. She regarded them stormily. There was silence. Then suddenly her fear had gone. In its place was an immense, soul-searing pity that pricked the tears into her eyes. They were so wretched. They were so hopeless. A mass of thin faces: angular cheekbones, puckered lips; faces contorted with misery, pain and hunger; eyes, dark with fear and despair, looked into hers. They were remnants of humanity, half-men dressed in rags, caked in dust, running with lice; animals more than men, and the cages in which they were penned around the arena were those of brutes. She could have wept openly that human creatures could be so wretched. With an effort, she tightened her lips, took command again. The fear had gone, yes; but she knew she must still cow them with her authority.

"You should be ashamed of yourselves," she said, berating them like an irate mother scolding a crowd of naughty children. "All this noise and all this mess!" Mess! She waved her arms to indicate the bodies and blood the battle had left behind. "The Governor sent me in here to find out what it was all about. Now, if you clean up this courtyard and promise to behave in future, I'll ask him to deal leniently with you this time." She tried to keep her eyes away from the still figures of the dead. She knew she must focus their attention until all the desperate violence had seeped away. "Now what is your grievance?" she snapped. "Why did you start fighting like this?"

There was no answer. Several hung their heads in shame.

"I want you to appoint a spokesman, then," she went on. "He can tell me what the trouble is. And then you can start cleaning up this courtyard at once. Now go over in that corner and appoint your spokesman. I'll wait here."

The convicts trooped over into the corner she indicated and talked among themselves. A few moments later, one of the taller men of slightly better physique approached. Like the others, he was dressed in rags.

"My name is Feng," he said. "I am their spokesman."

While they swabbed up the blood with rags, and moved the dead bodies into less spectacular positions, Gladys listened to his story. Later she learned that he had once been a Buddhist priest; he had been convicted of theft from the other priests of the temple and sentenced to eight years in gaol. He explained that no one really knew why, or how, the riot had started. They were allowed the chopper—he indicated the axe which Gladys still carried—for an hour every day to cut up their food. Someone had quarrelled over its possession, someone else had joined in, and suddenly, without anyone knowing exactly why, the volcano of passion had erupted and a lava of blood flowed everywhere. He could not explain this strange occurrence. Perhaps it was that many of the men had been there for many years, he said. As she knew, unless their friends or relatives sent in food, they starved. It was hard to sit up against a wall and starve to death while other men ate. Sometimes they took one of their number out into the square and executed him. That terror hung over many heads. He could not explain the outbreak, but the walls were high and the doors were strong; they never saw the outside world, women or the mountains, a tree in blossom or a friendly face; sometimes the spirit grew so oppressed that it burst out of a man in a wild tumult of violence. That, he thought, is what had occurred. They were all very sorry.

"What do you do all day in here?" asked Gladys seriously.

"Do? There is nothing to do."

"No occupation of any sort?"

"None!"

"But a man must have work, something to do. I shall see the Governor about it."

It was at that moment she became conscious that the Governor and his retinue were behind her. She did not find out until later that there was a small opening towards the end of the tunnel through which they had heard everything. The noise of the riot had died, and they had now thought it safe to enter and take an official part in the peace treaty.

The Governor bowed to Gladys.

"You have done well," he said gratefully. "We must thank you."

"It's disgraceful," she said bitterly. "These men are locked up here week after week, year after year, with nothing to do. Nothing to do at all!"

"I do not understand." His bewilderment was rather ludicrous.

Gladys could, however, sense his gratitude and decided to press her point. "Of course you have riots if they've nothing to occupy their time, year after year. You must find them occupations."

The Governor was still completely puzzled. "Occupations?" he repeated.

"They must have work to do. We must get looms so they can weave cloth; we must find them all sorts of jobs so that they can earn a little money and buy food, and get back a little self-respect."

The Governor nodded. Whether he agreed or not she could not tell. "We will discuss it later," he said amiably.

"I have promised them there will be no reprisals," she said.

The Governor nodded again. A few corpses were rarely the subject of an official inquiry, or even an embarrassment to the Chinese penal system. "As long as there is no recurrence," he said, "we shall forget all about it."

"That is good," said Gladys. She turned to Feng. "I'm going now, but I shall come back. I promise I will do all I can to help you."

She saw upon her the dark eyes of the priest who was a thief. "Thank you," he said. "Thank you, Ai-weh-deh."

She did not know at the time what the word "Ai-weh-deh" meant. That evening she asked Lu-Yung-Cheng when he returned from the long walk he had so suddenly decided to take.

"Ai-weh-deh?" he said curiously. "It means the virtuous one."

She was known as Ai-weh-deh for all her remaining years in China.

CHAPTER SEVEN

THE EPISODE in the prison raised Gladys's prestige considerably in Yangcheng. Becoming official foot inspector had given her some importance, but stopping a gaol riot had conferred honour of a different sort altogether. She noticed that merchants standing in their shop doorways who had ignored her for so long, now bowed politely as she passed. Her two soldiers were as pleased about the affair as if they had received a rise in pay. She had gained much 'face'.

She did not forget her promise to the prisoners, either. The Governor, at heart, was an educated, kindly man, and in the years that followed became a good friend of hers. If the condition of his prison was abysmal, it was because the conditions in all Chinese prisons were dreadful. If only to prevent more riots breaking out he was perfectly willing to accept suggestions from Gladys. No large-scale reform could be accomplished; there was no money in the yamen funds allotted to the improvement of prisons. Gladys had no money either, but she did manage to get a couple of old looms from friends of the Governor, and a supply of yarn. She obtained cotton cloth and set the prisoners to making the puttees which were worn in Shansi, and a miller's wheel, so they could grind grain and make a few cash out of that work. She visited them regularly: almost every day when she was in Yangcheng, taught them facts about hygiene, and read them stories. Whimsically she thought to herself that they were the only parishioners she was always certain of finding 'at home'. She managed to get some domesticated rabbits and they kept them in hutches and bred from them. But perhaps her greatest triumph came when the Governor's old school friend, a scholar of some repute, visited Yangcheng.

"He is a Christian," said the Governor importantly. "Perhaps I could prevail upon him to preach in your Mission."

"A good idea," said Gladys at once. "And I'll tell you what. Why don't we have all your convicts down to listen to him?"

"You mean allow the convicts out of gaol!" The Governor was very perturbed. "That is impossible!"

"Why is it impossible? Some of them have never left that courtyard for ten years or more. It would be a great event for them. Do them all good!"

"But they're convicts . . . !"

"You could guard them. It would flatter your old friend, too—if he's a good Christian, that is?"

From the moment Gladys stopped the riot in his gaol, the Governor had regarded her with some awe. At least on that occasion *her* religion had worked; his had not! Reluctantly, after a little more persuasion, he agreed to let them out for this one occasion.

Gladys never forgot the Sunday the convicts came to church. Manacled together with heavy chains, they were marched down the main street and out of the West Gate. The people lined the roads to stare at them. Outside the gate, with the windy mountain world falling and rising all about them, the whole troop halted instinctively and stared with a bewildering hunger at the scene; for two whole minutes the soldiers who were guarding them allowed them to stand, murmuring together, and look out at freedom. Then they marched down the narrow street to the Inn of Eight Happinesses, filed through the courtyard, and into the old ancestral hall at the far end, which had now been converted into a mission hall.

They sat on the floor while the portly, beaming friend of the Governor preached to them solidly for three long hours. It was perhaps the most blissful church service ever conducted in the province of Shansi. At the end of it, through their spokesman, the convicts thanked Gladys gravely for allowing them this privilege, and with chains jangling marched back to gaol.

It was also in her second year at Yangcheng that she had her first small altercation with the Mandarin. She had just returned from a foot inspection tour into the mountains,

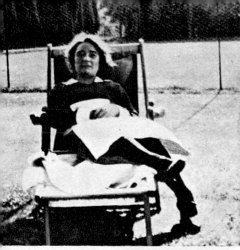

Gladys Aylward,
London parlourmaid

Gladys Aylward,
China missionary
for 20 years

With some of her converts at prayer over Mrs Lawson's coffin.

With some of the children before they crossed the mountains to Sian

One of the 'children', Lian Ai, sent Gladys Aylward this picture, taken on her wedding day

Bandaged feet. One of Gladys Aylward's first duties as Foot Inspector was to break down the centuries-old custom

and was walking down the main street rehearsing the speech she was going to make to him. As her employer, she decided he should know about these things and put a stop to them. "Excellency," she was going to say, with reluctance, but with some firmness, "I wish to discuss with you the status of women." She would pause there to let that point sink in. "Is it right," she would continue, "that a man is allowed to beat his wife? Is it right that a husband has the power to sell his wife, even to kill his wife? As a most loyal and obedient employee, these things have been brought forcibly to my notice in my journeys into the mountain villages. Respectfully, I would like to know what you intend to do about these matters? I know they are of immemorial origin, but that does not make them any less repellent."

She halted in mid-thought when she saw the woman sitting on the pavement with her feet in the roadway. The woman was swarthy, coarse, dirty. Heavy silver earrings dangled from her ear lobes. Silver and jade pins were stuck in her hair; she wore a silver necklace and embossed bracelets; her baggy trousers were secured at the ankle by bright green puttees. The puttees first attracted Gladys's attention. Although they were a normal part of Shansi dress, she had never seen them of that colour before; she thought at once that the woman must come from a village which she had never visited, that she had not even heard about. Gladys walked towards her intending to find the answer to these questions. As she approached she saw that a child leant against the woman's knee; an appalling, sickly scrap of a child, clad in a dirty bit of loincloth; it had legs like stalks, a swollen belly which told of malnutrition, and its head and body were covered with running sores. Gladys was horrified. Its condition made it impossible even to tell its sex. The pleasantries stopped in her throat.

"Woman, you have no right to sit on the side of the road with a child in that condition," she said sternly.

The woman's dark eyes flicked up at her insolently. "Mind your own business," she said.

"It is my business," said Gladys indignantly, remembering her official status as foot inspector. "You let the baking sun pour on that child's head much longer, and it will die!"

"What has it got to do with you whether it dies or not?" sneered the woman. "If it does I'll soon get another one."

Gladys glared down at her. She guessed from her manner that the woman was not the child's mother. She remembered vaguely that she had heard about people like this. Child dealers? That was it; people who bought and sold children. In the Shansi mountains they were thought of as devils; mentioned only in whispers.

The woman's next remark confirmed her thoughts. She said provocatively, "Would you like it? You can have it for two dollars."

Gladys realized at once that, as far as current market prices went, the price was cheap. A pretty girl, suitable as a bride, would cost ninety dollars at least; even a young female child would fetch ten dollars. But who would want this sick and weakly infant?

"I haven't got two dollars," she retorted. "It's sick and likely to die, and it will take two more dollars to bury it; and that makes four dollars."

The woman pulled a face. Her eyes were hard. "You can have it for a dollar and a half, then."

"I haven't got a dollar and a half, and I don't want the child, anyway."

She walked away, the woman's jeering laughter following her. No one else passing along the street had bothered to listen to their conversation. But, as she walked towards the yamen, a surge of indignation began to rise inside her, indignation which did not quieten even though, as usual, it was an hour before she was granted an audience with the Mandarin. By the time the gong boomed, and the soldier pushed open the great door to admit her into the presence, she was aching to tell him about the child-dealer. She knew, however, that you could not immediately protest to a Mandarin, no matter how serious your complaint. Courtesies came first. She bowed low before the imperious scarlet-robed figure, obeying the ancient ritual of the small official addressing the high and mighty.

"Are you well?" she asked.

"Yes, I am well. You are well?"

"Yes, I am well. Have you eaten your food?"

"Yes, I have eaten my food. Have you eaten your food?"

"Thank you, yes. Are your old relations well?"

"Yes, my old ones are very well."

This went on for about a minute, and then, the courtesies over, she handed him the slip of paper containing her report. It was a very brief report, because in the very early days, before she had learnt to write in Chinese, she had to get someone to write the Chinese characters for her. Her reports, in fact, were masterpieces of simplicity. This one read:

'Gladys Aylward has been to Chowtsun. Gladys Aylward has come back from Chowtsun.'

The names of the district or village might alter with each trip, but her written reports did not. All the details of her work she gave him verbally. A smile creased the Mandarin's mouth as he took the paper. Seeing him thus in his bright scarlet robes, with high collar, scarlet cap and wide-sweeping sleeves, it always took her some seconds to get over her feeling of awe.

"You have things to tell me," he said.

Gladys answered: "What do you do with dealers in children?"

The dark, thin eyebrows lifted slightly. "I do not understand you."

"A few yards away from this yamen, a woman tried to sell me a child for two dollars. What do you do about that?"

Gladys knew intuitively that her question worried him. He walked to the end of the chamber and back before replying. Then he said: "You do not do anything."

"But I don't understand," said Gladys. "It's wrong!"

"If she is indeed a child-dealer she belongs to a gang of wicked and desperate people. If you interfere with them, they commit horrible crimes. It is better you forget all about it. It has nothing to do with you."

99

"But . . ."

"Now tell me what you have done in the district of Chowtsun."

It was a command, and Gladys outlined the women she had seen, the speeches she had made. It took half an hour. When she had finished, the Mandarin nodded his head. He picked up the small hammer and rapped the gong. It was the signal for the doors to be opened; the interview was over. As she turned to go, he stayed her with a gesture of his hand.

"About the child-dealer. The law says that Ai-weh-deh is to put her head in the air and pass on the other side of the road. And you will not repeat my words to anyone! Go!"

The doors were open. Gladys walked towards them. She was deeply disappointed in this man for whom she felt so much respect. She turned in the doorway.

"I have to inform you," she said, "that I did not come to China only to observe your laws. I came for the love of Jesus Christ, and I shall act upon the principles of His teaching, no matter what you say."

It was a well-timed exit. Before the surprised Mandarin had time to reply she had gone. Months later, when she was on terms of much greater intimacy, he reminded her of that meeting. He told her that his friendship and his respect for her had stemmed from that action. It was the first time in his term of office that any person, man or woman, had dared to question his authority as Mandarin. It was certainly the first time in his life that any woman had spoken to him in such a fashion.

Gladys walked swiftly down the main street. The woman was still there. When she saw Gladys she called out, "Lady with the heart of pity! Here you are again. I will sell you the child for a shilling."

Gladys stopped and stared at her. "I haven't got a shilling."

"Then how much would you give for it?"

"I haven't any money; and what would I do with the child?"

"But you do want it, don't you?"

Gladys started to dispute the remark, then suddenly stopped. She did want the child.

"How much would you give?" said the woman in a wheedling tone.

Gladys reached inside her jacket pocket. She had a few coppers cash there, in value equal to about ninepence. She took it out.

"I'll give you this ninepence, but not a penny more."

The woman cupped her hand to take the money. "She is yours." She stood up and hurried off down the street. Gladys looked down at the child. Its age was indeterminate: roughly between four and six years old, she reckoned.

"Come with me!" she said. The child made no move. It seemed to comprehend little. Gladys took it by the scruff of the neck and led it along the main street, through the gate and back to the inn. Inside the main room it ran to the darkest corner and crouched there, terrified. Gladys fetched in the cook, Yang, to see what she had brought home.

He regarded the nalf-naked sickly mite in silence for a few seconds. "Well, you've done a fine thing," he said. "What d'you want such a child for? It will die very quickly."

"Give it some food," said Gladys. "Poor little thing; it looks nearly dead already."

Yang fetched a bowl of millet and placed it on the floor near the child, who eyed it hungrily, then rushed out, grabbed the bowl and retreated to its corner to scoop the food into its mouth with its fingers.

"We shall have trouble with this child," said Yang. Gladys noticed that at least he had said '*we*'. That gave her a little more confidence.

For three weeks the infant reacted exactly like a wild animal. It allowed no one to touch it; it bit and scratched and screamed if any attempt was made to wash or dress or interfere with it in the slightest; it ran out of the house at the first opportunity and refused to come back, preferring to eat and sleep in a corner of the courtyard. Gladys despaired of ever turning it into something even resembling a human being. It was a girl child, a wild, dark-eyed outcast, hating everyone.

After three weeks of effort, Gladys realized that she was defeated. She knew that she would have to hand over the child to someone better equipped than herself to see what they could do. She came down the street towards the Inn one late afternoon with this thought in mind, and passed a young woman sitting in her doorway weeping over a small dead child which lay in her lap.

Gladys stopped and looked at her. Impulsively she said, "I have a child which you can have in exchange. There's no use in you crying over a dead body."

The woman's tear-stained eyes lifted to her. "I do not understand," she whispered.

"Give me your dead baby and I'll go and bury it," said Gladys. "The other child is at the Inn of Eight Happinesses. You go and fetch it."

The woman did not protest as Gladys took the dead baby out of her lap. Carrying it in her arms she walked back the way she had come. In Yangcheng, little ceremony was attached to the burying of new-born babies. You found a hole in the mountainside, pushed in the body, stopped up the entrance with stone and earth and the task was done. Sometimes around the deep, dry moat which encircled the city you would see the dogs nuzzling a bundle and knew that some new-born female child had been unceremoniously thrown there. Boy babies were treated as little gods; girl babies were unwanted.

When Gladys returned to the inn she found the woman waiting for her in the courtyard. Yang, beaming broadly, was standing behind her. The woman held Ninepence—for that is what Gladys had nicknamed her—by the hand. She was transformed. She now had a clean face and wore clean clothes. Gladys stared in astonishment. The woman smiled back at her. She led the little girl forward and slipped the child's hand into Gladys's.

"There is your child," she said. "She will love you always when she understands what you have done for her."

Gladys looked down at the small urchin by her side. Ninepence had come to stay.

. . . . .

Although she was christened with the Chinese name of Mei-en—Beautiful Grace—to Gladys her nickname was always 'Ninepence'. She did not learn about her past until many years later. As the months passed she grew into a pretty little girl, with all the charm and impudence of all little girls. And it was through Ninepence that the family increased. One afternoon she came scurrying into the courtyard, her black eyes popping in excitement.

"Is the food ready?" she called up to Gladys standing on the balcony.

"Nearly ready."

They had their evening meal in the late afternoon, so that they were ready for work when the muleteers arrived.

"Is it a nice meal?" asked Ninepence eagerly.

"Of course it's nice. Isn't it always nice?" Ninepence as a rule was not concerned about food. "Go on; run off and play. I'll call you when it's ready."

Ninepence looked up very seriously. "If I was willing to eat a little less of the meal, would you be willing to eat a little less also?"

Gladys had no idea what she was getting at. "Yes, of course."

"Then if we put the two 'lesses' in a basin, we'd have enough food for one more person, wouldn't we?"

"Ninepence," said Gladys severely, "what are you up to now?"

"Do you know," said Ninepence, frowning in concentration, "that there's a little boy outside the door who hasn't even got a little 'less' in his basin."

Gladys looked down at the small child in the middle of the large courtyard, a small, blue-uniformed figure with a very serious face.

"Ninepence," she said, "if you're willing to go without, I am too. We'll give it to this boy. Go and fetch him in."

Ninepence shouted out, and a ragged little urchin about

eight years old appeared from under the balcony. He blinked up at Gladys. He was in dirty rags, a male replica of Ninepence when she first arrived. Ninepence had discovered him begging on the streets. He ate his meal with relish and stayed with them for the next ten years. His nickname thereafter was always 'Less'.

He was old enough to tell Gladys his story. Bandits had raided his village in Horbay. They had killed the men and taken the women off with them. Less's mother had been pregnant. Her labour pains started on the forced march and the bandits left her behind in a ditch. How much of his mother's agony he comprehended, Gladys did not wish to think about, but he saw her die, and after tugging in vain at her clothes, left her to return to their village. It was in ashes. Only corpses lay in the ruins. He wandered away into the mountains, begged food, joined up with the muleteers on their journeys across the trails, and eventually reached Yangcheng. There, at the Inn of Eight Happinesses, he became the second child taken to the heart of Ai-weh-deh, the virtuous one.

The third child arrived in the spring of the next year. They had gone to wash their clothes in the first warm spell of bright weather, for in the spring the whole town washed its clothes on the rocks of the river bank a few hundred yards from the East Gate. Gladys was dutifully pounding the wet quilted garments with a piece of wood, hopeful at least that the lice would not dodge all her blows, when she heard Ninepence and Less calling behind her on the bank. She turned to look; they had a small child about two years old walking between them, holding their hands.

"What d'you want with him?" shouted Gladys. "Take him back to where he belongs, this very minute."

"But he doesn't belong to anybody," called Ninepence. "We've looked everywhere. There's no one else about."

Gladys glared at them from her perch. "Well, maybe he's wandered from the town, then. Somebody must own him."

"Can we take him home with us?" asked Ninepence hopefully, the real point of her anxiety now emerging.

"What!" said Gladys indignantly. "Indeed we can't! Do you think I want to be dragged up before the Mandarin for child-stealing? I've never heard of such a thing."

"But he really is lost," insisted Less. "We've looked everywhere."

"Wait until I've finished this washing, I'll find his parents all right."

But she did not find his parents. They searched along the banks, and up the hillside. There were no buildings nearby. They called aloud at the top of their voices. No one turned up to claim the child, and when they had done all they could they took him home with them and let him sleep at the Inn. Afterwards, even though they posted notices on the city gates, and the Mandarin sent the Town Crier around, no one wanted him.

So she was now responsible for three children. 'Bao-Bao', precious bundle, had joined the family. In the years which followed she was to become official parent to two more, and unofficial mother to children without number. In 1936, when the Yellow River flooded and refugees came up into the mountains, they brought with them a small boy called Francis, whom no one owned and no one wanted. And Lan-Hsiang was a small girl of eight, 'left over' from a law case in the Mandarin's court. She had no parents, and the Mandarin decided that it would be an excellent idea if she became a member of the family.

"Haven't I enough children?" said Gladys in some irritation.

"You are the best person to look after her," said the Mandarin with the smooth Oriental authority that permitted no argument.

It was the Governor of the Prison who solved the problem of their schooling. He had three children, and there was no school in Yangcheng. Children were taught at home, if they were taught at all.

"Therefore we must open a school here!" said the Prison Governor. "We can engage a teacher from Luan—if all the parents will make a small donation towards his salary."

So the school was started, and it was five years from the time it opened that Gladys discovered the story of Ninepence's past. She had grown up into a very pretty little girl, and brother Less watched over her like a mother bear. It was he who reported to Gladys that for two or three days in succession a man had waited outside the school for Ninepence and tried to talk to her, tried to take her arm on one occasion. He was very worried about it.

It worried Gladys also. She told him she would meet them out of school next day, and if the man showed up, Less could point him out to her. He was there all right, and although he did not try to molest the child with Gladys present, he looked at them with glinting, insolent eyes. Gladys didn't know what to do; so, as always in such cases, she went to see her old friend, the Mandarin.

"It is no use apprehending him unless we catch him in the act," said the Mandarin thoughtfully. "But I will have a soldier standing by outside the school every day, and if this man lays a hand on the girl again, she must scream and we will arrest him."

The man fell into the trap, poor accomplice that he was, the very next day. He caught Ninepence by the arm as she came out through the school door and tried to drag her off with him. Less, prowling in the rear, flew at him like an enraged bulldog and buried his teeth in his arm. The noise was tremendous. When the soldier ran up a few seconds later he had considerable difficulty in prising Less away. The man was removed to prison. The Mandarin opened the inquiry next day and the interesting story was revealed. The man who was trying to kidnap Ninepence was no more than an agent for a wicked uncle. So simple was his approach that the only way of taking Ninepence he could think of was to drag her off after school. Apparently, Ninepence's mother had been very happy with her husband and baby daughter. But her husband had died, and mother-in-law, not wanting a female child, had married off mother and daughter into another family. There Ninepence's mother had also died, leaving her as an unwanted female child in a household without blood relations at all. She had been given away, passed through many hands before the child-dealer had met Gladys in the main street of Yang-cheng.

The fact that the 'foreign devil' had bought Ninepence and was looking after her quickly filtered back to the grandmother at their mountain farm in a village many miles from Yangcheng. They made no move to take her back; of what use was a female child to anyone? Chinese philosophy regarding female children followed an ancient tradition. The birth of a girl child was looked upon as a disaster, and neighbours and relatives commented acidly upon the misfortune. Unloved by everyone except the unfortunate mother, who had no rights in the matter anyway, the child was often killed at birth. If left to live, it would drudge and slave and be married off as quickly as possible. As soon as it was betrothed it was looked upon as belonging to another family. Time and money therefore were only wasted upon a girl child; who would want to lavish love and affection upon a girl who would shortly belong to someone else! If a woman did not give a man a son, she was quickly discarded for a second, a third, or fourth wife who could remedy the error. When a boy was born, now that was different! An ancient Chinese poet wrote 825 years before Christ:

> . . . And sceptres shall be given them for their toys,
> And when they cry, what music in the noise!
> These shall yet don the scarlet aprons grand
> And be the kings and princes of the land. . . .

Even when the muleteers talked to Gladys about their families, she quickly noted that the baby girls were not even counted as members. A man might have two daughters and four sons, but when she questioned him about the number of children he possessed, he would say proudly, "I have four children."

If, therefore, Ninepence's wicked uncle had managed to spirit her away, it is doubtful whether Gladys would have found redress at law. What had happened was quite simple. Grandmother and grandfather had died, leaving a farm and money with only two people in line of inheritance: the wicked uncle and Ninepence. What would have happened to Ninepence had she been kidnapped it is unpleasant even to consider. But now, his design revealed, he was about to contest Gladys's claim to the child in the Mandarin's court.

The Mandarin informed Gladys of the case against her after hearing the preliminary evidence; she would have to appear in court to defend her claim to Ninepence.

"But what can I do? I know nothing about Chinese court procedure," she protested.

The Mandarin looked very bland and impassive. "Before you speak, you will look at me," he said urbanely. "You will say only 'Yes' or 'No'. If I shake my head slightly you will say 'No'. If I nod my head slightly you will say 'Yes'. You understand?"

"Yes, I understand; but I can't lose Ninepence now! She belongs to me. I love her. I've looked after her all these years."

"She will not be taken from you," said the Mandarin quietly. "I am the judge in this matter, and I can promise you that. But these things must be done properly. When you are summoned, you will come to the court and do as I say."

The day of the inquiry arrived. The messenger from the yamen brought in the red paper, and Gladys went off to the court. She listened to the long, legal speeches of the lawyers appearing for the wicked uncle. She was asked many questions herself, and looked carefully for the slight guidance of the Mandarin's head before she answered any of them.

The case lasted a fortnight, and it was several days after that before the Mandarin announced his considered decision.

Ai-weh-deh was appointed official guardian of Ninepence. Her grandparents had left land and money. This would be divided, one half to Ai-weh-deh as legal guardian, one half to the wicked uncle; Ai-weh-deh could have which half she desired—the land or the money. That was his decision, and the wicked uncle seemed satisfied by it.

Land was useless to Gladys, but the money, which came to almost 200 dollars, represented a small fortune.

It was all saved for Ninepence; some of it was spent on her education and the rest reserved for her dowry when she married.

CHAPTER EIGHT

THE FRIENDSHIP between the Mandarin of Yangcheng and the tiny ex-parlourmaid from Belgrave Square is probably one of the oddest in the entire history of Eastern and Western relationships. Although she spoke the language as fluently as a native, it was years before she managed to dig down through the layers of his mind. He was enigmatic. He regarded her urbanely, his fine thin face, with its high cheekbones and thin, dark, almond eyes, always impassive. A glossy pigtail dropped from under the round silk cap; the gowns he wore were embroidered in wide scrolls of many colours, inevitably beautiful: scarlet, blue, green, gold. To Gladys he always looked as if, by some miracle of time, he had just stepped down from an antique Chinese scroll. His was a feudal society. From his yamen, civic authority was administered in much the same manner as it had been dispensed in the time of Confucius. His aides and counsellors bore ancient and honourable titles which defined their interest in transport, sanitation, roads, water and household duties.

In one of the inner courts was the place of the women. They were not wives, or even concubines, but slave-girls, young and lovely creatures purchased with yamen funds for the ancient and honourable delights of love. Gladys was not shocked when she understood the implications of the women's court. It was a custom which dated back many hundreds of years; everything was very proper. They were watched over by the older women, most of whom had themselves been yamen maidens, and whose daughters would grow up and continue in the same service. They were gay and enchanting girls, singing songs, playing instruments and learning dances; not secluded like harem women of the East, but able to trip through the bazaars fingering the soft bales of silk, and buying the combs and cheap jewelled ornaments they adored. Gladys had many friends amongst them, and often, when she was visiting the Mandarin, she would walk through to the women's court to chat and drink tea with them. There is little doubt that at first, to the Mandarin of Yangcheng, Gladys Aylward was as alien a species as a creature from the moon. She was a female, which meant that in the eyes of man she was socially and intellectually less than dust. Nevertheless, as news of her exploits reached him, and as, over the months, she continually bombarded him with applications, supplications, admonitions and near-threats, she loomed as astonishingly as a new planet thrust into his orbit. Indeed, as their contacts and acquaintanceship increased, the Mandarin of Yangcheng found, to his growing astonishment, that not only was she becoming an adviser of sorts, but also a friend. By immemorial Chinese standards, he was a highly intelligent man, but his background was circumscribed by the contemplative scholarship of a formal education.

Gladys blew into his yamen with the winds of the world around her ears. To him, she was worldly and foreign. She never forgot his first gentle admonition after she had delivered herself of a particularly impassioned piece of Christian propaganda. "Ai-weh-deh," he said softly, "you send your missionaries into our land, which is older by far in civilization than yours. You see us as a nation of heathens and barbarians, do you not?"

She tilted her head, looked up at him with inquiring eyes. She was rapidly becoming aware that this intellectual sparring in flowery and formal language was as integral a part of Chinese social relations as taking tea together.

"Not by any means," she said.

The Mandarin placed his slender hands in the wide silken sleeves of his robe.

"We have produced great art and great philosophy. The Mandarin speech of China is more beautiful and descriptive than any other in the world. Our poets were singing when Britain was but a rocky outpost on the edge of the known world and America was inhabited solely by red-skinned aborigines. Yet you come to teach us a new faith? I find it very strange."

She did not miss the gentle mockery in his voice, and as usual she was always willing to argue with him. It was not, however, until many years later that she realized she was a witness of the end of a Chinese era which had lasted for forty centuries.

In the near future the torrent of Communist retribution bearing its driftwood of Western habits and thought would flood Old China; the Mandarin and his like were to become as extinct as the dodo or the dinosaur. For thousands of years the Confucian scholar, not the dialectical Commissar, had been the civil servant of China. Caste or birth played but a small part in the scheme of things. They were rulers by virtue of learning, and they controlled the destinies of a quarter of the entire human race. The rise to respect and authority of any scholar was the result of years of intense learning, and the examination hall was the proving ground of his skill and intellectual superiority.

Of this Gladys was to hear in their long conversations through those ten sunlit years. With a smile and a polite gesture meant to absolve her from any feeling of guilt at belonging to a society as rude and barbaric as that of the West, he told her of his own education. She learnt something of the endless toil which had confronted him before he became Mandarin of Yangcheng.

Born of a reasonably well-to-do family in a small town in North China, for the first seven years of his life he had been allowed to run wild. In the long, hot summers, with the other boys he had scoured the rivers and streams, splashed in the shallows, flown his scarlet kite high against the blue sky, and played the ancient game of catching grasshoppers and locusts and stringing them on slender reeds. He had seen the coloured lanterns bobbing in the dark at weddings and funerals, at the harvest and the threshing time; he had played shuttlecock and gambled with copper cash, imitating his elders, and every year he had looked forward to the fourteen-day celebrations of the New Year.

At six years old, his father had consulted the astrologists to discover a propitious day for the commencement of his school life, and when that day was chosen the hours of his young summer were over. On school morning, smartly dressed in blue gown, red outside jacket, yellow trousers and navy cap with a scarlet tassel, his head newly shaved, the glossy queue plaited and hung down his back, he presented himself to his schoolmaster. He opened his first school book. It was a primer on the importance of filial duty, of the nature of man, of the need for education. Because the book was printed with three characters on each line, it is known as the 'Three Character Classic'; it contains 500 separate characters each of which must be learnt by heart. From sunrise to sunset, with intervals for meals, he and his school-fellows worked. Only the writing lessons provided intervals in this prodigious work of memory, and a lesson consisted of copying thousands of different characters on to rice-paper with a brush of sable or fox hair, copying and re-copying hundreds of times until they were indelibly printed on his mind. A study of the 'Three Character Classic' in the old days was as far as thousands of Chinese schoolboys ever advanced towards an education. The book was first introduced as a primer of learning a thousand years ago and has been used unchanged ever since. A study of six such books comprises the education of any boy intended for a scholastic career.

Because his parents were moderately well-to-do, and because he coveted the empire of scholarship which by diligence and practice he knew could be gathered within the bony frontiers of his skull, the Mandarin decided to continue with his studies. The basis of all his learning was Confucius. "What Confucius teaches is true: what is contrary to his teaching is false: what he does not teach is unnecessary." And there were four more immense classic volumes of Confucian philosophy to be absorbed.

In all their discussions of Chinese philosophy and ritual one salient fact inevitably disturbed Gladys. Why had these carefully regulated codes of social behaviour, this fine sifting of pure thought by the wisest sages of China down from generation to generation, not produced a society fit for gods to walk in? Why, at the very moment of their discussion, were there in every province warring armies, jealous and ambitious men lusting for power. "Why?" she repeated. "Why?"

He spread long, delicate hands. "The scholar and the soldier exist. One cannot theorize them out of existence. One hopes that eventually the perfect man will evolve . . ."

He never tired of explaining the Chinese conception of the 'Princely Man'.

"The second of the four classic volumes deals with this paragon. The book is called 'True Man'. It was compiled by a grandson of Confucius in the year of your calendar some three hundred and thirty-eight years before your Christian prophet was born.

"In this book the conception of a perfect man is depicted, who in all circumstances preserves a golden roundness of character and is thus a model and a standard of virtue to all succeeding generations. The perfect man is never satisfied with himself. He that is satisfied is not perfect!"

"It seems to me," said Gladys, "that the only concern of Confucius and your other Sages was how to pattern life on earth. We in the West believe in life after death. We believe in a God-like spirit in man which is always present. Are your prophets willing to die for their beliefs?"

The Mandarin of Yangcheng picked up a pale yellow lotus flower from the shallow vase in which it floated, and looked at the waxen texture of the blossom. " 'I love life and I love justice,' " he quoted softly, " 'but if I cannot preserve both I would rather give up life and hold fast to justice. Although I love life, there is that which I love more than life. Although I hate death, there is that which I hate more than death.'

"That was written by Mencius," he said, "a teacher who lived two hundred years later than Confucius. In greatness he is second only to the master himself. He believed that man was naturally good: 'All men are naturally virtuous,' he wrote, 'just as water naturally flows downwards; the evil of the world contaminates them.' "

The Mandarin replaced the lotus blossom on the water and delicately flicked a spot of water from his finger-tips.

"It is necessary to study these great books diligently and commit them to memory before approaching the examination hall," he said. "One must acquire a literary style and elegant penmanship; one must be skilled in poetry and faultlessly accurate, for a single mistake will lose a degree. Lastly, for your examination, one must study the Sacred Edict of K'ang-hsi and commit it entirely to memory. If you pass this examination, you attain the rank of 'Cultural Talent', but for your more advanced degrees there are five more volumes to be memorized and understood: the Five Classics, accepted by the Chinese people as the noblest words of mankind since the beginning of time, leaving nothing to be added, nothing subtracted."

"You give most of your life just to learning a lot of old books?" said Gladys.

"I understand that much of your own religion is based upon an old book," said the Mandarin politely, "but it is true that a lifetime can be extended in scholarship. Some do not become Finished Scholars until they are past three score years and ten."

"But what about the outside world?" said Gladys. "Geography, science, literature, history, mathematics, the philosophy of other countries?"

The Mandarin lifted his shoulders delicately. "As far as the Chinese scholar is concerned such things do not exist. They are outside the boundaries of our knowledge and are considered redundant."

In all her conversation with the Mandarin, Gladys never left his presence with a feeling of inferiority or inadequacy. She realized that there was a balance between her practical knowledge and his classical scholarship. Although the teachings of Confucius had permeated down to the humblest peasant in the fields, she possessed a practical faith which was endowed with a spiritual power and a glory beyond the analytical philosophy of Confucius.

In China three religions have met, and become embedded in the daily ritual of life: Confucianism, Buddhism and

Taoism. A household will worship in the ancestral hall where the tablets to the honourable dead are placed in accordance with the precepts of Confucius; they will also burn incense on the shrine of Buddha; and for a propitious day on which to start a new scholar at school, to hold a marriage, a celebration or a funeral they will consult a Taoist priest.

Gladys Aylward brought a new religion; she travelled the bare mountains in that wild region, experiencing perhaps the greatest joy ever known to a Christian missionary, for they were simple peasants she moved among. She met none of the sophisticated resistance, the disillusion and despair of the West; this was a virgin land. She brought a simple faith to uncomplicated people, a faith which answered their needs; a faith which many embraced as devoutly as did those early Anglo-Saxons when the monks of Benedict and Gregory came to their forest clearings, bearing the reassurance that there was, indeed, an infinite Being of goodness, faith and love existing outside the shell of their mortal world.

Yet to her, also, came moments of doubt and indecision. She remembered one night, after a long conversation with the Mandarin, when both had stood on the balcony at the back of his yamen with the mountain falling away almost sheerly beneath, and the sinking sun reddening the whole wild panorama of peaks before them. The peace of that moment had stayed with her even when she reached the courtyard of the Inn of Eight Happinesses and mounted to her room. She paused on the balcony, looked down into the courtyard where the mules bunched darkly together, moved occasionally, snorted and whisked their tails. The moon was rising, its light spilling into the cool, fresh mountain sky, brilliant with stars. From the doorway of the downstairs room a fan of yellow light from the castor-oil lamps spread across the level, beaten earth. The gate was shut; the inn was full. She went down into the courtyard, into the muleteers' room, smelly and warm, and there was a hush as the men saw her. They chatted for a few moments, then she sat on the edge of the k'ang and began, as she almost always began: "Once upon a time, long ago in a far-off country called Israel, there lived a man named Jesus Christ. . . ."

She glanced up and saw the light from the flickering oil lamps accentuating and strengthening the features of the men gathered around her. They were simple, kindly peasants, almost as close to nature as the animals with which they journeyed. She knew that their eyes would glisten, their faces quicken with interest as she continued with the story of the faith and strength which had had the power to send seven crusades of armoured knights across Europe to the Holy Land; which had assuaged the agony of Jeanne d'Arc as her slender body flamed into a human torch, and which had morticed the stones upon which the civilization of the West still stood. She wondered if, in the years to come, any remnant of the faith she preached would stay with them, and be of help to them in their troubles.

She looked at Hsi-Lien, the simple muleteer, one of the first of her converts, and one of her friends. He had been in charge of the very first mule-team she had hauled into the courtyard, the man who had fled in terror at the sight of Jeannie Lawson. They had had many a good laugh about that occasion afterwards. His home was only a day's journey away, at Chowtsun. But did *he* really understand? Would this faith he had accepted stand him in good stead in a time of trial? Could she just as wisely have told him about Robinson Crusoe and Little Red Riding Hood? They were also stories. Was the catalyst that turned a legend into a religion only human pain and desperation?

Looking back in the years that followed, she sometimes wondered what she should have done about Hsi-Lien. If she could have seen into the future, discerned the terrible tragedy which would befall him, what would she have done? Would she, for his own sake, have sent him out, through the city gates, down the mountainside, and away for ever from the Inn of Eight Happinesses?

CHAPTER NINE

To GLADYS AYLWARD, those early years in Yangcheng were peaceful and unhurried. There was time to think, time to sleep, time to pray. The big events stood out in the years; she did not forget them.

There was the time when the Yellow River flooded, drowning hundreds of people, making thousands homeless, and the refugees trooped back up into the mountains, passing in long streams through Yangcheng and on to Tsehchow, Chin Shui and the other cities of the province. There was the time when the Yellow River, bordering the western boundary of Shansi, froze over and Communist troops from Yenan and the province of Shensi walked across the ice. It was a 'three-coat' winter that year, the coldest in living memory. You always judged a winter by the number of quilted coats you had to wear, and a 'three-coat' winter was cold enough to freeze the tea in the pot. There was heavy fighting around the capital T'ai-Yuan far to the north, and the Communist troops infiltrated through the passes as far south as Yangcheng. The posse of resident soldiers under the Mandarin's control elected, at that moment, to chase bandits far from the city; they returned, looking a little sheepish, only when the Communists' three-day occupation was over. The Communists' advance was little more than a reconnaissance in force; they did no damage in the city, although they inflicted much elsewhere; they were not seen again until the Japanese arrived.

There was the time in 1936 when Gladys decided that she would become a Chinese citizen. She wanted nothing to cut her off from the people, and it was better to be a 'Chinese foreigner' than simply a 'Foreign devil'. With the help of the Mandarin she sent off her papers, completed all the formalities and became a naturalized Chinese. It made no difference to her work, or to her relationship with the townsfolk of Yangcheng, but it made her feel as if she belonged to this background.

There was one sadness. Her old friend Mrs Smith from the Tsehchow mission, on the way to pay her a visit, was taken ill half way between Tsehchow and Yangcheng. The coolies in charge of her mule litter were uncertain whether they should press on to Yangcheng or return to Tsehchow; eventually they decided to go on to Yangcheng. The old lady was delirious when she arrived, and died that night without recovering consciousness. Gladys missed old Mrs Smith, who had been a good friend to her. It was her death that brought new missionaries, the Davises, to Tsehchow, one year later, and Gladys made the journey from Yangcheng to welcome them.

She enjoyed immensely these occasional visits to Tsehchow. It lay on the plain, and although a walled city also, it was much larger than Yangcheng. It was one of the great trading centres of South Shansi, terminus for the caravans of small, pouting-lipped, tawny-golden camels, which brought down silks and cloths and tobaccos from Pekin and the northern territories, and took back on the return journey coal and iron goods, chinaware and cotton wool, humped up from the Yellow River and through the Shansi mountains by the mule trains. It was spring when she arrived, and around the city the apricot and prune trees, the peach and persimmon were in bloom. From the walls, on one side, you looked down into the narrow, choked streets of the old city; on the other, across the patchwork fields of growing crops: maize and mustard seed, cotton, millet, alfalfa and the dark green, tall-stemmed Kaoliang, to the blue-peaked mountains nine miles away.

Jean Davis, a bonnie Scottish lass from Perthshire, never forgot her first sight of Gladys ". . . a wee thin thing with great, dark, staring eyes," she said, "who rattled away in the Shansi dialect as if she'd been born in the district."

It was true; Gladys had not merely learnt the language; she had embedded herself in it like a stone in a fruit. The language had grown around her. She never wrote it very well, but in its idiomatic forms she spoke, thought and dreamt in Shansi dialect; there were no language barriers at all between her and the people with whom she lived.

The arrival of the Davis family—husband, wife and small son—to live at a mission only two days' journey away across the mountains was a piece of great good fortune for Gladys. They became staunch friends, united in their interests and their work. David and Jean, when they settled down, also dressed and 'lived' Chinese. David Davis was a lean, hard young Welshman of thirty-three. Like Gladys, he also visited the loneliest villages to start Christian communities; their parish, through which they roamed individually, covered more than 5,000 square miles. In many of the isolated villages the peasants had never seen a white man before, let alone a white woman!

David Davis was a man of courage and determination. He had lived in China many years before, and had had occasion to demonstrate this determination. Born on a farm in South Wales, he had served in the Royal Flying Corps during the last years of the First World War, gone back to Wales to work in the docks at Cardiff at the end of it, and experienced years of the slump-despondent twenties. Eventually he went to China to serve in the International Customs; it was this experience that convinced him he must take up missionary work. He had always been a God-fearing man, but it was the sight of the desperate poverty, ignorance and need of the Chinese coolie that clinched his determination. The International Customs post at which he was stationed was based on the River Yangtse; the river fed at its source by the Himalayan snows, and of such fabulous power that a 20,000-horse-power gunboat trying to thrust up through its gorges could proceed at no more than walking pace. A considerable amount of gun-running went on through David Davis's customs post; the Communist troops who held the territories farther up-river were willing to pay large sums for arms and ammunition. Many of his fellow customs officers —and they were of various nationalities—were prepared to close a judicious eye to this traffic. David Davis kept both eyes wide open. He did not think it part of his duty to aid the Communists to get arms. On one occasion he discovered a considerable store of rifles and machine-guns concealed on a ship bound up-river. He confiscated the cargo and handed it over to the International Authorities. From that time onwards he was an unpopular man in Communist eyes, for they had spies everywhere.

They captured him with superb effrontery during the visit of a British gunboat three days before David's tour of duty as a custom's official was due to expire. The commander of the ship was dining with him in his bungalow that evening, when the Communist troops came quickly down from the mountains on either side of the river and set up enfilading artillery and machine-gun points on either bank. They ordered the naval commander back to his ship, now immobilized under the muzzles of their guns. David Davis they took to a house higher up the hill and in undramatic, oriental fashion, informed him he would be executed next morning. At first light the following day they took out a Chinese they had also made prisoner and cut off his head on the lawn, apparently to convince David Davis that there was no hope for him. At almost the same moment a British merchant ship, with sandbagged decks, and guns rigged everywhere, summoned the night before by the gunboat's radio, came steaming slowly up-river against the current, indulging in that particular form of gallantry and intimidation obviously taught as part of the curriculum of the Royal Navy.

Artillery deployed around the house where David Davis was held captive, opened up at once and jetting plumes of water made pretty patterns around the merchant ship. This burst of fire revealed the artillery's whereabouts. The British merchant ship returned the fire with all armament, and the impassive orientals became considerably more mobile as trees and bushes, bodies and parts of the house erupted skywards around them. The naval commander's gunboat chose this psychological moment to slip its anchor, and its 4.7 shells came lobbing into the front garden further to inconvenience the Communist gunners. It was during this confusion that David Davis decided his presence was not really necessary and made a quick exit through the back door. No one noticed his departure, and he was up the mountainside and into the wild country beyond without dignity, but with a great deal of speed. When he came down to civilization three days later, much farther down-river, he learnt that several sailors had been killed and wounded in the action, but that both vessels had managed to escape downstream. His time in the International Customs had expired, and he returned to England.

His return to China as a missionary started off in the same dangerously theatrical way. Unlike Gladys, who had taken a month to get from Tientsin to Shansi, most of the way by mule, the Davis family came by train to Pao Ai Hornan, a city to the south of the Yellow River, and then travelled north by mule litter through the mountains to Tsehchow. Their baggage was supposed to follow them. When it did not arrive, David Davis returned to the Yellow River to see what was the matter. Nothing was the matter that a little exertion would not cure. With a couple of muleteers he loaded his baggage on to a mule train and set off on the return journey. In a lonely stretch of the mountain country, a dozen bandits popped up from behind rocks and David Davis had the uncomfortable experience of seeing a German Mauser revolver pointed precisely at his stomach. In his travelling case the bandits found his cut-throat razor, and used it to slash open the other boxes. With the loot fast on their horses, an argument broke out amongst them concerning the disposal of David Davis. Some of the bandits saw in his capture an ideal opportunity for demanding a ransom; others insisted that it was better to destroy the evidence—shoot him and drop his body into a ravine. But eventually, after some squabbling, a man who appeared to be the leader turned to him and yelled, "Go!" David gratefully scrambled away as fast as he could. From a high point nearby, he watched them ride away with all the possessions he had so slowly accumulated and brought out to China. But at least his wife was not yet a widow.

So the years passed. Sometimes Gladys did not see the Davises for months at a time, for it was a long journey from

Yangcheng, and her work took her out mainly to the lonelier regions. That she left a mark in those places there is little doubt; even today, if one walked through some of those isolated villages, the songs the men and women would be singing as they worked in the fields would be Christian hymns. She made many converts amongst them and Christianity altered the lives of those who embraced it completely.

To the peasants, Christianity was not a foreign doctrine of imperialism; to the women particularly it brought a new life. They had rights in the household; no longer were they, or their daughters, sold out of hand, or replaced by second and third wives. The idols were burnt. A family became a unit, working together, not ruled by a supreme male. It is quite obvious that Gladys Aylward was successful in her work because she was different. On one occasion her mother received a letter from a Chinese friend Gladys knew. It ran:

> When your precious daughter came to China my wife first saw her, and then I talked with her, and found that she is a missionary we need in China. She won't mind the bitternesses, difficulties and poverties, but preach the Gospel all the places in the south of Shansi. Most foreigners come to China not purely for preaching the Gospel, and most of them are very comfortable, and therefore very few people in China believe Jesus Christ. Because the people see that it is not same what saying in the Bible when they have it compared.

Gladys lived her frugal, happy life according to 'the same what saying in the Bible.' She did not know, and no one in Yangcheng ever dreamt, that war would engulf them soon; she did not know that the Japanese were in power in Manchuria, and would drive down the age-old routes of the Mongol conquerors. They knew in Yangcheng that there was friction in the outside world, that war-lords in every province were conspiring for power. Occasionally a detachment of northern troops would pass through the city, but they had little contact with the average citizen. And indeed, who would wish to fight over a small mountain city like Yangcheng? There were finer silks and rarer treasures in Pekin and the cities to the south. No doubt the monks of Monte Cassino could have argued in the same fashion!

The muleteers who carried news and gossip were not experts in political matters. It was only when the caravans passing southwards began to mention that the people in Luan were worried about a Japanese attack, that the people of Yangcheng discovered that the Japanese had even invaded northern Shansi. Even when news of battles fought far to the north reached them, no one could bring themselves to believe that they would be affected. And so it was on that spring morning of 1938, when the little silver planes came buzzing in over the mountains, everyone ran out of their houses to watch them, for many had never seen an aeroplane before, and these looked so pretty, swooping down out of the sun.

Gladys did not run out of the Inn because, at the time, with the cook and four converts, she was kneeling in prayer in an upstairs room. She did not hear the aeroplanes until the last minute, and then the whole world turned into a roaring, jumbled, falling, confused chaos which ended in blackness. The people in the streets of Yangcheng were still waving and shouting as the pointed metal cylinders fell from the bellies of the aircraft and plummeted down into the town, and their shouts turned to screams of pain and horror as chunks of flying masonry and hissing shrapnel ricocheted amongst them. The aircraft droned up and down, very low, swooping out over the valley and then back again. It was almost impossible to miss. One bomb, however, did miss. It screamed over the buttress of the city walls and struck one corner of the roof of the Inn of Eight Happinesses. Nine people in the roadway outside were killed at once. In the upstairs room where Gladys, Yang and the others were praying, the floor canted suddenly sideways and they slid and fell downwards in a welter of timber, tiles, dust and plaster, to be buried amongst this debris in the room below.

Gladys did not remember losing consciousness; she only remembered hearing faint voices, and then slowly realizing that she was lying face downwards with a great weight pressing on her back. She felt no pain, but her breathing was difficult. She could hear voices nearby saying, "Praise the Lord, praise the Lord!" and her quick thought was: 'This is no time to be praising the Lord. Why don't they do something to get me out? Why don't they get me out!'

Then she heard a voice she recognized vaguely shouting, "They're there, I know they're there! Under the rubble!"

It seemed hours before Gladys felt the debris being hauled away. At last they got to her. A heavy beam pinned her down; it was a miracle she had not been killed. She felt bruised and sick, but she dusted down her clothes and helped to pull out the cook and the others. Yang was most un-Christian in his speech and general behaviour. He was using words which Gladys never knew existed in the Shansi dialect. The women were frightened. All of them were suffering from cuts and bruises, but none was seriously injured. The aeroplanes had gone, but now there was panic and confusion everywhere.

One man was hopping from foot to foot. "In the town it is dreadful," he was crying. "Everywhere is blocked; all are killed; it is dreadful, dreadful!"

"We must go and see what we can do, then," said Gladys grimly. "Now stop that caterwauling and go and lend a hand!"

In her bedroom she kept her medicine chest. It contained one large bottle of Lysol (broken), one bottle of permanganate of potash crystals, a tin of boracic powder, and cotton wool—plenty of cotton wool. She rapidly tore her two sheets into bandage-sized strips and set off for the East Gate.

Nothing in her life before had quite prepared her for the sight which confronted her. The walls and gate were untouched, but the centre of the town appeared completely pulverized. Dead and dying, wounded and bomb-shocked lay everywhere, for the streets had been crowded. The main street was littered with masonry; bodies were half buried beneath it; people still trapped were screaming for help. For a second or two she paused at the gate, quailing momentarily in the face of the task ahead. What could she do with her few silly bandages and the little bottle of permanganate? But the sense of futility passed in a second. A sudden hardness and determination completely physical in effect pervaded her. To the chattering group of onlookers at the gate she became suddenly authoritative.

"I need all of you," she snapped angrily. The surprised townsmen stared at her, then obediently followed her instructions. "Now get to work. You must all help. You two men clear that rubble over there; someone is buried. You three, go and get buckets of water—hot water. You, one, two, three, four, five—you'll clear the main street so that there's a clear passage. All the dead you'll carry outside the gates. Understand? Now, let's start working at once."

Into the confusion of rubble and masonry and human pain, Ai-weh-deh contrived to insert some modicum of common sense and first aid. A woman lay only a few yards from her, blood streaming from her head. She looked up with agonized eyes. Gladys knelt beside her, plastered a huge piece of cotton wool on to the wound and tore off a strip of bandage to hold it in place. She was not badly hurt.

"There you are, dear. Now you lie there for a few minutes until you feel better and then get up and go home. D'you understand?"

The woman nodded gently. The terror went out of her eyes. "Yes," she said weakly, and there was a note of utter relief in her voice.

"Where do you live?"

"Outside the walls in the Street of Three Swans."

"D'you think you could walk there if I got someone to help you?"

"I'll try."

Gladys called over one of the men tugging at the rubble.

"Listen to me," she said. "In a minute or two this woman will feel strong enough to walk. You'll take her down to her house in the Street of Three Swans. If she cannot walk you will carry her. Make her comfortable in her house, then come back here; there is more work to be done. You understand?"

The man nodded. "Yes, Ai-weh-deh," he said humbly. He helped the woman to her feet, and with her arm round his neck they stumbled off. Gladys moved on.

The first two men uncovered a shopkeeper from the rubble of the first house. They called her over. One look was enough to tell her that he was dead.

"Carry the body outside the walls. Then come back and continue with the work."

In the distance of ten yards she dressed the wounds of twelve people. A pail of hot water had appeared and she emptied a few crystals from her precious bottle of permanganate into it. This she dabbed on as a rough antiseptic. She kept coming across groups of bomb-shocked, pathetic survivors; all of them she coaxed or threatened into action. Her shrill voice echoed through the ruins:

"You three men, get down that hole. Someone's there for certain; can't you hear them calling out? And you others search that building—see that no one is in there."

Her face streaked with dust and tears and sweat, her mouth set in a firm and fanatical line, her tunic stained with blood, she worked steadily on, bandaging and splinting, and sponging with her bucket of permanganate, and once or twice, though she tried to control herself, sobbing quietly to herself when she happened upon a wounded or dead or mutilated child. But nothing stopped her working. In the late afternoon, with a sinking heart, she realized that she was still only three-quarters of the way up the main street. On the steps of the yamen an old man was sitting, his head on his hands. He was covered with dust, but otherwise appeared unhurt. As Gladys clambered over the rubble, he raised his head and looked at her with dull eyes.

"And so God is still alive," he croaked. "You're still here."

"I'm not God and they can't kill Him," snapped Gladys. "What are you doing, old man, sitting down when there is work to be done?"

"I have been working," he said wearily. "They are all still working over there."

Gladys looked in the direction he pointed. At the corner

127

among the broken masonry she saw her old friend, the Prison Governor. She went to meet him.

He was dazed and dirty. "Ai-weh-deh?" he said wearily. "I knew that if you were not dead you would be somewhere in the middle of it." He drew the sleeve of his jacket across his brow, leaving a dirty mark.

"You've got people trying to help?" asked Gladys.

"All the prisoners," said the Governor. "They are doing very well."

Even as he spoke, Feng, the Buddhist priest, appeared round the corner carrying a wounded man on his back. He smiled at Gladys as he carried his burden past her.

"We're putting the wounded back into the yamen," explained the Governor dispiritedly. "There are so many of them. How much longer can we go on like this?"

"Until the job's finished," declared Gladys impatiently. "But we must put some organization into our relief work. We must get the wounded to shelter, the dead buried and the city cleaned up. Where is the Mandarin?"

"He is in the yamen, helping there."

"Let's go and talk to him."

They picked their way over the debris and found the Mandarin still in scarlet gown talking to a group of worried officials. At the sight of Gladys he dismissed the others, and sat down to talk to her. He agreed with all she said. Half an hour later the 'relief committee' was functioning. It consisted of the Mandarin, the Prison Governor, Gladys and Lu Tchen, a shrewd little merchant. Caked with dust and sweat and blood they sat round a table to formulate plans for the relief of their city. They had no experience; no disaster in history could be compared with this. Long centuries ago the men of Yangcheng had built their walls wisely and well. They had smoothed the outer face with great square stones, carefully locked and dovetailed into place, and built a second wall behind it. They had filled the space between with a solid core of granite and made it so wide and strong at the top that a horse and cart could be driven along it. If cannon were hauled over the mountains, they were thick enough to sustain a cannonade, and against such puny things as arrows, spears and catapulted boulders they were quite impregnable. But death which plummeted down from the heavens—that would obviously be sent by God, and against it there would be no defence. Thus they had reasoned. And their fine walls had made a tight basket into which the Japanese bombers had dropped their bombs with neat precision, certain that the blast within those narrow confines would create the maximum havoc.

"We must use the muleteers," said Gladys. "We must stop them at the gates of the city, tell them to stable their beasts where they can outside the city, then they must work with us to clear the rubble. There are still people alive under the ruins. We must get them out and clear the main road."

"There are hundreds of homeless, and many wounded," said the Governor despondently.

"The temple of Lang Quai and the temple of the Buddhists in the city centre are unharmed," said the Mandarin. "In one the homeless can live, in the other we can put the wounded."

"We must pool the food supplies, start a communal kitchen and get the cooks to prepare food," said Gladys.

"The merchants will give food and cloth to the hungry and homeless," added Lu Tchen.

"Women must be enlisted to nurse the wounded," said Gladys, "although I am afraid many will die. The Town Crier must go round and make these announcements. He should also tell people who have relatives in the country to go out and stay with them."

"I will see that the muleteers and my prisoners clear the main street from the East to the West Gate," said the Governor. "Unless we do this all mule trains will come to a halt on either side of the town."

The Mandarin nodded agreement, but still appeared worried. "I have other disturbing news," he said. "Reports have reached me that the Japanese have captured Luan and are advancing on Tsehchow. From Tsehchow they will almost certainly march towards Yangcheng. I understand that they are not a merciful people."

"Well, we've several days before they arrive," said Gladys quickly. "We ought not to waste any more time."

The clearance squads were organized. The muleteers, the prisoners and the townspeople picked up the lumps of masonry from the main street and tossed them back on to the ruins of the houses and shops which lined it. The wounded were carried to the temple of the Buddhists, and there Gladys Aylward with many helpers bathed them in her purple wash of permanganate, roughly splinted broken limbs, tore up more sheets to make bandages, comforted as best she could those who were about to die, and sent runners off to fetch relatives of the wounded who could be moved. A huge pit was dug outside the West Gate close to an ancient cemetery and the dead were buried. Yang superintended a squad of other cooks from neighbouring inns so that no one went hungry. That night a hundred flickering lamps burned within the thick walls of Yangcheng as the work progressed, and every muleteer—after his long journey—worked until he staggered from exhaustion. There was abroad a spirit of comradeship in adversity which in later years so many other citizens of bombed cities all round the world were to experience. A brotherhood in despair; a unity which brought from the deep recesses of the human spirit an unsuspected fortitude which was both a comfort and a victory.

The dawn came up in a great flush of crimson, and the air was cool and clean, while outside the walls the cocks crowed and the dogs barked as they did every morning during the first hour. Inside the walls only the pariah dogs nosed at the rubble in search of food, and no children laughed. The smoke which rose slowly into the clear sky was the smoke from smouldering buildings. It was still smouldering five days later when the victorious troops of Nippon, in their light khaki uniforms and packs, came up over the mountain path from Tsehchow and entered a deserted city through the East Gate.

CHAPTER TEN

THE JAPANESE entered a deserted city, for stories of their ruthlessness had preceded them. Even in Yangcheng the news of their bombings and brutalities was current gossip. Out to the lonely villages and the mountain caves the people streamed, taking what possessions they could carry with them. The Governor of the prison and his guards assembled the convicts in chains and marched them off to an isolated mountain village; the Mandarin, his wives and family moved to another tiny hamlet nearby; and Gladys with her small Christian community of about forty people left for Bei Chai Chuang, a tiny walled village of eight houses, which lay several miles away to the south behind the mountain flanking the main mule trail.

Bei Chai Chuang lay on the side of a high peak like a swallow's nest on a sloping roof. No road led to it and the rocky terrain over which one passed to reach it left no track across the mountains. In the hollows and clefts out of the wind, the villagers grew millet and maize, cotton wool and linseed; they tended their chickens and pigs, sheep and cows, and in season trapped the mountain partridge and pheasants. It was a frugal, simple mode of existence. No Japanese soldier ever discovered Bei Chai Chuang and lived to reveal its whereabouts. No Japanese soldier ever moved far from his main force in those mountains during that cruel war, for every farmer was a guerilla fighter and showed small mercy to those he considered despoilers of his country.

Gladys had many old friends in the village. She was always welcome there, and on this occasion the farmers, even with the many mouths to feed in her group, were hospitable and listened with horror to their stories of the bombing. They stayed at Bei Chai Chuang for over a week, and then further news reached them that the Japanese Army had passed through the city and disappeared down the trail.

Gladys decided to go back to recover some property. She had left the deeds of the house and various passes and papers buried in a box in the courtyard. On second thoughts she decided that Bei Chai Chuang was a safer place for them than Yangcheng.

It took her several hours to reach Yangcheng, and she approached it cautiously. As she came closer she could see that the West Gate was shut; she skirted the wall, clambering round the narrow apron of rock which dropped sheerly to the valley below, on the yamen side of the city, until she reached the East Gate. The houses outside the city were completely deserted; an air of eerie stillness seemed to hang over the entire town. It was late afternoon and the shadows were long when she walked down the narrow alleyway to the Inn of Eight Happinesses. The inn sign still creaked in the wind, and it needed a new coat of paint. She went from room to room; it was as they had left it; the corner of the bombed building gaped to the sky. She took a piece of stick and began to grub in the earth in one corner of the courtyard to find the box. She had almost uncovered it when she sensed rather than heard movement at the entrance to the courtyard. She turned in alarm. In the doorway, in his dirty tunic and trousers and round black hat, stood the water-carrier. She knew him quite well. He was an old man with a goatee beard, and a thin, sly face. She didn't like him; she knew he was a thief and she considered him a wicked old man. She wondered if he had stayed there during the short Japanese occupation. She wouldn't have put it past him; it would provide him with an ideal opportunity for looting.

"When are you leaving?" he asked in his scraped tin voice.

She frowned at him. "Why should I leave? This is my home. I shall sleep here or with one of my neighbours."

"There are no neighbours. Everyone who has come back is in the town behind gates which are locked and barred. You won't get in."

"What does that matter? I can sleep here."

She was annoyed by his attitude. What business was it of

his where she went and what she did? She scraped away the last of the dirt and lifted her deed-box out of the hole. She opened the lid and examined the contents, wondering if the flimsy bits of paper were really worth preserving. With a war starting, nothing was going to be of much value.

"The Japanese are coming back," said the water-carrier, chuckling like an old peahen.

Gladys stared at him for a moment without speaking.

"Are you trying to frighten me?" she said coldly. "Because you won't."

"They are already at the West Gate," he said with a snigger.

"Why haven't you gone, then?" retorted Gladys.

"They won't hurt me. They won't bother with a poor old man. And they're at the West Gate, I tell you!"

"Rubbish!" began Gladys, and as if the word was a cue for sound, at that precise moment a terrific explosion came from the other end of the town. It was so sudden and so startling that she dropped her box and ran. She scurried through the courtyard entrance, and as she ran a succession of other explosions added to her speed. She sped up the alleyway to the East Gate. It was locked and barred. It was no use going along the track eastwards; that led to Tsehchow, which must be in enemy hands. Bei Chai Chuang lay to the south-west. She had to skirt the wall again and go in that direction. She wasted no more time but clawed her way over the boulders in the shadow of the wall. The firing continued. It was almost dusk, and as she rounded the last buttress, she came to an abrupt halt.

A battle was joined at the West Gate. Beneath it, about fifty Japanese soldiers in light khaki uniforms were sprawled behind rocks, or out in the open, shooting up at the walls above the gate. On top of the wall she could see Chinese Nationalist soldiers firing back, and occasionally tossing down a hand grenade which exploded with a loud bang. Gladys felt a small icy hand reach up from her stomach and grip her heart. The small cemetery in which they had so recently interred the bombed dead lay between her and the battle. She crept quickly into the shelter of its mounds and tombstones. She crouched there, thinking that of all the places she might have chosen to hide in, a graveyard, a place of the dead, was the most inauspicious. "But *I'm* not dead yet!" she told herself determinedly. Somehow, she had to worm through that battle and make off along the mule trail to the west. If she waited until darkness she would not be able to see, and she guessed that the main Japanese Army was not far behind this patrol. They might even choose this very graveyard to bivouac for the night. That was a perturbing thought. There was more chance of slipping through this advance guard than the main body of troops. These troops were so busy engaging the Chinese that they were paying no attention to their rear. That suggested a solution. If she walked quietly round behind them, they might not even see her. She had to go very close to them, though, for a high mountain face cut off any chance of progress on the right hand side.

Beyond the trail on the other side was a small field of green wheat almost two feet tall. Gladys felt certain that if she could reach its shelter she would be safe. She stood, blew out her pent-up breath, and walked quickly forward. She skirted behind the ranks of Japanese soldiers, determined to run for it if one sprang up in front of her or from behind a boulder. Nearing her objective, she could contain herself no longer, and with a mad run threw herself head first into the wheat field. She crawled rapidly away, heedless of the stones and gravel bruising her hands. She reached the falling slope of the mountainside on the other side of the field, and hidden from view, scampered along until she came again to the main track leading westwards. It led downwards until it closed into a narrow, steep-sided gorge, a mile from the city, which cut for some distance through the mountains. Both sides were sheer. In bad weather a rushing river streamed along the rocky bed, but in fine weather—as it was now—the bed of the stream was used as a highway, and the high rocky path hacked into the cliffside ignored. 'Supposing,' she thought with a sudden spurt of panic, 'I meet another party of Japanese in the gorge, I shall be trapped. Which route will they use? The river bed or the high path?"

She stood there while the panic ebbed and left her. Now she was not frightened, only conscious that she needed aid. "You'll have to help me, Lord," she said aloud. She closed her eyes and began to spin in a small circle, saying: "Whichever path I face when I stop, I shall take. D'you hear me, Lord? Whichever path I face when I stop turning, I shall go along." She spun until she felt giddy and stopped. She faced directly up towards the high path cut out of the side of the gorge overhead. She scrambled up and hurried along it, By now the long shadows of the setting sun filled the canyon, making it a chill and eerie place.

She had gone perhaps half a mile, almost half way, almost to the place where the gorge swung sharply to the left, when she heard unmistakable noises from ahead and below. It was the sound of an army on the march. The noise of wheels and feet and hooves clattering over stones. She threw herself flat on her stomach and peered over the edge of the canyon. A feeling of utter relief that she had chosen the right path flooded through her. Part of the imperial army of Nippon was passing below! They came slowly up the river bed, a long column of soldiers. They passed fifty feet below her, and she counted heads. There were about 500 in the battalion, with pack mules, and mule-drawn light artillery. She geussed that the guns would soon be trained on the gates of Yangcheng. She wondered what would happen when those gates burst inwards. The consideration depressed her. The soldiers picked their way through the gloom of the gorge, and Gladys let them rumble out of sight before she risked getting to her feet to run onwards.

Breathlessly, she reached the place where the high track came down to join the river bed, scrambled across it and picked her way up the mountainside. When she reached the ridge she could feel her heart pumping heavily. It was almost dark; stars were pricking out high above the peaks. She felt the cold breeze on her face, but the sense of relief at escaping from the enemy in the gorge exhilarated her. She headed along the ridge in the direction of Bei Chai Chuang, and realized that she would never reach it in the darkness; but the fact that she would have to sleep on the mountain-side did not trouble her.

Next morning in the village she told them what had occurred at Yangcheng. Many had relatives whom they thought might have been unwise enough to return to the city, and they were worried. But there was nothing they could do. The Bei Chai Chuang men made daily reconnais-sances towards Yangcheng, and on the fifth day returned with good news. The gates were open; the Town Crier was parading along the tracks outside the city, banging his gong and shouting, "Will all citizens return and clear their courtyards?"

Gladys's small band were delighted. Obviously the Japanese had retreated towards Tsehchow; now they could return to their homes. She was less confident, not liking the sound of the order, 'Clear your courtyards!' She had never, in all her years in Yangcheng, heard that particular pro-clamation. On the other hand, they had never before been invaded by the Japanese!

She insisted that all her band remained in the village until she had investigated. With one of the Bei Chai Chuang women accompanying her, she made the journey over the mountains again and down to the city. From the heights she looked down at the old walls and was suddenly afraid. As they clambered down the rocks towards the mule trail she became more and more certain that horror lay inside those old walls. Intuitively she felt it in her bones, in the dryness of her mouth. The absence of movement, the absence of noise, the absence of rising smoke, the absence of life, all coagulated into a frightening sense of physical oppression.

The West Gate was open and they walked slowly under the arch, every step confirming her intuition. It was a city of the dead. A city of hollow-eyed corpses piled along the main street, and in every alleyway. Most had been bayon-eted; very few shot. All along the streets, in the temples, in the bazaars, the bodies crouched or lay, some twisted grotesquely, others with a foot or a hand stretching into

the air; women and children, too. In the angular, disinterested rigidity of death, the bodies clogged the city,
and the dogs, the horrible pariah dogs, had become
cannibals upon the surfeit of flesh. The air smelt of death.
With a set face Gladys walked along the main street. She
shed no tears. No tears would come. These bodies were
past pity or tears; one could not weep for corpses in a
charnel house. Her emotions were frozen into a tight
kernel of horror inside her.

A small crowd huddled outside the yamen. She pushed
her way through, and in the inner chamber discovered the
Mandarin. His face was grey.

"They must be buried," she said flatly.

He nodded, passing a thin hand across his brow. Like
Gladys, he had arrived at Yangcheng from his mountain
hideout only that morning. He had seen and heard what
had occurred. With no sign of the Japanese in the city,
many of the townsfolk had come back into Yangcheng to
pick up their lives where they had left off. It was then that
Chinese guerilla troops had retreated into the city attacked
by the Japanese advance guard. As the Mandarin explained
the sequence of tragedy, Gladys nodded. She had seen the
opening skirmishes of that action. Infuriated at resistance,
at being denied access, the Japanese had contained the city
until their main army arrived, then beaten in the gates.
With systematic fury they had butchered every man, woman
and child they found within. Not even Genghis Khan could
have slaughtered so ruthlessly, and Yangcheng in past
centuries had seen the blades of his warriors.

A huge pit was dug outside the West Gate at the edge of
the cemetery which already contained the victims of the
bombings. The dead were heaped into it. In the courtyard
of the Inn of Eight Happinesses Gladys found three more
bodies sprawled. She helped to bury them on the mountainside some distance away. She stayed until late afternoon in
the city but, suddenly overwhelmed by the tragedy which
grew into a great sickness in her mind, she could stand it no
longer; abruptly she decided not to spend the night in
Yangcheng, but to return at once to Bei Chai Chuang. She

walked back through the town, past the grisly procession of citizens carrying their dead to the pit, and out under the West Gate, and her sorrow was scarcely bearable.

From the mountain above she looked back at the town which had been such a well-loved home for so many years. With the sun low, the roofless pagodas were black silhouettes against the sky; the dereliction was masked in shadow. The walls still sloped up, strong and elegant as ever. It looked a whole city, a remote mountain city of peace and beauty built by ancient, skilled hands; but she knew that everything had changed. What she saw was only a shell, a husk; in two short weeks the city she loved had sickened and died.

She might return and live in that city; perhaps she would rebuild the roof of the Inn; but it would never be the same again. No cleansing, or rebuilding, could ever remove the memory of its death, or erase these recent horrors from her mind. The time of peace was over. This remote and windswept territory she had come to know and adore was now a battlefield. With a deep sigh she turned away and went on slowly over the mountains towards the village of Bei Chai Chuang.

. . . . .

As usual, she was up just after dawn. Ten days had passed since the sacking of Yangcheng. She walked round the balcony and down the stone steps into the courtyard, leaving the room she shared with ten other women and the children. In the kitchen she gulped down the steaming bowl of millet with her chopsticks, swallowed scaldingly hot twig tea from a small china bowl. Outside the house it was cool, for the sun was still not above the peaks, and there was a fragrance and a sharpness in the air. She stood for a moment breathing deeply, looking down into the valley, and across at the distant heights. Then she hurried over to her improvised hospital to start the day's work. As she walked into the cave, the ten patients turned up their heads to greet her.

She was brisk and cheerful, and as much like all

those intimidating nurses she remembered from her childhood as she could manage. "Good morning," she said. "Have you slept well? Time to give you all your medicine."

The hospital cave lay within the village wall. The wall itself was built so closely into the contour of the mountainside that from a distance you could not separate the natural from the man-erected stone. The mountain peak loomed above it like a cliff, and below the village the ground fell away sharply.

Into the side of the mountain, within the wall in the centre of the village, was the cave. Usually the men of Bei Chai Chuang used it as a stable for their animals, and when the heavy winter snows came they packed all their livestock into its shelter. With their help Gladys cleaned it out and made it her hospital. The sacking of Yangcheng had made this a humanitarian necessity. Many wounded had dragged themselves, or been carried to refuge in the village. She did not know it at the moment, but in the next few weeks there were going to be many casualties needing attention. Japanese aeroplanes, on patrol, machine-gunned and bombed whenever the inclination took them, and patrols of soldiers fired at any villager they saw working in the fields or on the mountainside. Francis, one of her children, caught in the open by an attacking plane, received a bullet through his hand and lost three of his fingers.

News soon spread of the improvised hospital at Bei Chai Chuang operated by Ai-weh-deh, and the sick and wounded crawled towards it. Most of the injured suffered from gunshot wounds. These she treated as best she could in primitive but effective fashion. She had castor oil, sulphur, the inevitable permanganate of potash, and a metal syringe given to her in Tsehchow which was almost as big as the syringe with which her father squirted his rose trees in the garden at Edmonton.

In the cave, Chung Ru Mai, the Bible Woman, a visitor from Tsehchow trapped by the sudden Japanese advance, boiled the water and allowed the crystals to dissolve. Gladys carefully filled her syringe and turned to the first patient. He was a young farmer from the fields near Yangcheng. A bullet had passed through the calf of his leg. He smiled as she approached and pulled up the blue cotton trouser leg.

"Hold the bowl underneath," directed Gladys.

Syringing the wounds with permanganate was her standby treatment. It proved an effective remedy, for only one of her patients died. He was also a young farmer. A Japanese bullet had smashed his elbow and glanced off into his stomach. Not all her patience and care and syringing could save him.

That spring offensive of the Japanese down the ancient Shansi mule trails towards the Yellow River was obviously only a preliminary foray. In the early autumn their forces evacuated Tsehchow and pulled back as far as Luan. Their limited offensives in North China during those early months of the war were experimental probes into difficult terrain. In the spring and early summer they moved into the mountains, following the old trade routes, overcoming any pockets of resistance with the ruthlessness and barbarity which had characterized every enemy from the north since the days of the earliest Mongol invasions. After passing through Yangcheng they pressed on as far as Chowtsun. Here they captured many people, including Hsi-Lien, the muleteer whom Gladys knew so well. With a rapid advance patrol they had surprised him at home with his family, his wife and three children. Grinning, the stocky Japanese soldiers prodded him outside. "Here is a good strong muleteer," they said. "You will serve as an ammunition carrier and no harm will come to you and your family. You understand?"

"But I cannot," faltered Hsi-Lien. "I am a Christian. I am a pacifist. If I carried your bullets, I would be helping in your war. I cannot do it."

They took him before an officer and Hsi-Lien repeated his beliefs, and affirmed his refusal to aid them.

"In that case," said the Japanese officer pleasantly, "we will show you how we treat Christians who refuse to co-operate."

They tied him to a post outside his own home, barricaded the door so that his wife and three children could not get out and then set fire to the house. They jeered at him as the screams of the trapped woman and children drove Hsi-Lien to the verge of madness. They left him tied there while the flames still burnt and retreated back to Yangcheng to practise butchery on a larger if not more dramatic scale within the city walls. When night fell his neighbours crept down from the hills and released him. Demented, out of his mind with despair, he made for the mountains. He had heard that Gladys was at Bei Chai Chuang.

He burst in upon her as she was preparing her syringe and her castor oil, her sulphur and her permanganate of potash for the wounded. He was incoherent with grief and was some hours before they could extract the story from him. Gladys listened in silence. There was little she could do to comfort him, but at least they could inter the bodies of his family in Christian burial. A small party, Gladys, the Bible Woman, two strong farmers and the desolate Hsi-Lien set off back over the mountains towards Chowtsun. They came down out of the mountains at dawn and, with a few villagers, gathered in the courtyard heaped high with blackened embers.

Gladys stood on a heap of stones, raised a little above the others. They bowed their heads as she read aloud from her Bible: "*Let not your heart be troubled; ye believe in God, believe also in me. In my Father's house are many mansions: if it were not so, I would have told you. I go to prepare a place for you. And if I go and prepare a place for you, I will come again, and receive you unto myself; that where I am, there ye may be also. And whither I go ye know, and the way ye know.*

She looked at Hsi-Lien, the muleteer, who stood with head bowed, the tears running down his cheeks, a man now without son, daughter, wife or home, and her heart went out to him in pity. When she rode back over the mountains to Bei Chai Chuang, she took him with her.

.   .   .   .   .   .

Through the autumn, winter and the early spring of

1939, Gladys divided her time between Bei Chai Chuang, Yangcheng and the villages in the province where she had established small Christian communities.

Her job as a foot inspector had ended. It was a luxury occupation which did not survive the bombing. There were more important things to do than inspect feet. The Inn of Eight Happinesses also was failing. The mule traffic along the ancient route had almost stopped, for with Luan in enemy hands they could go no farther than Tsehchow. On this curtailed route a few of her old muleteer acquaintances still called, but Yang, the cook, had disappeared, and with him much of the spirit of the place had gone. When the Japanese first invaded Yangcheng he had gone back to his native village in the mountains. He did not return. What happened to him Gladys never discovered, but news reached her that he was dead. She never found out how he died. He was an old man and it could have been from natural causes, but, somehow, she could not quite believe this. He was such a rebellious, impatient old fellow that the idea of his taking to his bed and quietly passing away was completely alien to his temperament. She was deeply distressed by the news; he had been a staunch friend when she most needed friendship.

These days she was always short of money. From time to time her mother sent a money order, and with the rate of exchange so high a few shillings would last her for months. Not that money mattered very much, for she was a tradition in the region by now, and among the Chinese, in those troubled years, when you had food or shelter you shared it with those in need.

In that spring of 1939 the news that the Japanese were moving in through the mountains again, sent a wind of panic blowing through the streets of Yangcheng. Reluctant to abandon their homes and their livelihoods the people had slowly returned, hoping that some miracle might prevent another Japanese advance. They reasoned that the first disaster could have been bad luck; it might never happen again. The orders of the Chinese Nationalist Commander in the district destroyed all their illusions. His dictum, supported by the High Command, was harsh. "A scorched earth policy!" he said. "Burn your crops. Leave your houses roofless. Let there be no shelter for the invaders anywhere!" In despair the peasants watched the soldiers burning the stalks of the green millet and maize upon which their very existence depended. "But what shall we do?" they pleaded. "How can we live without grain?"

"Take to the hills," was the reply. "Live in the caves and mountains, and grow your crops in every fold or valley where you find fertile earth. Prey on the invader like locusts! Kill his men! Steal his supplies! Take the rifles from his dead and turn them against the Japanese. Only in this way can we save China."

Gladys looked ruefully at the gaping roof; the bomb and the winter weather had made a scorched earth policy quite redundant. The Mandarin was very troubled, however. He called her to see him. "This policy of destruction is difficult. We have done almost everything that the soldiers desired, but there is this Pagoda of the Scorpion."

"What about it?" said Gladys. "Ugly old place!"

"As you may know, there is a legend attached to its history. Hundreds of years ago, so it is said, a giant scorpion roamed these mountains destroying many people. While it was sleeping, the people brought great blocks of stone and built the pagoda around and over it, imprisoning it for ever. Now the townspeople are afraid that if they destroy the Pagoda the scorpion will escape."

Gladys blew out her breath in exasperation. "D'you mean to say you believe *that* old wives' tale?"

He smiled, "No, I do not believe it; that is why I wish you and your Christians to accept the task of pulling it down!"

"With the greatest of pleasure," said Gladys briskly, with the slightly self-righteous satisfaction of a good Christian allowed to destroy a work of idolatry. "I'll get the men in from Bei Chai Chuang, too. We'll start on that horrible heathen temple first thing tomorrow morning."

"When you have finished," said the Mandarin, "I am giving a feast which I would like you to attend. It will probably be the last ever held in the town of Yangcheng as we are leaving little that is useful and I have something to say that I wish you to hear."

Next morning, several dozen healthy Christians attacked the Pagoda of the Scorpion with a variety of implements. It did not take them very long to pry the stones apart and raze it to the ground. When the Mandarin's feast was held, Gladys, to her surprise, found that although as usual she was the only woman present—that had been her privilege for many years—on this occasion she was sitting next to the Mandarin in the seat of honour at his right hand. This had never happened before. All the important personages of Yangcheng were present: the Governor of the prison; two wealthy merchants, several officials, about a dozen in all. The meal was simple, unlike the sumptuous feasts she had enjoyed in early years, and which had lasted for hours.

Towards its close the Mandarin stood up and made his speech. He recalled how Ai-weh-deh had first come to Yangcheng; how she had worked for them; what she had done for the poor and the sick and the imprisoned; of the new faith called Christianity which she had brought with her, and which he had discussed with her many times. Gladys was puzzled by his references. He sounded so much like the chairman of a local committee back in England that she wondered, rather flippantly, if he was going to present her with an illuminated address or a silver teapot? But after speaking for some minutes he turned very gravely towards her, and said seriously: "I would like to embrace your faith, Ai-weh-deh. I would like to become a Christian!"

Around the table rose a murmur of astonishment. Gladys was so astounded that she could hardly speak. The guests nodded and smiled, and she knew that she was expected to reply. She got up and stuttered her surprise, her appreciation and her thanks. The Mandarin saw her confusion and helped her out. "We will talk of all the details later, Ai-weh-deh," he said. She subsided, realizing that she had made her most important convert since she came to China, and yet now hardly knew whether to believe it or not. The talk then turned to the approach of the Japanese. How they would evacuate the city. The Governor of the prison revealed his problem. When the enemy arrived the first time he had marched all his prisoners off into the country and kept them manacled in a cave in the mountainside. Feeding and guarding them had been most difficult; he did not think he could do it again. Should he release the prisoners or execute them?

The guests discussed his dilemma. There seemed general agreement that execution was the safer plan; there were murderers and desperate men among the convicts. Only Gladys protested. Surely, there must be some better way? Why not release them on security or bail into the custody of their friends or relatives? They could be responsible for their behaviour. Yes, the Mandarin was in favour of that solution, and the Governor nodded agreement. He would try her plan, but if the Japanese came too close and there were convicts still without guarantor, he was afraid he would have to behead all who remained.

On the East and West Gates next day, notices were posted proclaiming this procedure; stating that friends and relatives could come and claim a prisoner if they would guarantee his future behaviour, and pay ninety cents as a token of good faith. The Town Crier was sent round the streets to shout identical instructions.

Gladys visited the gaol next day. The response had been reasonable, but there were still twelve prisoners left with no friends or relatives to claim them. As she entered the dismal courtyard, Feng, the Buddhist priest, and another man, Sheng-Li, with whom she had had many conversations, came forward to greet her. By local standards Sheng-Li was an educated man. He could read and write, and was well acquainted with Chinese finance. So well-versed had he been in this particular art that he had forged a *tucheng*, a stone seal used by most wealthy men to stamp their official papers. Each bears its own distinctive markings. Sheng-Li had forged the tucheng of a wealthy merchant, and by using it discreetly had made a pleasant income until his deception was discovered.

He was a jolly little man, and Gladys was very fond of

him. He had been sentenced to fifteen years in prison which occasionally made him rather sad. Now, on impulse, she said she would act as his guarantor. She paid over the ninety cents and the reprieved Sheng-Li skipped nimbly beside her, but as she prepared to leave the courtyard she was dramatically aware of the dejected eyes of Feng trying not to look towards her. She sighed in resignation. Of what use was friendship if an extra ninety cents could not be found? "I will be guarantor for Feng also," she said, and her reward was immediate in every line and muscle of the man's face. He said nothing; he did not have to speak; happiness and gratitude radiated from him. Followed by the two freemen, she went back to the Inn of Eight Happinesses and began to make arrangements for their departure for Bei Chai Chuang. This time she intended to be out well before the Japanese arrived.

Next morning she went to take leave of the Mandarin and the Governor of the prison. The Governor was still disturbed; he had eight prisoners left, two of them condemned murderers, and no guarantors had yet come forward to take them off his hands.

"How did they commit murder?" she asked.

"In the Green Pagoda," said the Governor, "the idols had valuable jewels in their ears and eyes. They were caught in the act of prying them out by one of the priests. They murdered him while trying to escape!"

"Um!" said Gladys contemplatively. She decided she would not feel particularly happy with those two around.

She went to see the remaining convicts in the prison. Eight dejected pairs of eyes stared up at her. She questioned them all and learned that each one had relatives living in outlying villages, but that there was no chance whatsoever of the news of the amnesty reaching these villages before the Japanese arrived. She said "Um!" to herself three or four times, and considered the risk, before she turned to the Governor.

"I can't pay ninety cents for each of these men; I haven't that much money, but if you agree, they can come with me and I'll be responsible for their behaviour. I'll send messengers to their relatives in each village as soon as I reach Bei Chai Chuang, and as I get the securities I'll send them off."

The Governor nodded; not only was he in full agreement with any solution to his dilemma, but also firmly convinced by now of the rightness of most of Ai-weh-deh's decisions. The official in charge of the women's court also came to see her with a problem. One of the young slave girls, Sualan, was troubling him. She was very young and pretty and gay, and almost of marriageable age, and as the yamen was moving, and this time the women were dispersing to many villages, he did not know what to do with her. All the officials had their wives and concubines to attend to; there was not time to marry Sualan off; it was not fair that she should be left alone and unchaperoned after living such a sheltered life in the women's court; and she being so young and pretty and gay, and men being the creatures they were . . .

"All right," said Gladys resignedly, "she can come with me and my criminals, and I'll look after her. It'll be quite a new experience for her. For me too, I expect," she added.

So they set off for Bei Chai Chuang, Gladys and her band of Christians, and Sualan the pretty slave-girl, and the small gang of convicted thieves, rogues and murderers, trailing not uncheerfully in the rear. The convicts gave her no trouble whatsoever. They remained peaceably at Bei Chai Chuang, while messengers went out to their villages to obtain the pledges of responsibility from their relatives. Eventually only Feng and Sheng-Li remained, and they stayed with her for a very long time.

·   ·   ·   ·   ·

She was in Bei Chai Chuang when the news reached her in the early spring that one of her Christian converts in a village close to the town of Chin Shui had been attacked by bandits. Although in reality a poor man, a rumour had reached the bandits that he possessed a hidden hoard of gold; the sort of childish rumour, in fact, which would stimulate simple-minded robbers. They swept down from the mountains, broke into his home and tortured him in an effort to make him reveal the whereabouts of the mythical treasure.

With Timothy, a nine-year-old orphan boy who had also joined the ever-growing troop of children at the Inn, and Wan Yü, a seventeen-year-old girl who lived in a village not far from Chin Shui and wished to visit her mother, Gladys set off to see if she could help him. They found the peasant in his home. He was very sick; the bandits had burned him horribly with red-hot irons. She dressed his burns and made him as comfortable as she could. It was a quiet village in a hidden valley and the terraced fields were still green with spring corn. They stayed there for more than a week; it was peaceful and serene and Gladys enjoyed the short holiday. Chin Shui was two and a half days' travel away, Yangcheng even farther. Each morning she climbed a nearby hill and sat on the top looking at the clouds and the far-stretching mountains, forgetful of the war. But her days of serenity were shortlived. A messenger came running—literally running—from the small Christian Mission she had set up at Chin Shui. The Japanese had entered Yangcheng for a second time, and were expected to sweep on into Chin Shui any day now. There were 200 refugees in the Mission. Could she come and help at once?

She scrambled her few belongings together and set off with Timothy and Wan Yü. They spent the first night at Chersin, a small village, and listened that night to a heavy thunderstorm beating on the tiles. It delayed their departure next morning, as the road was impassable with slippery mud, but as soon as the hot sun began to dry it out, they set off again. Chersin was no more than two miles behind them when they heard the noise of an aeroplane, and saw it beginning to circle above their heads. They ran for shelter. Flat on the ground, they heard the bombs whistle down in the distance and explode, and with mixed feelings, Gladys realized that it was Chin Shui, their destination still a day's journey ahead of them, that was under attack.

They arrived next morning in time to witness the now almost familiar pattern being repeated. All the citizens were assembled in the courtyard of a large temple in the centre of the city, and here the Mandarin of Chin Shui was making his announcement. The city had been bombed, therefore they could expect the enemy to follow up the bombing. Everyone must leave the town not later than first light the next day.

As she listened to his voice, this tall thin figure in his Mandarin's robes standing on the grey stone steps of the temple, the pagoda roofs and the city wall framed behind him, the hot blue sky and the mountains beyond, she realized how often through the centuries such a scene must have been enacted. The invaders invariably came from the north, bringing blood and death and destruction. The people fled to the mountains; crept back again when the enemy had gone, to bury their dead and rebuild their homes. It had happened to generation after generation. If not a foreign invader, then it was some upstart warlord. In ten years' time, who would remember on which day the Japanese had attacked, and who had been killed, and what damage done? Yes, the mother who lost her son, and the widow mourning her husband—they would remember. But soon they, too, would grow old and forget, and the eternal pattern of birth and death, sowing and harvesting would be re-established. You could not eradicate this life; wipe it out, burn it out, or kill it out. The human species was as fecund as lice and harder to annihilate. It was then she realized that God had fashioned them well, these mountain people. For her part she would never abandon them; they were now as much a necessity to her as the skin on her body.

In a letter sent home that year to her mother on a grubby scrap of paper, she wrote: 'Do not wish me out of this or in any way seek to get me out, for I will not be got out while this trial is on. These are my people; God has given them to me, and I will live or die with them for Him and His Glory.'

In London, that year, the summer was hot and soporific, and the people waited for war. The dragonflies glided on brilliant wings above the smooth, gloss-bright surface of the River Thames and the people dug trenches in the parks as shelter against the other wings which would soon spread in the sky. Winston Churchill rumbled in his belly with frustration, and awaited the years of greatness when he would rally the British Commonwealth with immemorial language.

Perhaps it was not so very strange that the words of the small woman writing from the depths of China should carry the same echoes of the New Testament in her letters. 'Do not wish me out of this or in any way seek to get me out, for I will not be got out while this trial is on.'

CHAPTER ELEVEN

THAT NIGHT in the courtyard of the small Mission house at Chin Shui, Gladys made her decision. They also must flee if the enemy were advancing. Yangcheng was already overrun; they could not go back there; therefore, she must endeavour to get back to Bei Chai Chuang with Timothy and Wan Yü, where her friends and the rest of the children were waiting. These days there was safety only with people you knew and could trust. Chinese bandits were joining with larger formations, recruiting from the homeless villagers, becoming, in effect, guerilla forces. All were lawless and savage, and when the inclination took them, they could be crueller to their own people than the Japanese. Gladys knew that if she took to the mountains she could, at least, avoid the advancing Japanese. Against other enemies they would have to take their chance.

It was odd, she reflected, how medieval this warfare was proving. The weapons were modern, yes, but this was not a conflict of swift manœuvre, of sudden surprise; the terrain militated against scientific principles of warfare; this was a cutlass, cut-throat war. The sullen enemy marched by day; a city was woken by a voice crying a midnight warning at its gates, and if it was defended, sack and rapine were visited upon it. No Geneva Convention protected soldier or civilian, no international laws preserved any humanitarian decencies. The human beast had broken out of its zoo.

At first light next morning Gladys, Wan Yü and Timothy left the Mission and walked out through the East Gate carrying their bundles. The darkness still clung to the valleys; but the sky was lightening rapidly above the peaks ahead, and the cocks were brazenly warning the city that both day and the Japanese were advancing.

They had walked no more than 300 yards when Gladys felt the stirrings of a strange uneasiness in her mind. She

151

began to worry. They had two miles to cover before they could reach the rocky shelter of the mountains, and some instinctive sense, some mental telepathy winked a series of warning signals along the corridors of her brain. There was no visual reason for the oppression of fear she suddenly experienced, but she believed implicitly in her intuitions. They said "Stop!" Supposing the Japanese had patrols operating on either side of their advancing troops? Supposing they were trapped in a gorge by these patrols? It had almost happened to her outside Yangcheng. She frowned at Timothy and Wan Yü.

"We're going back," she announced loudly.

They looked at her in astonishment.

"But why?" protested Wan Yü.

"I don't know. But we are!" she answered in a voice which had made its mind up very firmly. She grabbed Timothy's hand, turned on her heel and marched briskly back towards the city gates, tugging him along behind her.

"We can go and stay at my village," said Wan Yü eagerly, hurrying after her. "It lies in a valley out through the West Gate. My brother will look after us. He is a very nice man."

"All right, we'll go and stay there," said Gladys. "I just have an idea it's too dangerous to try and get to Bei Chai Chuang just now."

They hurried back through the East Gate. The streets were boiling with people. Men, women and children carrying a miscellaneous collection of household goods streamed through the streets, making for the West Gate. As they scurried along with the crowd Gladys heard a voice behind her calling: "Ai-weh-deh! Ai-weh-deh!" She looked round. It was the postmaster, a small, eager, fussy individual whom she knew only slightly. He carried a bulky brown-paper parcel tied together with string.

"There are letters for you," he gabbled, thrusting the parcel at her. "They were sent on from Yangcheng. All the post-office documents and stamps are in it, too. Will you look after it for me?"

"But why can't you look after it yourself?" she demanded in an aggrieved voice. "Why tie my letters up with all your stuff?"

"It is necessary. You are the safest one."

"But it's not my job. I'm nothing to do with the post office," she began, and stopped in mid-sentence. At that moment from the gate by which they had just re-entered came the noise of a fusillade of shots and screams of terror. The Japanese advance troops had arrived! If her intuition had not been correct, they would have walked right into them! There was immediate panic; whereas everyone had been walking, now they were running. Larger baskets and bundles were jettisoned in a wild scramble for the West Gate. Men, women and children popped like rabbits from the burrows, from houses and alleyways and joined the confusion.

The postmaster—civic responsibility abandoned—dropped the parcel at Gladys's feet and ran for his life. Instinctively she stooped to pick it up. It was heavy, too big to carry under her arm; she struggled along carrying it in both arms on top of her bedding, determined not to abandon the precious letters from home. Timothy and Wan Yü scurried along beside her, carrying bundles of Bibles from the Mission, for they also were too precious to abandon.

Outside the West Gate the road ran parallel to the swift-flowing Chin River. There was a ford 300 yards from the city gate. Wan Yü's village lay across the river and far up in a steep valley on the other side. Most of the towns-people were making for the ford. Amid a swarm of them, Gladys, Wan Yü and Timothy waded the river. It was chest-deep to Gladys: she jettisoned her bedding and, balancing the post-office parcel on her head with one hand, she clutched Timothy with the other. In mid-stream she thought suddenly how ridiculous she must look; fleeing from the Japanese with a brown-paper parcel containing all the paraphernalia of the Chin Shui post office balanced on her head. But she did not stop to laugh. Safely across the river, their garments clinging clammily to their legs and bodies, they began to scramble up the mountainside, spurred on by the sound of rifle fire cracking through the city streets behind them.

There were no paths. They panted up through terraced fields to the broad valley, flanked by steep peaks, and continued up through millet patches. All that day they climbed, barely pausing to rest. The noise and confusion died away behind them. The valley stretched up for many miles, hemmed in all the way by mountains; there were villages at regular intervals with bushes and flowers everywhere, and the wheat was bright green in the patch-work pattern of terraces. Wan Yü's village lay almost at the top of the valley with only one other above it. At any other time the situation would have been idyllic, for from the village the valley sloped downwards to the Chin River, a winding, sun-glossy streak far below. Where the valley joined the deep cleft of the river bed, on the flat ground, stood the walled city they had just left, now in the hands of the Japanese.

Beyond, rising in blue banks and pinnacles, the mountains massed. In the sheltered valley terraces roses bloomed, furry-legged bees clung to the blossoms; pigs and chickens nosed and scratched in the hard-baked earth and grunted and clucked in industrious research. Each day, swooping overhead high in the sky, the eagles looked down with sharp eyes at the unfamiliar smoke rising from the villages, along the river banks and the lower slopes of the valley. It was high summer, and the conquerors from Nippon burned and looted and slaughtered. Using the ancient city of Chin Shui as base, they made daily forays into the countryside.

Blessed and bolstered by their State religion of Shintoism, believing that the antiquity of their State was greater than that of any other nation on earth; that their Emperor was descended directly from the gods; that they, as the children of the gods, had laid upon them a divine mission to 'save' the rest of mankind; that a Japanese soldier could do no wrong—were not all their wars holy wars?—they burned the green crops in the fields and raped old women and

154

girls, stole the livestock and shot down the peasants and civilians who crossed their path.

From a hole they had knocked in the outer wall of the courtyard Gladys Aylward could see the smoke and flame which revealed these happenings. They soon abandoned the thought of fleeing farther up the mountain and over into the empty country beyond if the enemy approached, for other people depended upon them.

In Wan Yü's house lived her old mother, her brother and his wife, but within a few hours of their arrival they were joined by many others fleeing from the Japanese. These were poor creatures to whom the house of Wan Yü's brother became a final haven. They could go no farther. They sheltered two blind old men, several grandfathers, four pregnant women, half a dozen children and several mothers with small babies. It was quite impossible to contemplate trooping farther across the mountains with such a party. Several were injured. Once again Gladys turned the house into an improvised nursing-home and dressing-station. She prayed, without much hope, that the Japanese would come no closer.

Practically every day their troops came out of their Chin Shui headquarters, systematically ravaging the seven villages which lay at intervals along the river bank. They made quite certain they were back inside the walls with the gates locked by nightfall. Almost every night, holding aloft their lanterns, Gladys and the farmers went down into the valley to aid dazed or wounded peasants. She knew that it was only a matter of time before the enemy turned their attention to the villages which lay farther up the valley, but as Wan Yü's house was so far away, Gladys hoped they would never reach them. Refugees were constantly moving through their village and on into the mountains beyond. As the weeks passed, as a small measure of safety, Gladys arranged a system of watchers to man the hole in the wall during the daylight hours.

Five weeks after they had entered Chin Shui, the Japanese started to raid the villages in the valley, and now they were pressing farther and farther afield. As the raids came closer,

Gladys realized that, even though the house was packed with old and sick, they could expect no mercy from the Japanese. Chinese guerilla bands were constantly attacking the enemy on these forays, and the Japanese treated each village as a possible hiding-place.

The news that the small woman who possessed a God with magical powers of protection lived in the village had reached many people, and a constant stream of suppliants was the result. On the afternoon that the Japanese came, she was tending one of the sick women in an upstairs room. Even before her door banged open she heard Wan Yü's shrill scream: "They're here, they're here!"

Gladys ran downstairs and across to the hole in the courtyard wall; she peered out. Theirs was the first house in the village; only a small temple about fifty yards away lay farther down the valley. She could hear the priests blowing horns, banging drums and offering up obeisances which were supposed to drive the Japanese away. As she watched, she saw a number of khaki-clad figures advance through the terraces and group near the temple. They talked among themselves. Some of them went towards the temple; others started towards Wan Yü's house. Inevitably the next place they entered would be this courtyard, unless she did something to prevent it. "Hide yourselves quickly," she shouted to Wan Yü. "I'll try and keep them out."

She ran to the front gate. She did not know what to do. She only knew she must stop them, even to the extent of going out and fighting them with her bare hands. If she appeared by herself, perhaps the sight of a 'foreign devil' in such an unusual place might occupy their attention for a time; perhaps they would forget the others? The outside door was solid, the latch of heavy iron, and as she got to it her courage ebbed away. She leant against the door, turning so that her back was braced against it for support. Her clenched hand went to her heart to try and stop its pounding. For perhaps ten seconds she stood there in a vacuum of weakness, fear and indecision reaching with desperate mental agony for strength. Then into the confusion of her mind with the clarity of an articulate voice burst the phrase: '*My grace is sufficient for you, because my strength is made perfect in your weakness.*' She stood up straight, and the feeling of panic seeped away from her. She turned, depressed the latch, swung open the heavy door and stepped out into the bright sunshine, abruptly aware of Wan Yü's piping voice from the balcony behind her.

"Ai-weh-deh, they've turned back! They're going down the valley! They're going away!"

She felt the sunshine warm on her face. She tried to call back to Wan Yü, but found the roof of her mouth too dry. Her legs felt weak; she sat down quickly on the threshold of the doorway and breathed slowly and deeply. When she went inside the old women were crying in relief.

The Japanese never returned to Wan Yü's village. The weeks passed and in the late summer they pulled back from Chin Shui, back along the trail to Yangcheng and then through to Tsehchow, where they spent the winter. When the news of their retirement reached Gladys, she went down to Chin Shui with Wan Yü and Timothy. She carried with her the brown-paper parcel containing the post-office equipment, and handed it over to the rather shamefaced official. She went out along the mule trail, over the mountains to Bei Chai Chuang, and then on again to Yangcheng and the Inn of Eight Happinesses.

She looked at it sadly. The roof still gaped where the bomb had struck; the Japanese had stabled their horses in what had once been the mission hall. It was filthy, but she made it as habitable as possible. The people came in from the caves and mountain villages and repaired their houses, and a thin flicker of life seemed to re-kindle in the old city. The Mandarin came back with his entourage and set up again in his yamen. The Governor of the prison returned with his soldiers. A few mule-trains drifted up from the south and a few shopkeepers reopened with a dwindling supply of commodities. But only when the heavy snows sealed the passes did anyone really feel safe in their beds.

In February, with the snow beginning to clear, Gladys decided she would visit the Davises in Tsehchow, even though it was occupied by the Japanese. She had had no word from them for many months, and she was worried. From reports which filtered through from Tsehchow she had heard that the Japanese were not ill-treating the inhabitants. The Mission and compound at Tsehchow lay outside the walls of the city, and although the Japanese kept a fairly strict surveillance on those passing through the gates, they could not, and did not, keep a check on the hundreds of peasants and refugees who were constantly milling around the city.

Gladys believed that she could pass as a humble Chinese peasant, and as she arrived at night, when even the boldest Japanese was locked within the city walls, it was a comparatively easy journey. She was welcomed warmly by Jean and David.

They told her they had not been badly treated. This was the second time they had lived under Japanese occupation, and so far they had not been molested. Periodically the Japanese searched the Mission, but they had not behaved over-objectionably. During the first occupation, apparently the enemy and the townspeople had got on quite well, David Davis told her. Individually, he had found that many of the officers were pleasant people, and to his surprise some of them, if not actually Christians, were interested in discussing Christianity. Sometimes Japanese soldiers would attend his Christian services. Nevertheless, although ostensibly Japan and Britain were still friendly nations, he could feel the antagonism.

He warned Gladys to be careful, very careful. He was glad of her appearance at this time, however, because he hoped she would help to run the Mission while he escorted two elderly European ladies who were still in Tsehchow out of the danger area and away to Chifu on the coast, a month's journey away. More and more now this area of Shansi was becoming a battlefield. There were guerillas in the mountains. The troops of the local warlord had been joined by Chiang Kai-shek's Nationalist troops; the whole of the territory was a porcupine of resistance points. Gladys had observed how poorly equipped were the Northern troops in those early days; at times her heart bled for them. They possessed no lack of courage; but there was never more than one rifle between four or five men. In battle they would wait until the rifleman died so that another could seize the weapon and continue the fight. When Chiang Kai-shek's troops arrived, better equipped, stiffened by the sturdy Northerners, they soon revealed to the Japanese that their rôle as military conquerors was going to be a bloody one indeed! Intermittently entering into the conflict were Communist troops from Sechwan, as busy attacking the Chinese Nationalists as the Japanese. It was a war of desperate attrition by all concerned in which no quarter was asked or given.

In the mission at Tsehchow, surrounded by a large walled compound. David Davis had tried to retain some aspect of neutrality. After he set off for the coast, Gladys found her hands very full, for there were well over a hundred orphans and refugee children housed in the Mission as well as many other adult refugees. She quickly lost her awe of the Japanese, and soon she was asking and receiving food from their Quartermasters. They were a constant puzzle; she could never reconcile their intermittent courtliness and kindness with their many acts of ferocity. Most of the Japanese soldiers were fond of children; Gladys never forgot the occasion when a party of them entered the compound with sacks of sugar, tipped them into three large water jars, and with shouts of laughter began to serve every child with the sweetened mixture. Gladys was grateful for that memory; the Japanese left few other happy ones behind. When they returned to Tsehchow after any military victory, the troops were given three days' holiday; the gates of the city were locked, and the orgies and saturnalia that went on within the walls would have shamed a medieval conqueror.

It was in the weeks before David Davis left for the coast

that there occurred the terrible scene which she was never able to forget, and from which came the injuries that were to trouble her for years. The Mission at Tsehchow was large and rambling; the men's and women's courts were far apart. David Davis lived with his family near the men's court; Gladys when she stayed with them quite close to the women's court. It was she, therefore, who first heard the screams and shouts when a party of Japanese soldiers and officers, who had crept in through the front gate, began to smash down the doors of the women's rooms around their courtyard; there were at least a hundred staying there—refugees, converts, visitors from outside villages. She raced from her room—she was still up, even though it was nearly midnight—and as she scurried along she could not think what was wrong.

As she ran in to the courtyard, a Japanese officer saw her, and snapped a command to a private carrying a rifle. Without warning, he swung the gun and crashed the butt against her head. She fell, barely conscious, realizing only that the rifle-butt was still clumping into her body, and that other Japanese soldiers were kicking her ruthlessly into unconsciousness. By the time David Davis, hearing the commotion, had left his wife's side, and raced to the women's courtyard, Gladys was lying like a limp bundle of rags on the ground.

David Davis stared aghast. There were at least thirty armed Japanese, intent on rape. with struggling, screaming women in various stages of undress. The knowledge which flashed through his mind, that any interference by him into this affair was provocatively dangerous, did not deter him for one second. Unarmed against thirty soldiers he knew that physically he stood little chance; but at that moment his dilemma was simple. How could he prevent this outrage? It came to him instinctively.

"Pray!" he bellowed to the women at the top of his voice. "Pray, all of you!"

The Japanese officer swung on him, a savage curse hissing through his thin lips, as he tugged his revolver from its holster. From pointblank range he levelled it at

David Davis and pulled the trigger. It was impossible to miss! David heard the *click* as the hammer fell, the *click-click-click* as the officer jerked the trigger viciously. Whether all rounds misfired, whether the pistol was faulty, or unloaded, David Davis will never know, but no bullet exploded into his body. Cursing, the officer reversed his grip on the revolver, and with the butt end hit him across the mouth as hard as he could. The impact knocked David Davis down; his cheek and mouth were slashed open. Groggily, like a boxer, he pushed himself up to his knees, blood dripping down his tunic; he could taste the warm saltiness in his mouth as he opened his lips again and shouted: "Pray! Pray, all of you!" He couldn't see, but he kept on shouting, "Pray! Pray!"

And now the women and girls were all down on their knees, their hands clasped together, praying loudly. It was a sight to affront and baffle even the most lascivious. The Japanese soldiers, who had stopped and turned at David Davis's entrance, stared stupidly, not knowing what to do. The officer yelled at them; they stood there sullenly. Then he shouted a second order, and the soldiers turned away, and shambled out of the courtyard; the officer stalked after them. A woman ran and closed the door; most of the girls wept with relief.

David Davis got up from his knees. He could feel the flesh of his cheek and mouth swelling, making it difficult to talk. "All right," he said to the women, "you are safe now. Go back to bed."

The women carried Gladys back to her room, and revived her with cold water. She got up next morning, feeling bruised and sore, and not quite certain what had happened. Although she suffered internal aches and pains for many months afterwards, she did not let them interfere with her work. While David was away, she continued to visit Yangcheng and all the isolated mountain villages where she had started small Christian communities. The Chinese calendar of six days a week did not include a Sunday, so that at each village, when she arrived, it was declared the sabbath, and hymns were sung and prayers offered up. In the village deep in the high mountains there was no change in their manner of living; little news of the war had penetrated in to them; but in the places nearer Tsehchow they lived in preparation for flight, their bundles about them. Babies were born, the sick and wounded attended.

In the spring there was heavy fighting around Tsehchow. The Nationalists threw in large forces, and the Japanese, assailed on every supply route and in every village, pulled back from the city towards Luan. Nationalist troops entered the city. It was two or three weeks after their occupation that the Bible Woman, Chung Ru Mai, came running into the Mission to tell her that four important men were asking to see her.

"Who are they?" she demanded. She remembered David Davis's warning that, at all costs, the neutrality of the Mission must be preserved.

"They're important men from the Nationalists," said the Bible Woman.

"Well, send them away; they can't come in here."

The Bible Woman went off, to return a few minutes later with the information that they still wanted to see her. "You'll have to see them," she said. "They want somewhere to stay."

"If they think they can stay in our Mission, they're mad!" said Gladys heatedly.

"They're important people," said Chung Ru Mai.

"Oh, are they? We'll soon see about that." She scurried out of the door to find them.

The four men in civilian clothes were standing in the compound outside the Mission door. They were young, and in some indefinable way different from all the other men she had met during her stay in China, but she hardly spared a second to notice this difference. They bowed, greeting her with the polite ceremony that is a civilized part of any Chinese meeting. She snapped brusquely: "I'm sorry, but you can't come in here. This is a Mission compound and we must observe our neutrality. You'll have to leave at once."

The leader of the party was a young Chinese with a dignity rather like that of the Mandarin—the only person of real dignity she had met in China—and about his upright figure and unsmiling face was an authority she had not met before.

"We are sorry to cause you trouble," he said. "We thought you might help us."

Gladys frowned at him. "How can I help you? You're fighting a war. This land belongs to God. Will you please leave?"

The young man inclined his head slightly, and his companions turned away. Gladys noticed the dark, shining hair brushed up from the high pale forehead, the dark almond-shaped eyes under black eyebrows, the clear golden skin, ears set close to a well-shaped head.

The other three men were already moving towards the compound door. He said quietly. "We are sorry to offend you, but when we were in Chungking, the Generalissimo said, 'If you want someone you can trust, go to the Christian Church.'"

Gladys looked at him sharply. "What are you to do with the Generalissimo?"

"We are his representatives. We believed that you would be on the side of China."

There was a gentle rebuke in his calm voice which slightly disconcerted her. She hesitated for a second. "Perhaps you'd better come in and talk to me. If you leave the other three behind."

He smiled. "Thank you." The others disappeared through the gate.

Seated opposite her in the Mission, he told her that they were members of Generalissimo Chiang Kai-shek's Intelligence Service. The position in Shansi was confused, and they had been sent to find out what was happening. It was an area vital to the defence of China. If they could blunt the prongs of the Japanese attack anywhere, it would be here, where the terrain gave little help to a better-equipped adversary, where lines of communication were easy to cut, and where, at the foot of the peaks, flowed the mighty barrier of the Yellow River. "The cost of mountain conquest," he said, "can be made prohibitive, by small forces of determined men, operating from the provocative superiority of altitude." As he explained these theories in his pure Mandarin Chinese, he stared at her all the time with dark brown eyes. He added at the end, quite simply: "Will you help China?"

Gladys drew in her breath deeply. She had not expected such a plain question. "I'm Chinese—naturalized Chinese," she said slowly, hesitating, trying to choose her words, "and I care deeply what happens to this country."

"Does God insist on neutrality in all things?" he asked gently. "Is He not against evil?"

"Yes . . . but . . ." It was most unlike her to be hesitant. She did not understand it.

"Japanese intentions in China are evil, are they not?" he continued. "China is fighting to the death in an effort to prevent this evil spreading. China *must* win this war."

She had never thought very seriously or precisely about the ethics of the conflict which had margined the past two years of her life. She had looked upon the war as a man-inflicted epidemic; she hated the Japanese, but the hatred was not motivated by patriotism. It was odd that this gentle-voiced young man should force her to confront these issues. At length she compromised. "I will help you as far as my conscience will allow me."

He stood up and bowed. "That is most kind of you," he said softly. "I will call again and talk with you further, if I may."

She went with him to the gate of the compound; she walked thoughtfully back to the Mission. It was rather strange; she had lived in such a rough, rude society that she had forgotten that anyone could be as gentle and charming as this young man; she had almost forgotten the existence of men in relation to women.

It was a week before he called again. The Japanese had been driven even farther back towards Luan, and large forces of the Nationalists were now grouped around Tseh-chow. The Chinese General and his staff had set up their headquarters in the city. He came upon some small pretext to see if his men could attend services at the Mission. She said she would be glad if they did. Several Japanese Christians had attended the services when their forces had occupied the city. She noticed his eyebrows lift, saw the quick, angry dart of his eyes. She felt her colour rising.

"That is what I came to China for: to preach the Gospel of Christ," she said sharply.

He inclined his head in a small bow: it was a constant gesture of his, and there was a dignity and apology attached to the action which never failed to soothe her indignation. He asked her many questions. He told her about himself; he had been educated in Pekin, trained at the Central Military Academy in Nanking; how he had travelled all over China; and above all how he yearned for a China, strong and free and incorruptible. He stood up then, almost as if afraid that he had talked too much. As he bowed goodbye to her, and asked if he might come and talk to her again, she became aware, through some indefinable nuance of his speech, that he had called to see *her*! The thought flew in suddenly upon her, sitting in her mind like a small coloured bird on a May branch. She shook her head in disbelief. It disturbed her. When he had gone, she went across to the cracked mirror in the corner of her room and stared at herself. Her eyes were large and dark, and although her skin was tanned by the sun, the years had chiselled only a few faint lines from their corners; but how sombre was the dark blue, high-necked tunic. Unthinkingly, she plucked a white flower from the vase in the corner and stuck it in her hair. She found herself looking forward to his next call with an odd stirring of interest.

He came the evening before she was setting off for three isolated villages deep in the mountains, a very lonely and difficult trek. She laughed and told him about it, wondering why he seemed perturbed as she described her route.

"Aren't there bandits in those mountains?" he asked.

"Yes, lots of bandits!"

"And you mean to travel alone?"

"But I usually travel alone."

"It must be very dangerous, and the passes are high and steep; if you fell and broke a leg or injured yourself you could lie there for days and no one would ever find you."

Gladys looked at him with puzzled eyes. In all the years she had been in China, no one had ever professed the slightest concern for her personal safety. Now this charming, good-looking young man seemed seriously worried. It was very unusual. She decided she liked it.

"I shall be all right," she said. "I am capable of looking after myself."

"Please take care," he said. "Please take care."

She was a week out in the mountain country, and when she got back, Linnan, for she knew his name by now, was waiting for her. His relief was quite plain.

"But I've made these journeys a hundred times," protested Gladys in genuine amazement. "There's really nothing to worry about at all." That a young Colonel of Intelligence should be bothered about someone as inconsequential as Ai-weh-deh amused her; it was also very flattering.

His visits became more and more regular. They became good friends. They were the same age; both had eager, inquisitive minds; in the evenings they would often walk through the narrow streets of Tsehchow, past the dark bazaars hung with Chinese lanterns, past the fortune tellers, and the storytellers, the food stalls, the silk merchants and the soldiers gossiping and laughing. They would walk in the fields around the old walled city, and see the moon setting behind the tall temples and tiled pagodas. He talked to her about China; he told her of its traditions and culture, of its beauty and its spirit; he opened for her a new window on a country she thought she knew intimately already, and yet, after he talked, she realized she hardly knew it at all.

Each time they met, in the weeks that followed, the

immense gulf between their separate worlds grew narrower. His voice fascinated her; she had grown so used to the harsh mountain dialect that the age-old music of his classical and flowing Mandarin was an endless delight. One evening, as he rose to leave, he bowed as usual, but his eyes in the soft lamplight held an awareness, an intimacy she had not seen before. She said goodnight abruptly. It was then she began to wonder if she was attractive; if there was still in her face and body the indefinable mystery that draws a man to a woman? She was a missionary dedicated to God. But He had also made her a woman full of the natural tides and forces which stir womankind. If she was falling in love, she reasoned, then it was God who allowed it to happen.

She had returned from a long trip into the mountains when the other thing arose. In two of the villages she had found Japanese troops billeted. She had paid small attention to their presence and had gone about her business ignoring them. She told Linnan about it when she returned. He was very interested, and questioned her closely about the number of troops, what weapons they had, where they were situated. The next time she went into territory occupied by the Japanese she made more careful note of their numbers and their armaments, knowing that her reports would please him. He had stirred in her a latent patriotism for her adopted country; and now after these months she was almost as fervent a patriot as he. It was a subject so closely allied to her evangelistic zeal that she wondered why she had never felt it before.

The idea of a new, noble China rising out of the rubble of war, out of the debris of a corrupt, inefficient and outworn society, was a topic which created endless stimulation between them. She came to believe implicitly that anything that could hasten the defeat of the Japanese, quickening the moulding of a new country built upon Christianity and a better society for the poor and the deprived, was of paramount importance. If she could spy for the Nationalist troops, bring them back information of military value, pass through the Japanese lines unhindered and unwatched, and so help to defeat the common enemy, then she would do these things. How much of this activity was due to her desire to please Linnan, and how much a desire to serve China, she did not try to disentangle. She knew that in the bitterness of this war she was equipped with a faith, and now with a purpose.

CHAPTER TWELVE

WHEN DAVID DAVIS returned to Tsehchow, both he and his wife, Jean, noticed that something was different about Gladys. Although they knew and liked Linnan, and welcomed his frequent visits to the Mission, they did not ascribe his meetings with her and their constant jubilance and laughter to anything more than friendship. Indeed, David Davis thought he detected in the gayness of Gladys's laughter a touch of hysteria. She had been working too hard, he decided.

"What you need," said David seriously, "is a holiday, a rest cure. And I know just the place for you. At Lingchuang the Christians are holding a small conference next week. Why don't you go and help them? There's been little bombing there and, as far as I know, no fighting. It's an odd little town like Yangcheng. You'll like it."

Gladys smiled to herself. Lately she found she was often smiling to herself. She agreed to go. She was perfectly aware by now that she was deeply in love—a love which was an intimacy of the senses more potent than any physical encounter. And because she had never been in love before, and had never expected to be, and because for ten years she had laboured diligently for her Christian God, eating the plain food of the mountains, drinking the cold water of the streams, sleeping on the hard brick k'angs, resolutely disciplining her thin body to the hard work and the long days, this mental and physical feeling of well-being was an intoxication of the spirit; she did not think that God would grudge her this small holiday of her affections. She set off for Lingchuang feeling very happy. With her went the Bible Woman, Chung Ru Mai, Timothy and Sualan. They loaded their possessions on to a small mule-drawn, two-wheeled wooden cart—the roads around Tsehchow made the use of that sort of vehicle possible—and urged the animal across the plain. Late that afternoon, with the sun already dipping rapidly towards the mountain peaks and the city only three or four miles away, they heard a familiar sound which had so often presaged death and destruction. They saw the silver planes droning down from the hot, haze-hidden sky, heard the scream of the bombs and the dull, ground-shaking thuds. They could do nothing but watch anxiously. Timothy and Sualan, climbing a little way up the mountain to get a better view, shouted excitely one to the other. The Bible Woman and Gladys regarded each other with serious faces. The Japanese were bombing Lingchuang. The war had arrived. So much for the rest cure!

The planes bombed leisurely for perhaps fifteen minutes and then flew away again. Gladys took the mule's head and urged it forward.

It was dark when they reached the city. The damage was not as bad as they had expected. Even the inhabitants of Lingchuang had learnt by experience that you did not run into the streets when a bombing plane came over. You crouched in a cellar or in the shelter of the walls and prayed very sincerely to your ancestors to protect you. The Christian Mission was undamaged except for a few windows blasted out; the cook's dough for the evening meal had been blown out with them; he was very angry at its disappearance and swore it had been stolen.

Undaunted by the bombing, the people from the villages were already arriving for the conference, and next day the usual work of instruction began. Each day at practically the same hour the Japanese planes flew over, and the bombs fell, and the work of Christian instruction was interrupted again and again by the necessity of burying the dead and comforting the living within the city, but the conference went on and the Mission itself was undamaged. Then late on what was to be the last night of the conference a strange rumour reached them: an unknown army was approaching the town. Japanese? Bandit? Communist? No one seemed to know. Gladys suspected it would be Japanese. This daily bombing before an army entered was strictly in accordance with their military strategy. The conference was over, anyway, and people made preparations to leave. It was one thing to live in a Japanese-occupied town, but quite another to be in residence when a victorious army first arrived; far better to be in the mountains at such a time. The village elders, for it was mainly of these that the conference consisted, decided to leave at dawn the next day. Everyone lay down to rest, baggage by their side, but for some reason Gladys could not sleep. She turned, and changed position, but sleep eluded her. Alarming thoughts chased each other through her brain; it was imperative, she decided, that they leave the city at first light; she did not want a repetition of what had happened at Chin Shui; they *must* be out early. The thought oppressed her so much that eventually, unable to stand it any longer, she got up and roused the Bible Woman, Timothy and Sualan.

"We're leaving," she said. "We're leaving straight away!"

The others did not protest; they were docile towards her sudden whims and fancies by now.

Her action awoke an evangelist from T'sehchow, who had come to the conference with his wife and two children. He overheard the whispered conversation, and looked up with anxious, inquisitive eyes.

"You can't get out; the city gates will still be locked. They won't open them until dawn."

"Then we shall be first out," she said firmly. "Come on, Sualan, Timothy; pack your things together."

Two other men from nearby villages lying on the floor a few yards away were also disturbed by the movements. They sat up. "We'll come with you, too," they mumbled.

Their decision obviously influenced the evangelist. He prodded his wife awake. His two sleepy-eyed children sat up and looked reproachfully at Gladys.

"It may be only a false alarm," she said. "But I've got a feeling I want to be first out of those gates when they open."

"It is three hours at least before dawn," protested the evangelist.

Gladys drew a deep breath. "I can't explain it, but I know

we're going to be first out," she said firmly. "There's no need for you to come unless you want to."

By the time the party filed out of the Mission house into the dark, chilly streets of the town it had grown by the addition of a young Chinese doctor, his old mother, his wife and baby. They had been visiting relatives in Ling-chuang, and, being Christians, had sought shelter at the Mission when the bombing started. The streets were empty. Timothy's cough echoed eerily. They reached the massive gate with its green-tiled pagoda roof, and paused in the black shadow. As the villagers had warned, it was locked. They crouched in a small huddle in the roadway against the heavy woodwork. Between the roofs behind them they could see the bright stars. It was cold and quiet; no lights showed in the city. The children quickly fell asleep again. The adults dozed off. Only Gladys kept awake. She put out her hand and touched the rough texture of the gate. It was wooden and solid, built to withstand any attack that the ancient town-dweller could visualize. She wondered vaguely why this desire to leave the city had so suddenly seized her? Would it not have been better if she had let them all sleep longer? After all, there had been no confirmation of the approach of an enemy. The Mandarin had made no official statement. No one had been warned to leave. It was purely her own intuition. Oh, well, she had to be satisfied with that.

The warmth of her padded jacket, the dark security of the wooden door against her back must have lulled her into a doze. She was awakened by the sound of the cocks shrieking that dawn was near. She opened her eyes. It was getting light and the gateman was busy with his locks and bolts, grumbling querulously at the human cargo in his way. Now a large crowd of people filled the roadway behind them, all anxious to leave the city as soon as the gates opened. Intuition had obviously been widespread during the night. The massive gates swung back on their hinges. A murmur of appreciation rose as the road leading to the mountains was revealed. The children laughed. They had not expected such excitement. The road stretched ahead of them, three miles of flattish country flanked by wheat fields before the track swooped abruptly up into the shelter of the craggy peaks.

Gladys felt her heart lighten as they marched along. A steady stream of refugees was moving out of the city gates behind them, and the sun shot golden searchlights through the notched ridges of the mountains. They were perhaps a mile from the city when they saw the stream of refugees falling back on either side, and for one moment of panic Gladys thought that the enemy was behind them. Then she saw that the horsemen galloping towards the mountains were Chinese cavalry, the pride of the Nationalist armies. They were a fine sight: a full squadron in grey uniforms and peaked caps, stirrups rattling, leathers creaking, swords bumping, as they pounded along. It was a sight to stir the blood. They were grouped in squadron formation, about twenty horsemen galloping together, then a space of about thirty yards, and then another division. The children screeched with delight as they galloped past, raising a cloud of dust, the drumming hooves making the earth tremble. Gladys wondered why the faces of the horsemen were so grim and intent. They were obviously bound on a mission of great importance. Then suddenly she knew! Above the pounding of the hooves on the baked earth came an overlaying noise—a shrill, insistent noise she knew so well. Into that moment of dreadful fear screamed the high-pitched, hysterical sound of diving aircraft. For a fraction of a second her muscles refused to act; her pupils dilated as she willed them back into action in the extreme moment of urgency. She screamed at the children:

"Into the fields. Run, run! Into the fields! Throw yourselves flat!"

She cuffed and slapped Timothy and Sualan over the low stone wall that bordered the road, driving them frantically into the wheat field like cattle, yelling fiendishly at them, as above the roaring engines came the metallic stutter of machine-guns. She threw herself down, covering her head with her arms as much to shut out the horror of the scene as to protect herself. The earth was churned. Horses screamed horribly. There was a great shout of utter agony, as the planes roared along the column of refugees and horsemen, massacring all beneath them. Spotting aircraft had obviously noted the entry of the Chinese cavalry into Lingchuang the evening before. An elementary military mind could define that they would seek the shelter of the mountains at first light. So it was. The planes came in over the mountains, zoomed down upon the city and roared along the line of cavalry and refugees, scything them with machine-gun bullets. Dead and dying horses, men, women and children collapsed like puppets with the wire suddenly released. They choked the road. Riderless horses, heads thrown high, eyes bloodshot, leapt the low wall, crashed frenziedly through the wheat field. The shrieks and the panic were more terrible than anything Gladys had ever heard before. Over the city and along the road of twisted, agony-ridden bodies the planes roared again and again. To Gladys, fingers buried deep in the ground, it seemed a lifetime that she lay there. Then the silver planes turned in a wide circle to examine the carnage, and droned away, dwindling to invisible specks in the sky.

She stood up, trembling. The scene, familiar perhaps to a cavalryman of past centuries, was to Gladys Aylward, Christian missionary and woman, as dreadful as any hell her imagination could conceive. Dead horses, dead men, women and children; gaping wounds, streaming blood, screams and cries and groans of agony. All around lay the mangled bits and pieces of their own possessions, bundles burst open and scattered in the corn as they had raced for cover. Riderless horses limped or galloped aimlessly across the nightmare scene. Timothy and Sualan clutched at her jacket, saying nothing. The two villagers, the evangelist, the doctor and woman looked expectantly towards her. They were dumb also. This sudden involvement in such carnage had frozen their resolution, even their instinct for self-preservation. Looking back along the heaps of bodies, they could see the chaos at the gates. Corpses of horses and humans had piled up and choked the exit; within the city, people were screaming and heaving to get out. Every impulse in Gladys's mind told her to fly to the mountains, to leave this ghastly battlefield and hide in the deep gorges away from the frightfulness. She stood mute. There were hundreds of wounded. The gate must be cleared!

She looked at the Chinese doctor, a thin young man, his scraggy neck pinched by a tight collar. He looked terrified, as well he might, she thought, for he had only just completed his training, and it had scarcely equipped him for an emergency such as this. She sucked in a great breath of air, and forced herself to act. To the two villagers she said: "You will take the women and children to the mountains. Wait for us there. The doctor and I will stay here to help. We'll join you this evening." She looked at the doctor as she spoke. He nodded nervously. The women and children scrambled their few possessions together and hurried off. Gladys waved them goodbye, and with the young doctor turned and hurried back towards the gateway. As they walked, she gathered every uninjured man, exhorting, threatening and scolding, in an attempt to muster a party to clear the gate. Dazed and blank-faced they followed her. Some, weeping beside the bodies of their dead, could not be cajoled into moving.

They reached the gate. The dead horses and humans and baggage were piled high, lifted in a grotesque barricade over which the townspeople were trying to clamber. Gladys, her spirit back now that she had a task to do, ran around shrilling instructions to her helpers. They heaved aside the bodies until a passageway was cleared. Then, with the doctor, she began to do what she could to help the wounded. Soldiers whose horses had been killed and who were themselves unhurt or only slightly wounded lent a hand. In the late afternoon other soldiers arrived to clear the mess. At this point, having done all she could, Gladys and the doctor felt they could leave. The military were busy digging pits for the dead, heaving the belongings, the pitiful bundles and bags, into a heap for later sorting.

Numbed, bloodstained, exhausted, Gladys and the young doctor walked slowly along the track towards the mountains. They were too tired to talk, too shattered to assess it in their minds. But, as she stumbled along, Gladys found tears running down her cheeks. She sniffed and snuffled for half an hour until the dust dried her eyes. Sheltering at a bend they found Chung Ru Mai, the doctor's wife, and his mother, the evangelist, his wife and children, Timothy and Sualan. The two countrymen had been home and returned. They had found their own people preparing to flee, and were about to rejoin them. Rumours and counter-rumours were everywhere. News of the carnage at Lingchuang had lit a powder-train of panic. Fighting was going on everywhere. Gladys realized that at that moment the only safe place was in the mountains, far from any town or village. It was not an unusual course to take; over the past two years she had spent many nights in the open or sheltering in caves. Between them, they carried enough grain to last for several days. After a short conference, the others decided that her suggestion was the best. There was little else to do; if this was a big Japanese offensive, the five towns—Tsehchow, Yangcheng, Chin Shui, Kaoping and Lingchuang—would soon be in their hands.

Weary and sick at heart, the little party moved off the road and up through the mountains, seeking sanctuary. They walked until it was dark, and then crouched under a rock. Next morning at first light they set off again. Most of the time the old lady grumbled and moaned; they were all suffering from shock, and even the tall mountains, craggy and silent, with narrow gorges and high, bare faces, gave them no sense of security. All next day they picked their way deep into the mountains; in the afternoon they discovered a large, dry cave half way up a steep slope. The children and the women were very tired and had no wish to go any farther, and black thunder clouds were massing overhead, filling the sky between the peaks with an ominous purple colour. As they crept into the cave the storm broke, and rain lashed down out of the sky. Sitting crouched inside, her arms round her knees, tired and miserable, Gladys watched the rain falling outside like a sheet of glass. On impulse she took the iron cooking-pot she had carried with her and let the water trickle into it. There

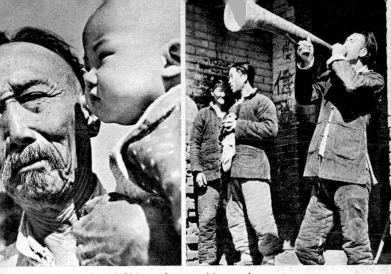

Local Chinese farmer with grandson
Town crier calling villagers to the west gate of Yangcheng

The village fruit market

Gladys Aylward tells a Bible story to the convicts at Chengtu

Happy ending in Shanghai for 'Ninepence' and her small son

Ai, Ai, 'ninepence' says, 'not call her that, she nice old lady, so now you know what I am in the eye of a child of 8.

Life is pitiful, death so familiar, suffering & pain so common, yet I would not be anywhere else.

Do not wish me out of this or in any way seek to get me out, for I will not be got out while this trial is on, These are my people, God have given them to me, & I will live or die with them for Him and His glory.

Photostat of part of a letter received by Miss Aylward's parents in Edmonton

The 'Small Woman's' certificate of Chinese naturalisation

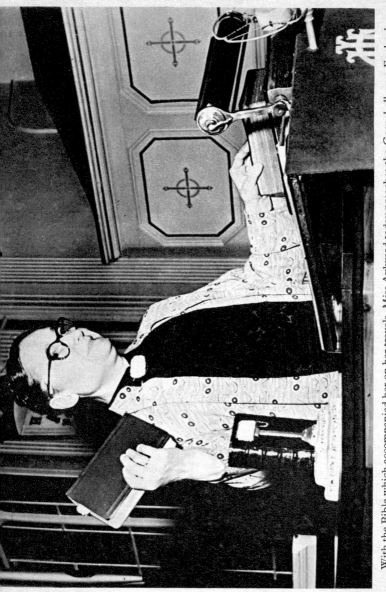

With the Bible which accompanied her on her travels, Miss Aylward today preaches the Gospel all over England

were dried sticks in the cave and animal dung. She broke up the sticks and piled them between the two low rocks. They blazed fiercely when she lit them, and the pot of water perched between the two rocks was soon boiling. She tipped coarse twig tea into the water, and in a few seconds they were all gathered round, sipping their bowls full of the steaming aromatic liquid. They added more sticks to the fire; in the gathering gloom their shadows licked at the roof and walls of the cave, and in this neanderthal setting their feeling of security slowly returned. In a second cooking-pot Gladys boiled their ration of millet, and they washed down the hot porridge with more cups of scalding tea. Food and drink in their bellies, a feeling of contentment seeped through them. Now they were weary; by the firelight, as the darkness grew, and the rain poured down with increasing fury, they lay down and slept on the warm, sandy floor of the cave.

For six weeks they lived in that cave, collecting dried rushes from the valley for their beds. The nearest supply of water was five miles away, but they saw in that factor an added safeguard. A village lay just beyond the well, where they bought eggs and grain. Their appearance caused no comment; refugees were commonplace by now. Their chief fear was the wolves which roamed in those mountains; practically every night they prowled outside the cave, and Gladys, the doctor and the evangelist took it in turns to keep watch. Usually, a well-flung stone was sufficient to scare them away, but if there were too many of them, or they seemed bolder than usual, they would light the fire, and watch the green, flinty eyes back away to a safe distance.

Back in Lingchuang, Linnan was concerned in a drama about which Gladys knew nothing. The Japanese had been defeated in their efforts to follow up their bombing of the cavalry, and the city was still in the Nationalists' hands. When Linnan heard of the disaster, he hurried to the city. He knew that Gladys had been visiting the Mission there, yet he had received no message from her. All they could tell him was that she had left at dawn on the morning of the attack and had not been seen since. As Colonel in charge of intelligence troops in the area, it was the duty of his men to sort the debris of the battle. On his table the second morning after he arrived in Lingchuang appeared a hymn-book. The soldiers, who did not really know what it was, had picked it up from a cornfield and brought it in for his examination. He recognized it instantly as belonging to Gladys. At once he was intensely worried. He went round questioning the soldiers who had buried the dead. As far as they could remember, they had not buried a foreigner. On two occasions when the soldiers were doubtful as to who lay in a certain grave, he ordered it to be reopened so that he could make sure himself. Then, with no sign of her body, and remembering her predilection for the wild mountains, he sent messengers to the surrounding villages asking for news of her. And at every opportunity he searched for her himself.

Gladys, in her far-off cave, knew nothing of all this. They had been sheltering for almost three weeks, and she was enjoying the feeling of security and peace. Often, because the old lady and the other woman either talked too much or grumbled too much, she would climb out along the valley, find a sheltered spot in the sun and read her Bible for hour after hour. One afternoon she was seated comfortably on a rock a mile away from the cave, and quite alone, when suddenly she was conscious of movement near her. She looked up, startled. She saw a farmer's boy of about fifteen or sixteen. He wore a straw hat, a torn blue jacket and trousers. Over his arm was a small basket containing half a dozen eggs. She was immediately on the alert. He stood there staring at her.

"Who are you?" she snapped.

It was a second or two before his lips moved. "I'm selling these eggs," he said.

Gladys's eyes narrowed at such an obvious lie. "Why are you selling them here?" she said sharply.

He stared at her stupidly. "I don't know."

"You don't wander across the mountains trying to sell eggs," she said suspiciously. "Do you?"

His eyes dropped. He shifted uncomfortably, but said nothing.

"You can go back and tell whoever you're spying for that we're all here," she said angrily.

It could be that the local bandit leader or a Communist group had got wind of the strangers in the neighbourhood, and this boy had been sent out to discover them. Probably they had offered some minor reward for information. She watched him clamber back up the mountainside before she hurried back to the cave. The others listened to her story with dismay. As it was then late afternoon, she said:

"We must leave first thing tomorrow morning and find a new place to hide."

As soon as it was light, she was impatient to be off, but the others dawdled. The old woman did not want to move at all, and said so. The doctor's wife had to breast-feed her baby. The evangelist's wife was slowly gathering her bits and pieces together. At last Gladys could stand it no longer.

"Look," she said, "I'll go on ahead, and wait for you at the end of the valley. Please hurry up."

She pointed in the direction she intended to take, and set off with Timothy. She knew that her departure might hurry them up a little, for neither the evangelist nor the doctor possessed any formidable qualities of leadership. They reached the end of the valley, and climbed a slight rise which led into the next. As they breasted the ridge, Gladys saw a sight which caused her to come to an abrupt halt. Spread out across the valley and advancing towards them was a line of horsemen, obviously searching. To Gladys it meant but one thing: they were seeking her party. She said quickly to Timothy:

"Run back and tell the others to go up the valley in the opposite direction. Tell them to go as far as they can, and hide."

Timothy's eyes were frightened. "But what about you?" he asked anxiously.

"If they get me, they'll probably be satisfied," said Gladys. She saw the small boy hesitating. "Now go on! Do as I tell you, Timothy!"

179

She watched him run back down the valley; then she turned towards the horsemen, walking boldly in their direction. While she was still some distance off, she shouted defiantly, "If it's me you want, here I am."

She knew the Communists usually shot first and established an identity afterwards; but now all feelings of fear had left her; she felt only anger that they should have been betrayed by a stupid small boy carrying a basket of eggs.

As her voice floated down-wind she saw the horseman in the centre point with his hand, and urge his mount into a trot and then into a gallop. As he clattered towards her she saw that he was a Chinese Nationalist officer. Only when he pulled up his horse in a flurry of dust and stamping hooves a few yards from her, tossed the reins over its head, swung out of the saddle and raced towards her, did she realize it was Linnan.

She clung briefly in his arms. In an agitated voice he told her what had occurred: how he had briefed everyone he could find in the countryside to keep a lookout for her, offering a reward if they found her. The farmer's boy had brought back the information he needed.

They went on to the cave, finding the others about to leave; they gathered around laughing and chattering in relief. Linnan gave them the news: sporadic fighting was going on everywhere. For the present it was better that they remained in the cave; they were safer there. He would arrange for food to be sent to them from time to time, and let them know when it was safe to return to Tsehchow or Yangcheng. Ownership of both cities was being contested savagely by both armies at that very moment. Indeed, during the next three weeks Gladys and the children often climbed up a nearby mountain to see, in the distance, the Japanese aircraft swooping down to bomb Tsehchow. But eventually it was the Japanese who were driven back, and when they did return to Tsehchow, it was still firmly in Chinese hands.

CHAPTER THIRTEEN

As SHE expected when she reached the mountain ridge, she could see the smoke of the Japanese cooking-fires below. The pale blue smoke spiralled slowly upwards against the clear evening sky. The enemy camp was hidden by a buttress of rock. She had done work like this many times through the summer months since she left the mountains and returned to Tsehchow. She held up her hand as a signal, and the young Nationalist officer scrambled up on to the ridge beside her. His feet dislodged a few scraps of rock, and she watched them pitch downwards to where the line of soldiers crouched against the mountainside, hugging their rifles. Carefully the officer scanned the valley below.

"You say there's about fifty of them?" he said quickly.

"I counted them as carefully as I could this morning," said Gladys. "I don't think I'll be more than a few out."

"They'll be moving out along the track towards Tsehchow tomorrow at first light, that is certain," said the young officer eagerly.

"They've got lookouts all round," said Gladys. "You'll have to be careful. One spotted me this morning as I crossed the ridge, but there was a valley in between. He couldn't do anything about it."

The man nodded. He was hardly listening any longer: his mind was automatically siting the machine-gun, placing his men to the best advantage along the valley so that no one would escape their fire. Gladys knew they would attack at first light, pouring down from either side in the natural bowl after the initial fusillade against the surprised Japanese. There were only thirty of them, but they were northern troops, tall, fierce young men who fought with a bitter courage and hatred. They would tear into the Japanese, and the battle would end in a bloody hand-to-hand encounter. The enemy would fight to the last man, and be wiped out to the last man. The Chinese would also suffer casualties. There would be blood on the valley floor, with bodies littering the rocks.

"You will go back now," said the officer, turning to her again. "You led us well, Ai-weh-deh."

"Yes, I'll go back now," she said wearily.

She had been walking since dawn. At first light she had left the little Christian community in Poren, a remote village in the mountains, and set off towards Yangcheng. On her journey she had seen the Japanese troops picking their way carefully along the dry river bed. She had known at once that they were very foolish to be so few in number and so deep in the mountains. She knew where to find Nationalist troops. She had detoured from her route and entered one of their camps, well hidden in the mountains. At her news an officer and thirty men were quickly detached to accompany her; she had an army authorization signed by the resident Chinese General in Tsehchow but it was usually unnecessary to show it: the leaders of most units of the Nationalist Army in that part of Shansi knew her very well. She knew the mountains in that area far better than most of the people who lived there, certainly far better than the troops. Years of wandering over the ridges and through the valleys by foot or on a mule, far from any habitation, had given her an expert knowledge of the South Shansi mountains.

It was not the first time she had used her ability on behalf of the Nationalists. There were no set positions in this cut-and-run warfare. The Japanese occupied the towns and tried to progress in force along recognizable lines of communication. The Nationalists lived in the mountains, adopting guerilla and scorched earth tactics.

With her Bible, Gladys moved through villages sometimes occupied by the Japanese, sometimes by the Nationalists. If they knew she was in the territory, the enemy ignored her; she was no different from the thousands of refugees wandering around the countryside. They were unaware that she took careful notice of their dispositions, that she passed this information back to the Nationalist troops, and even led them to where she knew the enemy would be. She knew exactly what she was doing, and was not ashamed of her actions. She was Chinese by adoption. Had she been in London, and England in danger, she would have acted in the same way. Her heart had reached the fighting stage, even though she could not entirely quieten her conscience.

It was almost dark when she returned to the village where she had first met the Nationalist troops. The village elder met her outside his house; a gentle old man in a faded blue robe; a straggle of white hairs on his chin; his eyes buried in an earthquake of wrinkles. "General Ley is here," he whispered. "He called to see me; he is an old friend. When he heard you might return, he waited. He is anxious to meet you."

She quickened her step. She had heard much of General Ley, but had never met him. He was a legendary figure in the province; a Roman Catholic priest, a European, though from what country he came she did not know. In these days you did not ask questions about anyone's background. She heard later that he was a Dutchman, but never obtained confirmation.

When the Japanese invaded Shansi he was not content to sit back and rely upon God's mercy. With militant Christian fury he had found weapons for his parishioners and struck back; now he was leader of a large guerilla force. They lived in the mountains, and fought the Japanese whenever and wherever they could. It was therefore with a tingle of anticipation that Gladys walked into the court-yard to meet this man who had managed to reconcile contemporary reality with his Christian conscience.

In the half-light she saw him standing there, feet astride, arms clasped behind his back, a sturdy figure of medium height, dressed in a long black robe. His short, cropped hair was blond; he had a strong, supple face; his mouth was determined yet fluid, and ready to smile; only his eyes, she thought, were sad, detached. He smiled, hand out-stretched. "Ai-weh-deh! We shall forget that you are a woman and I am a man; that you're a Protestant and I'm a Roman Catholic."

"We seem to have some things in common, General Ley," she said, with a returning smile.

"We have a common enemy," he said, suddenly sombre again. The laughter left his voice; his eyes were grave. "Come inside and let us talk. You must be tired and hungry."

As they scooped at their bowls of millet by the light of the flickering lamp, there was immediately between them that sense of warm friendship which so rarely illumines a first meeting. They talked of many things.

The main body of Ley's men were sheltering in caves some miles away. They were moving across to ambush the main trail between Tsehchow and Kaoping the next day. Their information was good.

"We shall kill many Japanese," he said in a flat voice. "We have a machine-gun. We shall cut them down as they pass."

Hearing him speak and listening to the weariness in his voice, it was not difficult for Gladys to divine his inner despair. It was not hard, not even intuitive, because the same conflict existed in her own heart. "We shall kill many Japanese," he said unemotionally; not as an ordinary military commander might have announced, "We shall cut their lines of communication!" or "We shall capture supplies!" or "We shall hit them hard!" He had gone straight to the heart of the matter.

"We shall kill many Japanese," he repeated.

Their eyes met across the lamp. The upward-striking, yellow light threw black shadows into his eye-sockets. She understood, and he knew she understood, this agonizing dilemma of his Christian conscience. She, too, in the quietness of her prayers had tried to find some clear path to follow.

Should he—should they—stand aside and let the forces of evil reach with black fingers into every corner of the province, or should he—should they—take up the sword, and in the name of God strike at the evil hand wherever it clutched? The policy of the Japanese was plain. For years they had operated their 'master' race policies in their northern colony of Korea. The Japanese were aristocrats, the Koreans serfs! No Korean was educated above an elementary level; no Korean ever held an administrative post of any importance; they were reduced to a proletarian and peasant level and kept there. Hitler was putting the same theories into operation on the other side of the world. The same treatment was already accorded those areas of North China in the enemy's grasp.

General Ley, the young Roman Catholic priest alone in his isolated Mission in South Shansi, had had to make his decision in consultation with his own conscience and his own God. He had gathered his flock in the courtyard of the Mission one clear, cold morning, and said, "We shall fight the enemy with the only weapon he understands. Force! We shall kill him when he sleeps, and when he is off-guard. We shall drive him out of our mountains, no matter what the cost."

His men, mainly his own converts, northerners, mountain people, bronzed-faced, their muscles hardened by their activity, an hereditary strain of banditry latent in their blood, were attached to him with a fanatical and ferocious devotion. He trained them in the arts of warfare. They struck with devastating speed, killed Japanese, captured supplies and arms, and retreated quickly into their mountains. This they had been doing for many months.

He sat on the rough brick k'ang in the elder's house and looked at her across the table. The corner of his mouth turned up ironically as he spoke. "A common cause—eh, Ai-weh-deh?"

She scraped the last few porridge grains of millet from the bottom of her bowl.

"General Ley?" she mused. "Why do they call you General?"

"The rank is purely honorary," he said, his mobile face slipping into a smile again. "The men prefer it that way. They have more face serving under a general. And it is a convenient *nom-de-guerre*."

She hesitated. "Aren't you frightened of being caught by

185

the Japanese?" She knew it to be a naïve question but one she had to ask.

"Often," he said. "Very often. Are you?"

"I hardly think about it."

"I have heard much about you, Ai-weh-deh," he said quietly.

"What have you heard?"

"At times you make journeys behind the Japanese lines to gather information for the Chinese armies. That is true, is it not?"

There was a ring of accusation in his voice, and she looked at him wonderingly.

"Yes," she said.

His eyes were fastened on hers. "Do you not feel that you are betraying the position that God has given you?" he demanded coldly.

"I don't understand." She looked at him in bewilderment, the anger slowly rising inside her. Then the words cascaded out.

"God recognizes the difference between right and wrong," she said stormily. "We can recognize the difference, can't we? The Japanese are wicked. Our Lord drove the moneylenders out from the Temple with whips. The Japanese sweep through our countryside looting, burning and killing. We must drive them out, too, with every means in our power. They are my people they kill; my people legally, morally, spiritually, and I shall go on doing what I can to protect and help them——"

She stopped suddenly in the middle of her tirade, conscious that he was smiling. "You did that on purpose," she said accusingly. Nevertheless she felt relieved.

He nodded slowly. "Yes." He paused, and she heard his breath expelled in a heavy sigh. "We ask ourselves these questions, Ai-weh-deh, do we not? And even though we answer them to our own satisfaction, even though we can clear our consciences at any man-made inquisition, we are still not quite certain how we would answer at the Courts of God. Are we, Ai-weh-deh?"

She did not answer. She knew he did not need an answer. He was examining his own conscience aloud.

"I am a Christian priest," he said slowly. "I am in this country to teach the ignorant and aid the sick, and bring the word of God to those who have never heard it. And yet on the battlefield I see the corpses of the men I have helped to kill—yes, killed myself with these own two hands." He jerked out his hands in a quick gesture of contempt. "Yet what is the use of neutrality? There is fighting in every part of the world, Ai-weh-deh, against a common enemy of evil, and unless every man takes up arms—spiritual, moral and physical arms—and fights in the best way he is equipped to fight, how can we ever defeat it? I am a man as well as a priest, Ai-weh-deh; a man! You know what they have done, Ai-weh-deh: how they have killed and looted and burned and raped. How can a Christian man stand by while it continues? I cannot, and I shall not!"

His voice was harsh and angry; his eyes glaring across the table into hers. Then, as quickly as it had risen, the anger died in him. He looked down at the hands still stretched before him, dropped them to his side, and wiped the palms against his gown with a downward movement as if to wipe out a stain. "The judgment must come later," he said wearily. His eyes lifted again after a moment of silence and a wry smile twisted his lips. "Mine is a religious order that believes in confession," he said quietly.

Gladys returned his look. "I understand," she said gently. She did not know what else to say, although she yearned for words that would reveal her sympathy and seal the bond between them. There was no way she knew of offering him comfort, other than the way he knew himself. No one else could carry, or share, his burden. There could be no syncretism between their faiths. Yet she also knew that from this meeting between them, two aliens far from their homelands, each would take a crumb of comfort. Because they were but two molecules of humanity swirling near each other for a fragment of time, in the bloody cockpit of war, their meeting was endowed with dignity

187

and a strength that neither would forget. She did not know, nor would she wish to have known, that in the years to follow, in every country, in every latitude and climate, such transient meetings of men and women for a few seconds, minutes, hours or days, was to be the commonplace of social behaviour; that the fabric of the long growing years, the slowly ripening acquaintanceships, the civilizing codes of conduct, were to be slashed to pieces by the exigencies of war. The few poignant moments before the battle, before the gas-chamber, before the take-off, before the embarkation leave, before the surgical operation, before the falling bomb, was all that millions of men and women were to have as solace on their short and bitter journeys to the grave. Yet, in these little meetings of kindred spirits, without a past to give them guidance or a future to give them hope, they would find a measure of peace and coherence to lend a reason to their dying; a faith to give some semblance of sanity to the farcical affairs of homo sapiens. Man, in all his wild adventures, riding his spinning globe between the cold stars towards eternity, had not, as yet, discovered a synthesism, an ersatz substitute for faith.

The wick burned low in the earthenware lamp. In the darkness General Ley left the house of the village elder, and with his long black gown flapping about his legs, climbed back through the mountains to rejoin his men. She met him twice after that, but there were many others present, and there was never time to do more than smile and exchange a greeting. It was many months later, in Tseh-chow, that she heard of his death. The Chinese had killed him, the report said, but both Nationalists and Communists disclaimed responsibility. He would answer well at his 'Courts of God', Gladys decided sadly.

The Chinese clung grimly to the territory around Tsehchow through the autumn, winter and into the early spring of 1940. It was during this period that Gladys became friendly with the Chinese General based in the city. Introduced by Linnan, she was made welcome at his house; after several of her exploits, he personally gave her the badge which established her identity with troops in the field. She often dined with him and his officers. He was an older man than Linnan, with a long and honourable battle record behind him. He had been present as a junior officer at the famous Shanghai Incident when, on the night of January 28th, 1932, the Japanese had sent companies of Marines marching across the boundary of the International Settlement and into the Chinese town of Chapei. He had been an officer of the Nineteenth Route Army which, with bitter gallantry, had so bloodily repulsed them. It was because of this unexpected resistance that Admiral Shiozawa of the Imperial Japanese Navy had sent in bombers to assist his Marines, an action which created world-wide horror, for Chapei was a civilian city.

The General smiled ironically as he recounted the incident to Gladys. "It is surprising how acquiescent a world conscience can become when an action becomes commonplace, is it not?" He was a wise and kindly man, considerate of his troops, and contemptuous of the graft, corruption and greed that existed among his superiors in the Kuomintang.

It was for Gladys a period of fluctuating and feverish activity. David Davis had left the previous autumn to take his wife and children, and one or two other remaining Europeans, out to the coast; without his help they would certainly not have got through safely. Gladys knew he would be back as soon as he could. She spent time in Yangcheng, time in Bei Chai Chuang, time roaming the countryside visiting her small communities of Christians, and in her travels amassing intelligence for the Chinese troops.

Few love affairs can have flourished in circumstances stranger than that of Gladys and Linnan. They met at odd moments in the mountains, in shattered villages, in the bombed towns. They talked at odd moments between battles and births and baptizings. They exchanged scraps of news, had a meal together, talked of the future they would build in the new China. His concern, his gentleness, his tenderness towards her never wavered, and for that she was eternally grateful. They discussed marriage; he was eager that they should marry at once, live together as man and wife as best they could, war or no war. It was Gladys who said, "No". The war had to be won first. Unconsciously foreshadowing Tito's guerillas, who punished severely any romantic deviation on the part of a partisan, she reiterated endlessly that the defeat of the enemy must come first. Marriage, their personal happiness, must wait. She wrote to her family in far-away England and told them that she was going to marry a Chinese, and hoped that they would understand. Her father wrote back and said that if her happiness would be secure with this man, they would be happy also. She read the letter in a cave in the mountains not far from Yangcheng where she had been visiting some of her Christians; how the letter had come up across the Yellow River and reached her in the mountains she could not imagine, but a messenger had brought it from Yangcheng. She wept a little as she read it, for all she had had to eat that day was a bowl of boiled green weeds plucked from the mountainside, and she was perhaps a little light-headed.

With the coming of spring, every day brought the Japanese closer to Tsehchow. They wanted that town very badly. In the fields and villages a few miles outside, the Chinese troops resisted them valiantly. A stream of wounded were passed back into Tsehchow; even the compound of the Mission was used as a dressing-station. Often Gladys went out with the bearers to bring in wounded men; they used doors torn from their hinges as stretchers.

Refugees packed into the Mission and streamed through the city every day. The Japanese were steadily bringing up reinforcements and applying heavy pressure. The noise of rifle and artillery fire was continuous.

In spite of all this, she was determined not to leave the city. She had lived so often under Japanese occupation that she felt she might protect her people from some of the worse excesses of their troops. She was worried about the children, however. From its inception, the Tsehchow Mission had always cared for orphans; there were always fifty to a hundred in residence, but the number had grown enormously during the past few months. Now there were over two hundred to be looked after.

She had known for some time that Madame Chiang Kai-shek had started a fund for war orphans, far away in Chungking. Orphans were collected from war-ravaged areas and sent to the ancient capital of Sian in Shensi and there fed, clothed and sheltered. They were given some schooling. During the winter Gladys had written, on impulse, to the authorities in Chungking asking if they could help her. She guessed, after the stout Chinese resistance of the past summer and autumn, that the Japanese would not be in pleasant mood when they re-entered Tsehchow, and she feared for the children.

A month later she got a reply. If the children could be brought to Sian, the Committee would gladly look after them. She decided that half of them must go at once. She briefed Tsin Pen Kuang, a convert, for the journey. With money and supplies he set off with a hundred children for the Yellow River, where they would cross and catch the railway to Sian. Their journey was uneventful, and five weeks later she heard that they had arrived safely. She also learned that Tsin Pen Kuang was returning so that he could convoy the remaining hundred children to Sian. With conditions at the Mission becoming more and more chaotic, she eagerly awaited his arrival. She did not know, and would not know until months later, that on the return journey he was captured by the Japanese, and presumably shot.

The morning that David Davis returned she was on her knees beside a wounded man in the Mission compound, a bowl of hot water by her side. She heard a voice behind her and recognized it at once. She turned and tried to smile a welcome, but found it impossible. Her thoughts translated themselves into words she would rather not have said. "Oh, David, why did you have to come back now? It's so dangerous!" she said. Yet, even as she spoke, she knew that nothing on earth could have prevented him returning to the place where he believed his duty lay. Now that he had evacuated his wife and children and the last remaining Europeans in Tsehchow, and taken them on the long journey to the coast, the Mission was his concern. At the port of Chifu he had left them in comparative safety in Japanese-occupied territory, and applied for permission to return to Tsehchow. It had been refused. Undaunted, he applied for permission to visit a neighbouring town. This he received. He had decided that, come what may, he was going back to his Mission. He set off with his pass to the neighbouring town, and 'disappeared'. He knew the Chinese people, and ways of living off the country. He avoided the main routes where he might find Japanese and travelled 'black' across country. It was more than a thousand miles, and it took him many weeks by a circuitous route. He walked every yard of the way. And he arrived to find his Mission packed with refugees and wounded soldiers, with a Japanese division fighting only a few miles away, and confusion everywhere. There was no time for Gladys to do more than exchange a few words with him; time was important, for she had decided that, at all costs, the remaining hundred children must be moved to safety. She was arranging that they should move back to Yang-cheng that very day. With a couple of women Mission workers in charge, she lined them up in a long procession, made a rough check that they all carried their bedding rolls, basins and chopsticks, and saw them out of the Mission gate—a long crocodile of singing, squalling children headed across the plain, bound for the mountains and the safety of Yangcheng.

That evening she held a small prayer meeting in the Mission Chapel. It broke up quite early, but she noticed one young soldier—they often attended the services—reluctant to go. He stood in the doorway fidgeting with his cap. She knew him quite well; he worked as an orderly on the General's staff. He was a youngster, shy and sincere.

"You're not in a hurry tonight," she said jocularly, as she went to close the door and see him out.

"I had to wait until the others had gone," he said mysteriously. "I have a message from the General." He produced an envelope from his breast pocket and handed it to her.

She frowned, tore it open, and scrutinized the simple page of foolscap. It was written by the Adjutant on behalf of the General.

> The Chinese forces in Tsehchow are on the point of retreating. The General would like you to accompany the Army, who will take you to safety. If you go with this orderly he will provide you with a horse, and lead you to a rendezvous.

Her expression grew even more severe. For some reason the letter angered her. It was presumptuous of the General to think that, at the first sight of danger, she would bolt for safety. She had been in danger many times during the past years. Although David had returned and the responsibility for the Mission was now nominally his, she still felt that her duty demanded her presence in Tsehchow. She grabbed the orderly's pencil and scribbled on the back of the letter, *Chi Tao Tu Pu Twai*, 'Christians never retreat!' She knew it was a rather extravagant gesture, but it relieved her annoyance.

"Take that back to your General," she said.

The orderly hesitated, then saluted, turned on his heel and strode off into the darkness.

Gladys lay on her bed and thought about the letter. So the Japanese were going to take the city? Well, she had lived under occupation before, and could do so again. There was still so much work to do—so much work to do! Fully dressed, for in those days of alarms and counter-alarms you never knew what the night might bring, she fell asleep.

It was the following afternoon that the orderly appeared again, his pale, thin face wearing a worried look. Gladys had just finished her midday meal of millet, and over her empty bowl she stared at him in astonishment.

"What have you come back for?" she asked.

He was flustered, agitated, stammering in his excitement. "The General pleads with you to come to safety at once.

He has sent me back with this message. The army is camped fifteen *li* away on the plain. I beg you, Ai-weh-deh, to accompany me."

His distress fitted a tiny feeling of uneasiness into her mind. She put down her bowl and stood up.

"Thank you for coming to tell me this," she said, "but as I have already told you, I will not go with the army, no matter what happens. If I stay in Tsehchow, or if I go into the mountains, it makes no difference."

To her this was quite logical. Although she might help the Nationalists with information, she still retained her very definite ideas about Christian properties.

She left him standing there, and walked away to go on with her work. Those of the Chinese wounded who could not walk were being loaded on to carts to be taken out of the city, and the walking wounded hobbled after them. The Japanese had no time for wounded, their own or the Chinese. Their own dead they collected in piles and cremated; the Chinese were convinced that they helped their own badly wounded men towards a Shinto heaven with a carefully placed bullet before quickly cremating them. To the Japanese, only the act of sending a small urn of ashes back to the homeland shrines seemed important. They tore the doors off the houses and the courtyard railings from the balconies to get wood for the pyres, and this utilitarian treatment of the dead shocked the Chinese violently. To them the dead should be revered. They believed that three souls belonged to the departed: one inhabiting the ancestral tablet, one the grave, and the third journeying out into the Unknown. More than ever they became convinced that they were fighting a nation of barbarians.

All that day the city of Tsehchow was evacuated. The Japanese had been thwarted for too long by the Chinese rearguard action to show any mercy towards those they suspected or disliked, and the city was by now almost deserted. Gladys had not had time to discuss the General's message even with David. She knew he would not leave the Mission until he was forced out of it. He, too, had lived under a Japanese occupation before, and thought he could endure it.

While they were gulping down some food at their midday break they exchanged a few sentences about the condition of the Mission, but there was no time for a long discussion. The place was packed with refugees; there must have been almost a thousand of them in the compound, and David Davis was trying to instil some sort of order into the confusion.

For many days now the rattle of small-arms and machine-gun fire, the duller thunder of mortars and heavy artillery had punctuated every waking and sleeping moment. Suddenly that evening it ceased! It was late and many people were already sleeping, but the very silence was in some strange manner ominous, terrifying. Gladys opened her window—the windows in the Mission were made of glass, unlike her paper windows in Yangcheng—and looked out into the dark courtyard. The very darkness seemed to breathe uneasily. She was annoyed at her own uneasiness and fear. "Why should you be frightened of silence?" she asked herself. "Supposing the Japanese do arrive. They *will* come; you know that. What about it? You've lived under their occupation before." But she knew, also, that she was opposing her intuition; the quick vital instinct that had served her so well in the past. Her instinct made her uneasy, as nervous as a deer drinking at a night pool lifting its head and scenting a tiger on the wind. She lay on her bed, fully dressed as usual, and closed her eyes. Weary from the long hours of organization and nursing, she dozed off. When the gravel rattled against her window-pane she awoke, startled.

She struggled up out of sleep, and got to the door. The wick of the castor-oil lamp still burning on the table gave a little illumination to the room.

"Who's there?" she called sharply.

She could not hear the reply, but recognized the voice as that of the General's orderly. She unbolted the door. He stood there, a dark shadow against the lighter sky. His voice was agitated.

"I have come to ask you to retreat with us at once, Ai-weh-deh," he said quickly.

Because she was a little frightened herself, her voice was irritable. "I've told you already I shall not retreat with the army," she snapped. "Why do you bother me at this time of night?"

He did not attempt to come into the room, but stood there, his voice full of appeal. "Whether you leave with us or not, you must leave. We have received certain information."

"What information?"

"The Japanese have put a price on your head."

"A price on my head!" She tried to laugh, but the laughter stuck in her throat. "What am I worth to anybody? The very idea's preposterous."

Without a word the orderly fumbled in his tunic pocket, produced a piece of paper and handed it to her. "Those leaflets are being pasted up in the villages outside Tsehchow. They will appear on the gates of this city tomorrow!"

She took it over to the lamp to read. The shadows danced across the small handbill, about eight by ten inches in size. Headed: "One hundred dollars reward!" it continued: "One hundred dollars reward will be paid by the Japanese Army for information leading to the capture, alive, of either of the three people listed below."

Gladys's eyes scanned the names. First was the Mandarin of Tsehchow; second was the name of a well-known business man notorious for his Nationalist sympathies. The third line simply read: "The Small Woman, known as Ai-weh-deh"!

CHAPTER FOURTEEN

HER IMMEDIATE reaction was that the whole affair was unbelievable. A hundred dollars; it was a small fortune! "They must be mad!" she exclaimed. "Offering a hundred dollars for me!"

The dark figure in the doorway did not move. "You must leave by the morning, Ai-weh-deh. I go now. You must leave as soon as the sun rises."

Gladys turned back to him, swayed by indecision now, unable to prevent a little maggot of fear suddenly moving in her brain.

"Thank you for bringing me this news," she said slowly. "I'll decide something or other; I don't know what."

He detected the note of anxiety in her voice. "I wish you well, Ai-weh-deh," he said gravely. Then he was gone into the darkness; she never saw him again.

She closed the door slowly behind him and walked back to the table. She examined the small poster more carefully. A hundred dollars! It was a vast sum of money to most of the inhabitants of Tsehchow. Without bitterness, she reflected that there were probably many amongst them who would betray her for half that sum. She did not think of consulting David Davis in her dilemma; for years now she had made her own decisions without help from anyone; she had not seen David for many months; and now that she was a woman with a price on her head, she did not want to involve him in her affairs. The air in the room felt oppressive. She went to a window and opened it. Darkness hung outside, thick and impenetrable; it was very quiet. "How can I run away in the face of the enemy?" she asked herself desperately, as a little short-wave station inside her head began to transmit small furtive words: 'Run! Run! Run for your life!'

It was obvious that the Japanese had heard of her intelligence work for the Nationalists. Someone had betrayed her. The enemy would have no scruples in squaring the account; nor would her sex offer protection. Yet she was still reluctant to leave. Her training, her heart and her spirit were all against abandoning her post in the face of the enemy. Yet she had seen many dreadful things these past years; the enemy were not above practising many of them on a Christian spy. Inside her head the furtive little voice repeated, 'If you stay, you will surely die. You know a prayer—a Chinese prayer—remember what it says.'

Yes, she knew the prayer well: many times she had repeated its message: 'If I must die, let me not be afraid of death; but let there be a meaning, oh God, to my dying.' The furtive voice was insistent. 'Will there be a meaning if you wait meekly like a sheep for the slaughter, for the Japanese to come and take you?' it said. 'You are a Chinese National. You are far from the land of your birth. Nothing can protect you. God would not have you stay.'

She did not know what to do, but on impulse reached out for her Bible. It lay on the table next to the leaflet. She flipped it open, then bent forward to read at random the line of Chinese characters. She had never read the passage before, and now she read it aloud in growing awe.

Flee ye, flee ye into the mountains! Dwell deeply in the hidden places because the King of Babylon has conceived a purpose against you!

"The King of Babylon has conceived a purpose against you!" she repeated aloud, wonderingly. If she wanted a sign, was this not it? *Flee ye, flee ye!* Yes, she knew now that she must leave at first light. She went to her little box in the corner and began to pull out all her papers and letters. They must be burnt before she left. Not a scrap of evidence of any sort must remain. She was still busy when dawn came, but she had completed her task. The sun was up when she went down into the compound, carrying her Bible and the small leaflet. One of the Chinese elders, a good Christian she had known for many years, was already taking a stroll in the sunlight. On impulse she held out the small square of paper to him. He took it, looked at it reflectively for a few moments, then lifted his eyes to her. His expression was grave.

"You should be out!" he said. "You should be away from here!"

"I'm going now," she replied. "I'm on my way to ask the gateman to get my mule ready."

As she crossed the wide compound to the front gate, she could feel the warmth of the sun on her back. Her feet in the thin shoes kicked up tiny spurts of dust. Mao, the gateman, was peering through the small spyhole in the door when she reached him.

"Mao," she said, "I'm leaving at once. Will you get my mule ready, please!"

His round, fat face turned slowly to meet hers. It was like a pumpkin, the same bright yellow colour, with wet currants for eyes. Usually it was creased in a grin, but now it was serious. His tight, round black hat seemed to constrict his forehead.

"You must look outside the door," he said. "It would be dangerous to leave now."

Gladys stepped past him. She put her eye to the small hole. It gave a view of the roadway which swung back to the left, cut off by the compound wall, and to the right where it rounded the city wall and entered the main gate. A party of Japanese soldiers were marching through the city gates. She stepped back from the peephole, fighting the surge of panic which rose in her throat. As she turned away she saw that for some unknown reason the cook, Mesang, had followed her across the compound. He pointed a stubby finger at her.

"You should be gone, you should be gone!" he called loudly.

She looked at him without answering, too stunned to speak. Then she turned and began to walk back across the compound, and as she walked the sense of panic—like the noise of a train approaching and increasing speed—began to roar inside her. Her feet moved more quickly, she broke into a trot, then abruptly she was running as fast as she could. The back gate was her objective, the back gate through which, by immemorial custom, they carried out the dead. The way to it lay through the courtyard, past David's quarters. As she raced through, she suddenly remembered his presence. On impulse she stopped, scooped up a handful of gravel, and hurled it at the glass panes. In a second he was at the window. He must have been in the process of dressing, because he was in his shirt sleeves. She could see his shoulders and head as he stared out at her through the glass. His voice came plainly.

"You're afraid, Gladys? Why are you afraid?"

Suddenly the blind panic had her in its grip again; without a word in reply, she ran for the back door. It was open, and she ran through. Outside lay the Strangers' Burying Ground, an open stretch of ground dotted with the humps of burial-mounds. Beyond was the shallow grass-grown moat which encircled the city, and away to the right stretched a large field of green wheat not fully grown but tall enough to hide her. All this she knew by heart and re-established in a quick perceptive flash as she dashed through the gate, but she also knew immediately that she had made one bad error of judgment. Although the front gate was closer to the city entrance, the route of escape from the back gate was overlooked by anyone advancing along the road for a much longer distance. Along the road, behind the detachment of soldiers she had seen proceeding into the city, were other companies marching at regulated intervals. She had raced right into their vision. The nearest body of troops was no more than a hundred yards away. She knew of their propensity for firing first and checking identities afterwards. Anyone who ran from them invited a fusillade! They loosed off round after round with the same sort of gleeful relish that a farmer's boy opens up at a running rabbit. If their shots found the target, rarely did they bother to go out of their way to inspect a corpse, or the wounds their bullets had inflicted. But she could not stop herself now; she was committed to flight, and this knowledge only increased her speed.

As she raced through the graveyard, she heard the soldiers shouting behind her; then she was conscious of the crack of rifles, the bee-whine ricochets as bullets glanced off the rocks around her. There was a pain in her chest, sweat in her eyes, but the edge of the moat was only a few yards away. She tried to spurt towards it but, almost on the brink, a fist punched her in the back. Instead of running, she was suddenly flat on her face, with the dust and grit in her mouth. She felt no pain, only an intense surprise. She knew a bullet had hit her somewhere. 'I'm dying,' she thought. 'So this is dying?' Then she became aware of a burning sensation across her shoulder-blades, and, with a quick return to common sense, realized that she was not dying at all, but soon might be, for bullets were still kicking up fountains of dust, and ricocheting from rocks all around her. The Japanese soldiers were using her prone figure for target practice. With intuitive reflex action, she reached up and tore open the cloth fastenings down the front of her heavily-padded coat. Her Bible had fallen with her; she could feel it pressing into her stomach beneath her. She wriggled out of her coat, sliding it down behind her like a sloughed skin; then, using the Bible as a sledge, she wormed her way forward, pushing with her toes and tearing at the earth with her hands. Panting, she reached the shallow moat and tumbled into it. Her back was burning now. Her heart thumped, as she listened to a shower of bullets spattering the discarded coat as the soldiers readjusted their aim. It gave her impetus. Doubled up, she scuttled along the moat until she could see the corn growing above her head. Carefully parting it, she burrowed among the pliable stalks, edging backwards so that she could lift up the slender stems and leave no telltale route of crushed wheat behind her.

In the middle of the field she felt fairly safe. She was sorry she had lost her coat, for all she wore underneath was a thin cotton vest, and even in the bright sun she shivered. Now she could feel the sting of the graze across her back The bullet had torn through her padded coat and skidded across the right shoulder-blade. Her exploring fingers located a thin runnel in her flesh, but it had bled little, so she was not worried. Her eyes were heavy, and she felt weak. She remembered that she had hardly slept at all the previous night. Birds sang in the bushes around the field and on the walls of the city. There was no other sound. It was quite peaceful. She curled up into a ball and yawned. Of a sudden, she felt tired, as if all will and enterprise had ebbed from her body. She closed her eyes.

She was surprised when she woke several hours later to find the sun high in the sky, and realized that she had fallen asleep. It seemed absurd, even foolhardy, to sleep in such a situation, and yet she was pleased because she felt so much better. She was frightened no longer. When darkness fell, she knew the Japanese would lock themselves inside the city. Therefore she had to wait until the sun set before she could make a break for the mountains. To occupy her time before dusk, she tunnelled through the corn to the farther edge of the field. As soon as the shadows were deep enough to give her shelter she slipped out of the wheat. She glanced back at the city walls. Not a soul moved in any direction as she hurried across the undulating fields towards the mountains.

It took her two days to reach the Inn of Eight Happinesses, and when she arrived she knew what she was going to do. As she picked her way up the rocky slopes, as the wind whipped her face on the ridges, as she stumbled down the steep inclines into the valleys, she examined all the courses which were left open to her. She arrived plainly at one decision. She must go! She must leave this part of Shansi altogether. After the bitter fighting of the past few months, the Japanese would not be merciful towards anyone they suspected. If they knew she was still in the territory, they might take hostages against her surrender. She thought of Hsi-Lien, and his wife and children burned alive. Suppose they did that to her friends or her children? She could not bear the thought for a moment. She would take the children—all of them—across the mountains to Sian and find refuge there. That was her decision as she came down the narrow road to the Inn.

The children were overjoyed to see her. They crowded around in the courtyard, laughing and chattering. The two

Mission workers who had looked after them told her that they begged grain from the Mandarin and all were well and fed. Gladys gathered them around her, a sea of brown, smiling, almond-eyed, dirty children, who knew her as their real, true and God-given mother.

"Ai-weh-deh!" they clamoured. "Ai-weh-deh has come to look after us."

"Tonight," she said, "I want you all to go to bed early. Tomorrow we're going for a walk across the mountains. A long, long walk!"

There was a burst of spontaneous cheering. A long walk to anywhere was an adventure.

"You must get up early and tie your bedding into a roll and take your bowls and chopsticks with you. Now off you go, all of you, and into bed early. Don't forget."

They disappeared into every hole and corner of the building and, as Gladys looked up sadly at the broken roof and the sagging balcony, she reflected that it was indeed all holes and corners. She sighed to herself and walked to the gate. Every house in the little street which led to the Inn was badly damaged. As she walked through the East Gate and along the main street which had been concerned with so many important happenings in her life, she felt a sense of overwhelming sadness for the derelict city. The yamen steps were deep in rubble. In the first courtyard she thought of the old splendour, the pomp and officialdom and all the ceremonial litter of thousands of years of courtly behaviour which had preceded those early meetings with the Mandarin. Now there was only one guard at the door of his small chamber. He recognized Gladys, grinned at her, pushed open the Mandarin's door and yelled: "It is she!"

As she went inside, Gladys reflected that in the old days such informality would have cost him his head.

The Mandarin came forward to greet her. He wore a plain blue robe and a black skullcap. For a passing moment Gladys regretfully recalled all those wonderful gowns of scarlet and gold. Even his long, glossy pigtail was now cropped to a stubby queue. All Chinese males had done this on Nationalist orders, for the Japanese had found ingenious ways of torturing men with long queues. They thought it uproariously funny to hang a man by his own pigtail.

"Ai-weh-deh," he said gently, "it is good to see you!"

"It is good to see you also," she replied.

She looked at him carefully. He was older. Scholarship had not mined those deep lines round his eyes and mouth. Like her, like all the Chinese people in southern Shansi, he had lived the past few years in an agony of doubt and fear. When the enemy came he had fled the city, carried on his civic business as best he could from a mountain village. When they left his city, he returned to its ruins. Neither the Communists nor the Japanese had any time for Mandarins; his life was in perpetual danger. But he smiled at her and inquired of her health, and her parents' health, and was anxious to help her. He listened gravely as she told him what had happened and of her decision to try to reach Sian across the mountains with the children. She could see that he was perturbed.

"I have heard that the Japanese armies are infiltrating through the mountain passes and have reached the Yellow River. You will have to cross their territory. It will be very dangerous."

"We shall stay away from all the known trails," she said. "We shall follow paths that the Japanese will never find."

"With a 'bei' of children?"

In Chinese numerology a 'bei' was a hundred; in actual fact, there were a few below that number.

"With a 'bei' of children," she said firmly. "I dare not leave one behind."

"That is true," he said sadly. He paused for a second. "You have money, food for the journey?"

"Neither."

He smiled, then chuckled aloud. "You have a faculty for facing the formidable, Ai-weh-deh, with a certitude and calm which I have envied ever since you came to Yang-cheng all those years ago."

"I've said it to you many times: 'God will provide'. Now you believe that, too?"

"On this occasion, at least, let the Mandarin of Yangcheng act as His agent. I can provide you with two *dhan* of millet, and two men to carry them for the first part of your journey. It will take you several weeks to reach Sian by the route you will have to travel—you understand that?"

"I know. I'm leaving at dawn tomorrow morning."

"May God help you," he said. "May the good fortune you deserve be yours."

They bowed low to each other; they were old friends saying farewell, and each wished to convey more of their innermost affection through something more than words. It was impossible; and also unnecessary.

She went back to the Inn. The children were stacked in rows on the k'angs once used by the muleteers. From the broken balcony she looked up at the star-filled sky and the familiar mountains. She knew in her heart that she was leaving Yangcheng, if not for ever, then for a very long time. Her mind swept back to that day she had first arrived, cheerfully ignorant of all that lay before her. So much work and toil, and yet so much happiness, had been compressed into those full and useful years; nothing could uproot or diminish those memories. She tried to console herself with the thought that there would be more work to do in Sian when she arrived, but it did not help much.

She wondered how David was faring. Had she known what was about to happen to him, it is probable that she would have returned at once to Tsehchow to try to be of some assistance. But she did not know. And it was to be many long years before she did hear the full story of David Davis.

Two weeks after the Japanese occupied Tsehchow they arrested him, and accused him of being a spy. Although it was precisely one year and four months before the Japanese declared war on the Allies, and David Davis was theoretically, therefore, a neutral, it made no difference whatsoever to his treatment. A thousand miles inside China theoretical scruples played small part in Japanese strategy. For some Oriental reason known only to themselves, they were determined to make him admit he was a spy. Their methods were quite simple. They starved him, kept him without sleep, and beat him viciously at regular intervals.

Two of his Christian converts they tied to beams and tortured in an effort to induce them to declare that David Davis had conspired against the Japanese. Both refused to condemn him. Both they killed. They were simple men; they could not understand why they were being tortured into confessing to an untruth, which they knew, and the Japanese knew, was an untruth. They died keeping faith. The Japanese had no grounds for suspicion regarding David, but he was a European and a Christian, and they distrusted both. Why had he come back to the Mission? Why had he allowed Chinese soldiers to frequent the Mission compound? Why had he spied for the Nationalists? Why? Why? Why? Day and night he was made to kneel facing a plain wall, and if he fell asleep he was woken every hour by blows.

For three months this treatment continued; they did not even dent his spirit or his determination. They knew about Gladys, but she was out of their reach. They had found a letter addressed to her from a certain Mr White, a journalist from *Time* magazine. Many months earlier he had crossed the Yellow River and penetrated up into Shansi in search of material. Because he had little of the language, and because the Nationalists were suspicious of him, he was eventually directed to Gladys. He wanted to know what was going on, who was fighting whom, if the Japanese were really committing atrocities. Gladys had helped him all she could. Months later he sent her a letter from Chungking, thanking her for her help in supplying him with details of Japanese atrocities. He had sent it to Tsehchow. Unknowingly, he might just as well have sent a death warrant. Gladys was away, David en route for Chifu. The letter was placed on David's desk and, during some periodic clearing-up process, it fell from the top down between the desk and the wall. Neither Gladys nor David in their destruction of all personal documents and letters had located it. When they searched the Mission for the last time the Japanese did not make that mistake. As soon as it was thrust in front of David's nose, he realized that if they ever caught Gladys it was the end of her. He declared that he knew nothing of either Mr White or the letter; which was true. He had been a thousand miles away at the coast when the visit had been made. But the Japanese were having none of his protestations of innocence. It was further proof of his guilt, they asserted. After three months of interrogation he was moved to a Chinese gaol at T'ai Yuan.

The inhuman treatment continued. He was placed in a steel cage with a concrete floor and concrete back wall with twenty other prisoners. It was a few feet square. They were jammed together in a hot, stinking mass with no means whatever of satisfying even the primary requirements of sanitation. Day and night an electric bulb glared down upon them. At dawn—they knew it was dawn because the warden would give a single order, 'Kneel'—they would kneel, facing the wall. They would stay in that position for hours; if they moved or spoke they were savagely beaten. Then they would get an order, 'Stand!' With heads bent, because the cell was too low for anyone to stand upright, they would crouch immobile. At night came the last order, 'Lie down!' and they would lie on the concrete floor in a packed, contorted row. Once every two or three days bowls of *kioliang* or maize would be passed in, and a little water. The prisoners would cram it into their mouths with their fingers. Every few days David Davis was taken out for questioning. He was told that if he admitted to being a spy he would at once be given better quarters and better treatment. He refused. He knew that they were trying to drive him mad; he also knew that while he was sane they could never defeat him. His resolution was a coil of steel inside him; the harder they twisted with their pliers of torture the more the coil contracted, and it contracted into a fist of solid indestructible metal. Even in the depths of his deepest physical misery there was a kind of exaltation in his suffering. If the Japanese had understood even vaguely the great mystique of Christianity, which had produced an unending succession of martyrs since that Good Friday when Jesus Christ was nailed to a Cross, they might have known that they were wasting their efforts. There was a core in the spirit of this man from the mountains of Wales which no physical degradation could destroy. For six months, filthy, lice-ridden, they kept him in this cell, heaped together with those other pitiful fragments of humanity. He saw neither sun nor moon, nor knew the passing of night into day, nor day into darkness.

At length it was the Japanese who admitted defeat. He was transferred into another cell which held only three prisoners; he was accorded slightly better treatment. He spent that time converting one of his fellow-prisoners to Christianity. Two years after he had been arrested he was sent to the coast to be repatriated as a civilian. There, while waiting for the last ship which was to take him homewards, he learnt that his wife Jean and his children were in a nearby camp. Forsaking any chance of repatriation, he hurried to see them. The boat sailed without him. His small daughter was ill with whooping cough. A complication which happens no more than once in ten thousand times had set in. In a few hours she was dead. He spent the rest of the war with Jean and the two boys in an internment camp nearby. Today he lives at Ely, a suburb of Cardiff, in a small house, running his own church and community. He carries scars on his face from his encounters with the Japanese. But no scars internally.

There is no malice or vengefulness in the soul of David Davis.

CHAPTER FIFTEEN

AT SUN-UP the young children were up and shouting, running round the courtyard, throwing their bundles of bedding at each other, playing 'Tag' and generally behaving in the normal way of young children all over the world. With the aid of the older ones, Gladys tried to sort them out and feed them. There were nearly twenty big girls, ages varying from thirteen to fifteen, Ninepence and Sualan amongst them: there were seven big boys aged between eleven and fifteen; the rest of the children varied from four to eight, wild, undisciplined, laughing, weeping, shouting little brats. In vain, she tried to tell them that they must save their energy for the long day ahead; she might just as usefully have told a stream to stop running. The two coolies from the Mandarin, carrying their shoulder-poles, a basket of millet suspended at either end, arrived at the front gate. Gladys said goodbye to the two Mission workers, to several other friends collected there; and, after one last look round the broken Inn, they were on their way, the children scampering ahead, dodging back through the gates of the city, shouting loudly that they could walk for ever and ever.

They followed the main trail southwards for several miles. Gladys possessed a whistle which she had obtained from a Japanese soldier months before, and she blew it occasionally to call the more adventurous little boys down from outcrops of rock, and twice to line them all up in rows for a roll call to see that no one was missing.

They stopped by a stream to boil millet in the iron pot which Gladys carried; she heaped the steaming grain into the basins as each child came up in turn for its helping. At the end of this serving there wasn't much left in the pot for her, and from that moment onwards that was the way things usually turned out. The children, revived after the meal, began to clamber about the rocks again, and made excited forays ahead, to lie in wait and ambush the main party. She gave up trying to keep them in order, but as the afternoon progressed, these minor expeditions became fewer and fewer, and soon she had four small ones hanging on to her coat, protesting that they were tired, and could they all go back to Yangcheng now? Gladys took it in turns with the older boys to carry them. She felt a little tired herself.

It was getting dark when they came to a mountain village she knew, and where she thought they might find shelter for the night. Not, she thought, that any householders would be particularly anxious to house a hundred noisy, dirty children. Help came from an unexpected quarter. An old Buddhist priest, in his bright saffron robes, stood on the steps of his temple as the Pied Piper of Yangcheng and her brood straggled past.

"Where are you going?" he called to Gladys.

"We are refugees on the way to Sian," she said.

He came down the steps and approached her, his small eyes almost lost in the maze of wrinkles and lines that creased his face.

"But what are you going to do with all these children, woman?" He sounded most disapproving.

"I'm looking for a place for us to sleep tonight."

"Then you can stay in the temple," he said abruptly. "All my brother priests are away. There is plenty of room. Tell them to come in. It will be warmer than the mountain-side."

The children needed no prompting. This was something like an adventure! It was dark in the temple, and there were gloomy recesses in which stone figures of the fat, bland, heavy-lidded Buddha resided. There were painted panels depicting the many tortures of sinners, but the children were too tired to notice them. They crowded round the iron pot when Gladys had finished cooking the millet, and when they had eaten, they curled up on their bedding and went fast asleep.

She did not sleep so easily. For one thing, the temple was alive with rats, who twittered in the darkness and ran over the sleeping children; and a small creeping doubt had entered her mind concerning the wisdom of starting this journey with so many small ones. Perhaps she was over-estimating her own ability? It was one thing to journey through the mountains alone; quite another to take a hundred children with you. The first day had been trouble-some enough, yet all the children were fresh, and she was crossing country she knew intimately. The older girls had not complained, but she could see that several of them had suffered already. They were completely unused to mountain walking; the feet of several of them had once been bound, and even many years free from the bindings was insufficient to turn them into healthy limbs able to withstand the drag and scrape of the rocky paths. For perhaps an hour the big boys tried to keep off the rats, then they also became too tired to persevere and fell asleep. Gladys lay on the hard floor; above her head the impassive sculptured face of the stone Buddha was illumined by a shaft of moonlight streaming downwards through some aperture high above. The more she thought about the future, the less she liked it, but there was no chance of retreat now; she had to go on.

The next day was a replica of the first. The children awoke refreshed, and with a complete lack of reverence began to explore the temple with shrill, admiring cries. The priest smiled urbanely; he did not seem to mind at all. He bowed when Gladys offered her thanks and wished her a safe journey to Sian.

They were far from any village when the next night caught them, and they huddled together in the shelter of a semicircle of rocks out of the wind. In the night there was a heavy mist and the children crept under their wet quilts, and next day they steamed and dried out when the sun rose. That afternoon they met a man on a mule travelling in the same direction as themselves. If they would come to his village, he said, he would be glad to find them shelter for the night. She accepted his offer gratefully. In his courtyard the children spread themselves out and scooped cooked millet out of their bowls until their bellies were full, then drank cupful after cupful of the hot twig tea. They still thought it was all a wonderful adventure. Even Gladys felt an immense sense of relief with another day safely past, and the Yellow River one day closer. She cupped her bowl between her hands, embracing the tiny warmth it offered, and chatted to the other girls.

"How many days will it take us to reach the Yellow River, Ai-weh-deh?" asked Sualan diffidently.

Although Gladys had never been through to the Yellow River, she knew the answer to that question without any trouble. "The muleteers on the normal track used to take five days. We're going right through the mountains. About twelve, I'd say."

"And we shan't see a single Japanese soldier the whole way?" asked Ninepence.

"I hope not," she answered.

She looked at the two girls as they chatted, the girl she had bought for ninepence, and the slave girl from the yamen. They were both exquisite little creatures with clear pale skins and blue-black shining hair. Even in their dusty padded coats their prettiness was still unimpaired. She thought wistfully how beautiful they would look in the ceremonial robes of China, wondering if they would ever know such luxury. How absurd that they should be forced to make this long journey to save their lives. She felt an unreasoning anger at the stupidity of all men that they should be the cause of this ordeal. She yawned. It was odd, this constant tiredness. "Probably the added responsibility of the children," she thought to herself, as she wrapped herself in her bedding quilt and lay down to sleep.

In the morning the two carriers of the millet had to return to Yangcheng. They had reached the limit of their province. However, the man they had met in the mountains proved a good friend; he provided them with another coolie who would carry what was left of the millet until it was finished, and even by rationing it did not look as if that would last another two days.

The next two nights were spent in the open. Two of the older boys, Teh and Liang, had obtained a pot of whitewash from a village along the way, and they went on ahead daubing a splash of white on to the rocks to mark the trail across the mountains. Sometimes they would write a text across a rock: *This is the way. Walk ye in it!* or *Fear ye not, little flock!* There were squeals of appreciation as the messages were translated to the young ones.

This was new country to Gladys, but she knew they were heading south by the direction of the sun. They were thirsty practically all the time, for the sun was hot and wells were only to be found in the villages. After the heavy wet mountain mists each morning they would gather round any drip from the rocks and moisten their tongues. The millet was used up now, and the carrier went back to his village. They had no more food, and the mountain stretched ahead of them, wild and barren, with few places of habitation. Often, when they climbed over virgin rock, the slopes were so steep that they had to form a human chain down the mountainside, and pass the younger children down from hand to hand. They cried when they fell down, and cried when they got tired. Often Gladys tried to rally them with a hymn, and when they reached a level patch of ground they would all march bravely along singing the chorus. Between them, the older children and Gladys were carrying practically all the bedding now, and often they would give one of the five or six-year-olds a pick-a-back ride for a short distance. There was rarely any moment when a small hand was not clutching at Gladys's jacket.

Seven nights out from Yangcheng found them camped in the heart of a mountainous region unknown to her. They had found a small trail which led southwards. It was not yet dark, but everyone was too exhausted to move farther. The thin, home-made cloth shoes, which everyone wore, were practically all worn out. The big girl's feet were cut and bleeding. Everyone was filthy, covered with dust and dirt; they had no food. Gladys raised her head to scan the party lying in huddled groups under the rocks. She did not like what she saw; unless they received food and help very soon, she was afraid of what might happen to them.

Suddenly she saw Teh and Liang, who were still acting as forward scouts, running back towards her. They were shouting something which she could not hear, but their obvious excitement presaged danger.

"Men!" they shouted. "Soldiers!"

Gladys froze in a moment of panic. She put her whistle into her mouth to blow the prearranged signal for the children to scatter, but she did not blow it. If they scattered into this wild terrain they might all be lost and would starve or die in the wilderness. And then, as the boys stumbled towards her, she saw men in uniform rounding a buttress of rock down the valley, and with a gasping sign of relief realized that they were Nationalist troops. The children had sighted them also. Their tiredness fell away and they bounded over the rocks to greet the newcomers. Gladys, with the girls, advanced more slowly, and as she walked suddenly heard the sound she dreaded more than any other. The noise of aircraft engines! With a thunder of sound that echoed throughout the valley, two Japanese fighters tore through a cleft in the mountains and hurtled across their heads. Although they must have been hundreds of feet up, their sudden appearance, the abrupt bull-roar of their engines sent a shock wave of panic through everyone in the valley.

She threw herself into the shelter of a rock, glimpsing from the corner of her eye that the girls were doing the same. She crouched, rigid, waiting for the rattle of machine-guns. None came. She looked up, as the planes disappeared, catching sight of the stubby wings, the Rising Sun insignia painted on the fuselage. But the airmen were obviously intent on something more important than machine-gunning Nationalist troops or refugees in the mountains. Gladys stood up and looked down the valley. The children had been well trained on their drill in the event of attack by aircraft. They were scrambling up from their hiding places. The Nationalist troops, who had also scattered wildly, were mixed up with the children. They rose from the rocks, laughing together.

There were about fifty soldiers, reinforcements from

Honan passing up country to join a Nationalist force farther north. Gladys met the young officer in charge, and explained their predicament, but the problem of the hungry children was being solved spontaneously. Soldiers were diving their hands into knapsacks, and bringing out treasures of sweet foods, and all round she could hear only the "Ahs!" and "Oohs!" and "Ohs!" of the delighted children.

The soldiers decided to camp in that spot for the night. They invited Gladys and her brood to stay with them and share their food. It was a feast! They had foodstuffs not seen in Shansi for years. The children sat round the small fires, stuffing themselves to bursting point. Even Gladys, for the first time on the journey, ate her fill. When the troops moved on at dawn the children waved them a sorrowful goodbye.

Each day now took on something of a nightmare complex. Strangely enough, the young children bore up well. They were used to little food; at night, no matter how hard the ground, they slept to a point of complete insensibility; and they woke refreshed and ready to play and gambol next morning. They charged up the mountains, lost their bowls and chopsticks, cried and protested, but they all remained healthy. Sualan, Ninepence, Lan Hsiang and the other girls were in a pitiful state. The sun had cracked their lips and burnt their faces. Their feet were blistered and sore, and they could only hobble a few hundred yards before they had to rest again.

Nevertheless, no one gave up, and they moved slowly onwards through the mountains. On the twelfth day they came out of the mountains and down through the foothills towards the Yellow River. As usual at this time, the small children's voices were a constant background of complaint.

"Ai-weh-deh, my feet hurt!"

"Ai-weh-deh, I'm hungry!"

"Ai-weh-deh, when shall we stop for the night?"

"Ai-weh-deh, will you carry me?"

"Down below," she said, "look over there; the village of

Yuan Ku; and beyond it, far away, look, the Yellow River!
See it shining in the sunshine!"

"But it is so far away, Ai-weh-deh. And we're so
hungry!"

"In the village of Yuan Ku they'll give us food, and then
we'll arrive at the Yellow River. And when we cross that
we'll all be safe. Now let's sing a song as we march down
to the town."

No band of shipwrecked mariners looking from a raft
with salt-bleared eyes at a friendly shore, no thirsty
travellers in the desert beholding an oasis, looked more
eagerly at that distant shining ribbon of water than Gladys
and the older children. The twelve days since they left
Yangcheng had been long and weary ones; now at last they
were in sight of relief.

They followed the road which led down from the foothills to the town. It had been badly bombed. Rubble
littered the streets and most of the houses were roofless.
There was an unaccountable silence about the place as they
approached. No dogs ran yapping to meet them. No
carriers or coolies moved in the streets. The children ran
from house to house, their shrill voices echoing in the
courtyards. There was no one there. It was deserted. Then
Liang and Teh, the faithful scouts still ahead of the party,
reported that they had found an old man. Gladys hurried
up to him. He was sitting against a tree in the sunshine, a
cone-shaped straw hat on his head, a few white hairs
straggling from his chin. His thin legs stuck out from the
blue cotton trousers. He had been asleep, and was querulous
at being woken.

"Old man, this is Yuan Ku, is it not?" she said loudly.

"Yes, this is Yuan Ku."

"But where are all the people? Why is the city deserted?"

"They've run away. The Japanese are coming, and
they've all run away."

A thin dribble of saliva ran down his chin. He was
toothless and his face was shrunken to the bone.

"Why haven't you gone? Why are you still here?"

"I'm too old to run. I'll sleep here in the sun until the

Japanese arrive, and if they kill me, who will care? All my sons are gone. All my family are broken like wheatstalks in the wind. I'll wait for the Japanese and spit at them."

"But where have all the people gone?"

"Across the Yellow River, away from the Japanese."

"Then we must go there, too. Are there boats?"

"There were boats once. Now I think you are too late." He cocked a rheumy old eye at the children crowding round him. "Where are all these children from? Where are they going?"

"We are refugees journeying to Sian," she said.

His lips curled contemptuously as he looked at her. "You are a fool, woman, to bother with all these children. The gods intended a woman to care for a handful of children, not an army."

Gladys had heard such philosophy in China before. It brushed over her head.

"How far is it to the river?"

"Three miles. Follow the road to the ferry, but you will not find a boat there. The Japanese are coming, and they will not leave their boats to be captured. Go back to the mountains, woman. They are the only safe places!"

"We are going to Sian," she said simply. She blew her whistle and the children lined up around her. It was Cheia's turn to be carried, so she humped him on her back. "As soon as we get to the river we shall bathe and wash our clothes," she said. "And we shall catch a boat and be safe on the other side. Goodbye, old man, and good luck!"

He did not turn his head to watch them go. He let it slump forward on his chest; he was asleep before they had turned the corner.

They trudged down the dusty path to the river edge. There were reeds along the bank, and little bays edged with sand where the children could splash and paddle in the shallows. They ran towards it, shouting and excited. The river was about a mile across, running swift and deep in the centre. But there were no boats, and no sign of any boats!

Sualan said quietly, "Where are the boats, Ai-weh-deh?"

"They must come across every now and then," she answered. "Perhaps we're too late today. We'll spend the night here on the river bank, so we'll be ready to go aboard the boat first thing tomorrow morning."

They crouched together in a hollow on the bank. A yellow moon rose above the Yellow River, peering down a great fan of silver to look at them. It was very beautiful, but she had no eyes for its beauty. Birds rustled uneasily in the reeds and occasionally a fish would ripple and leap, the splash disturbing the silver surface. It was quiet and peaceful, but she was much afraid. Where were the boats? Why were there no boats? Was the old man right? Had everyone fled across the river to avoid the Japanese? Were they trapped against this broad ribbon of water? She fell eventually into a deep but uneasy slumber, and dreamed that hordes of little yellow men in round steel helmets, carrying a large flag, bright with the scarlet-and-white insignia of a rising sun, were marching closer and closer.

When she awoke next morning the children were already playing in the shallows. The youngest were calling back, shouting: "Ai-weh-deh, we are hungry. When shall we have something to eat, Ai-weh-deh?"

"Soon," she called, "soon!"

She gathered the older boys around her. "We must look for food. Back in Yuan Ku, they must have left a few oddments. You must go back and search the houses. Look everywhere. We must find a little food."

The children went on playing in the shallows. The boys trailed off to look for food in the deserted town of Yuan Ku. Gladys sat on the bank and watched the sun climbing up the sky, reflected blindingly in the surface of the wide river. She felt sick. The children had still not got over their amazement at the sight of so large a river; and they explored and poked in the reeds and the shallows along the banks. But curiosity would not fill their bellies for long. 'If only a boat would come!' she thought. 'If only a boat would come!'

Three hours later the boys came back triumphant. They had scavenged through most of the houses in Yuan Ku, and each bore some small contribution: a few pounds of mouldy millet in the bottom of a rotting basket; a few dusty-looking, flat, hard cakes of dough from under a shop counter. It was all boiled in the communal pot over a fire of dried reeds, and the result ladled carefully into the forest of waving basins. There was not enough for Gladys or Sualan or the older boys, but the younger children were fed.

The sun rose high, and still no boat moved on the surface of the river. The boys went off to search for more food along the banks; there were a few scattered houses there. She sat quietly watching the children, half alert for the distant rifle fire that would herald the approach of the enemy. The boys came back with a few more scraps of food, which she hoarded for the next day. That night the children huddled together on the bank of the river and whimpered before they went to sleep.

"Ai-weh-deh, we're hungry."

"Ai-weh-deh, when are we going to cross the river? When are we going to cross the river, Ai-weh-deh?"

She comforted them as best she could, and one by one they dropped off to sleep. The cold, white moon came up from the opposite bank and sat in the sky looking at them. A little cold wind rustled in the reeds with a dry, thin rattle. Scarves of opalescent white mist hung above the surface. The water noises were soft, muted. Gladys lay on her back and looked up at the stars. Somehow, it was easier at night. In the sunshine the grim reality of that immense water barrier, the lack of food, the whimpering children, was a burden so heavy as to be almost insupportable. But at night the edges of the present and future were blurred; softened and eased by the slow falling through the peace which preceded sleep. There were a few short hours of forgetfulness before the hot ball of the sun lifted above the horizon and the yelling swarm of children raced for the water to splash and shout and greet the dawn. And, besides, tomorrow it might all be different. Tomorrow a boat might come.

They ate the last crumbs of food on the third day at the

bank of the Yellow River. The sun rose and the children grew tired of racing along the banks. She told them stories and they sang songs together, and her eyes were sore from staring at the water in search of a boat. As the sun went down again, they crept close to her so that she could touch them with her hands. On the morning of the fourth day even the youngest children had caught the mood of despair. It was then that Sualan said:

"Ai-weh-deh, do you remember telling us how Moses took the children of Israel to the waters of the Red Sea? And how God commanded the water to open and the Israelites crossed in safety?"

"Yes, I remember," she said gently.

"Then why does not God open the waters of the Yellow River for us to cross?"

She looked wearily at the pretty, childish face, the ingenuous wide eyes. "I am not Moses, Sualan," she said.

"But God is always God, Ai-weh-deh. You have told us so a hundred times. If He is God He can open the river for us."

For a moment she did not know what to say. How to tell a hungry child on the banks of an immense and wide-flowing river that miracles were not just for the asking. How to say, perhaps we are not worthy of a miracle. How to say, although I can face a mortal enemy wherever he may beset me, I cannot open these vast waters. I have no power other than the power of my own faith.

She said: "Let you and I kneel down and pray, Sualan. And perhaps soon our prayers will be answered."

. . . . .

The Chinese Nationalist officer commanding the platoon scouting on the wrong side of the river looked back at the section of men straggling along behind him. They were boys, all of them, boys pressed from hinterland villages: with rifles shoved into their hands, and ill-fitting uniforms on to their backs, quickly acquiring the ability to live off the land as an elementary part of their military and self-survival training. There were eight of them: unshaven, their heads closely cropped.

Oh, they would fight. If they ran into a probing Japanese patrol they would go to ground, and the bullets from their rifles would kick up tiny geysers of dust around the feet of the enemy. They would hold them for a while, unless the other patrol had a mortar. Or unless they whistled up one of their fighter planes to spray them out of existence with cannon-shells. They would hang on as best they could until nightfall, if possible. Nightfall would save them. Then they could signal their comrades on the far bank, and the precious boat camouflaged with reeds could be pushed out into the river and ferried across. Enough face would be saved by nightfall.

The young officer flicked a fly from his sweaty forehead and sucked in his breath.

His wandering thoughts suddenly jarred to a standstill. A noise! An odd noise! A far off, high pitched sound, wavering and uncertain. A plane? His men thought so; he watched them thumb back their helmets and roll their eyes round the cloudless sky in an effort to locate it. There had been an unusual lack of air activity up and down the Yellow River for the past week. Usually the Jap planes patrolled and fired at anything that moved, even firing bursts into the reed beds at the sides of the river, and occasionally loosing off a sustained burst into the river itself so that a momentary barrier of furious water heaved up in a wall of hissing intimidation.

And yet this sounded almost like singing. Faint and far-away, high and monotonous, the sexless piping of many children? He shook his head as though to clear it. The river at this point was a mile wide; there might be children left in the villages on the other side of the river. Perhaps they were teaching school; but would their voices carry this far? He mounted a slight rise in the bank, crawling carefully to the top. He raised himself to see better, and grunted in astonishment. He reached for his binoculars and focused. It was an astonishing sight. A great crowd of children were assembled on the bank, all seated in a circle and singing loudly. Some smaller ones were splashing and jumping in the shallows.

He motioned his men back with a hand signal. "Wait here," he said. "It may be a trick. Be alert."

The Japanese had driven refugees before them on many other occasions. And who were these children? All refugees had left this area days ago. The river was officially closed. As he walked along the bank, he could see that they were Chinese children all right. They saw him, the young ones, and raced towards him, gurgling and shouting with delight.

"Ai-weh-deh," they screamed, "here's a soldier. A soldier."

The young officer noticed the small woman sitting on the ground. She was thin, hungry looking. She got to her feet as he approached, and with a shock of surprise he realized that she was a foreigner.

"Are you mad?" he said. "Who are you?"

"We are refugees trying to reach Sian," she said simply.

Her Chinese was excellent, though she spoke with the heavy dialect of the north, but although she was small like his own countrywomen, and her hair dark, he knew she was a foreigner.

"This will soon be a battlefield. Don't you realize that?" he said.

"All China is a battlefield," she said wearily.

"Are you in charge of these children?"

"Yes, I am in charge of them. We are trying to cross the river."

He looked at her directly. She was quite a young woman. Her dark hair was scraped back into a bun, her clothes old and soiled; there were dark circles under her eyes, and her face had a sallow, unhealthy look.

"You are a foreigner?"

"Yes, I am a foreigner."

"For a foreigner you chose a strange occupation."

She looked steadily at him as he said, "I think I can get you a boat. It will need three journeys to take you all across, and it is dangerous. If a Japanese plane comes over when you are half way across there will be little hope."

"We *must* cross the river."

"You will probably manage to get food in the village on

222

the other side. The people do not like to leave their homes even when the Japanese come."

"I understand," she said. "It was like that with us in Yangcheng."

He walked to the river edge, inserted his fingers in his mouth and whistled loudly three times in a peculiar piercing fashion. From across the river came three answering whistles. Two little figures far away on the other bank pushed a boat into the water and began to scull it across.

"I cannot thank you enough," she said. "I thought it was the end of us when we couldn't cross the river."

The young officer noticed her sway a little as one of the children pushed against her.

He looked at her curiously. "You are ill," he said. "You should find a doctor. The Nationalist troops on the other side of the river will have a doctor."

"I am all right," she said. "When we get to Sian I shall be all right."

With shouts of glee the children filled the boat. The soldiers ferried them rapidly to the other side. They returned and more of the children piled in. On the third journey the soldier helped the foreign woman into the boat with the last group of children. His platoon had gathered round to help. As the boat moved away from the bank, he called his men to attention and gravely saluted. He called: "Good luck, foreigner!"

He turned to walk back along the bank to his platoon. As he walked he looked into the sky, and listened for the drone of Japanese planes. None came. It was curious about that foreigner. If this had been close to a large city or a settlement, he could have understood it, but wandering across a battlefield escorting an army of ragged Chinese children; that was, indeed, very curious.

CHAPTER SIXTEEN

THEY FOUND a village two or three miles back from the bank of the Yellow River and the people were hospitable to them. Although many hundreds of refugees had passed through, they still found food to spare for the children. The Village Elder apportioned so many to each house down the main street, and when their initial hunger was appeased the children scampered from house to house to see how the others were faring. Gladys heard their shrill questions. "What are you eating in your house?" "We've got *bingsies*. What have you got?" "We've got *mientiao*!" "Oh, rotten old mientiao. You can keep it!" "But we've got rice cakes as well, see!"

It was just as well, thought Gladys wearily—just as well they didn't bother where the next meal was coming from.

They stayed in the village only long enough to finish the food, and then moved on. If the Japanese were approaching the river she wished to get as far away from it as possible. They spent that night in the fields, and went on again next morning to the town of Mien Chih. It, too, was badly bombed, but an old woman directed her to a refugee organization. She found it situated in the old temple; there were cauldrons of steaming food; they were made welcome. And then the police arrived. The inspector was a fat and fussy little man bulging with a sense of his own dignity. He marched up to Gladys, and there was a touch of Alice in Wonderland about his conversation.

"I understand," he said, "that you say you have just crossed the Yellow River."

"Yes!"

"Then you are under arrest. You could not have crossed the Yellow River."

"Under arrest! But what for?"

"You say you crossed the Yellow River."

"Yes."

"No one else crossed with you?"

"No . . . only the children."

"If nobody else could get across, how did you get across?"

She shook her head in bewilderment. "We met a soldier who signalled a boat."

"You could not have met a soldier who signalled a boat. You could not have crossed the river. You are under arrest!" He pursed his lips seriously. This was obviously the most interesting crime he had had committed in his area for some time.

"You didn't expect me to stay there and wait for the Japanese, did you?" she said heatedly. "And if you arrest me, you'll have to arrest all the children too."

A little pucker of astonishment creased the blandly official face at this new complication.

"You mean to tell me you are in charge of all these children?"

"I am, and there's no one else to look after them." She was tired; it was late; and she wanted to rest. She tried wheedling.

"Why don't you leave us alone tonight? I'll come down to your yamen, or the police station, or wherever it is first thing tomorrow morning, and you can arrest me then."

The fat little policeman looked a little dubious. "I shall have to examine you before the Mandarin," he said importantly.

"Well, I shan't try and escape with all these children, shall I? I'll come down to the yamen tomorrow morning and you can ask all the questions you want."

He had to be satisfied with that. He went off into the growing darkness, and Gladys wearily spread out her bedding; it appeared that escaping officialdom was almost as difficult as escaping from the Japanese.

Next morning, with the children, at the head of her party, Gladys marched down to the yamen to be interrogated. The children were not allowed inside, and rumours that something awful was going to happen to Ai-weh-deh had spread among them. They stood in a block outside the front door, and as soon as she went inside kept up an increasing chant "Let her out! Let her out! Let her out!"

The Mandarin was a benign-looking elder who showed that he had little sympathy with the policeman, whose evidence was both repetitive and absurd.

"You say you crossed the Yellow River?"

"Yes."

"I say you did not!"

"But I tell you we did," Gladys protested. "How could I have got from Shansi to Honan unless I crossed the river?"

"Then how could you have crossed without a boat?"

"We crossed in a boat! A soldier signalled a boat!"

"Then you have committed a crime. You will please examine this document." From the hands of one of his orderlies he produced a massive and important-looking scroll, and handed it across.

Gladys scanned it. Among the seals and important looking hieroglyphics, she read that by decree of the General Commanding the Nationalist armies in that region, the Yellow River was closed to all traffic. No one could cross, or journey upon it. The order was dated five days previously.

"So that's why there were no boats," said Gladys. "I wondered why."

"Do you admit now that you have committed this crime?" thundered the little policeman.

"Of course I have," retorted Gladys angrily. "We are refugees from Shansi proceeding to Sian. There are a hundred children with me. You didn't expect us to wait on the other side to be killed, did you?"

Outside, the chant of the children went on monotonously. "Let her out! Let her out!" And now they had found the windows, and a dozen small faces were peering through, and tapping the panes with their fingers.

"Let her out! Let her out!"

The Mandarin had had enough. "It is plain," he said, "that if this woman has committed an offence it is of the smallest technical nature." He smiled at her. "If you can

226

control your children for a few minutes, I think I might be able to help you."

She went outside. A few sharp words and a few indiscriminate cuffs got the children into order. She went back to see the Mandarin. The policeman had disappeared.

"Every morning," he said, "a train leaves Mien Chih and travels along the river in the direction of Sian. It does not reach there because something has gone wrong with the line, but at least it will take you some distance on your journey."

"But we've no tickets and no money for tickets," said Gladys.

He looked at her gravely. "In Honan today," he said, "all trains are refugee trains. No one is expected to have tickets. Tomorrow morning go to the station with your children and get on the train."

Gladys thanked him, and took the children back to the refugee centre. That afternoon she led them all to a pond on the edge of the city, and they tried to wash off the worst of the dirt from their clothes and bodies. In the evening she assembled them in the courtyard and addressed them.

"You all know what a train is, don't you?" she said.

There was an excited babble of conversation. No, most of them didn't know what a train was. What was it? They'd never heard of such a thing.

Gladys demonstrated with sound effects, and "Oohs" and "Ahs!" of delighted anticipation greeted her description. Sualan, Ninepence, Teh, Liang, the older boys and girls were, on the surface, more sophisticated about the approaching experience. Of course, they had heard about trains. What was there to get excited about? But they were excited, nevertheless.

"Tomorrow you will line up with clean hands and faces, and anyone with a dirty face or dirty hands will not be allowed on that train." Her speech over, the children scattered, to play about and terrorize the other refugees in the temple, before clambering into their bedding, chattering eagerly of the wondrous experience that was to befall

227

them next day. They dropped off quickly into the sound sleep of the very young, and very innocent, within minutes of feeling their quilts around them.

They were all up at dawn next morning, eagerly tying up their bundles, scrambling to be first at the great stone basin full of water in the temple courtyard, so that faces and hands should be the requisite colour required by the omnipotent Ai-weh-deh. They lined up to have their basins filled with steaming millet, scooped the thick mixture into open mouths with dexterous chopsticks, and with astounding co-operation formed a long crocodile, before Gladys had even tied up her own bedding.

She thanked the women running the refugee centre, blew her whistle, and with a great laugh and cheer, and an explosion of chatter, they set off for the train. The station was a long raised piece of concrete three feet above the track. Any roof it possessed had been blasted away, long before, by falling bombs. A hundred yards from the platform the railway lines curved out of sight between a jumble of houses. It was upon this bend—on being told that from this direction the train would appear—that a hundred pairs of eyes were focused.

Gladys had lined them up in three straggling ranks. The air was tense with anticipation, and after a few minutes, far off, there came the noise of the train! One hundred children tensed, a little uneasy. Those were very strange noises. Such a whistling anger, such a terrifying rumble and hiss! Eyes twitched towards her and back to that fatal curve. Was Ai-weh-deh quite certain she was right about this 'train' thing? Even in the distance it sounded like the grandfather of all the dragons in the world. Supposing it gobbled them all up? The noise grew greater. Couplings clanked as buffers met; brakes screamed in steely anguish, and round the corner, steaming and blowing and snorting, came the hideous iron terror! There was one loud anguished squeal of utter terror from the children. The ranks dissolved: panic was contagious. Bundles, basins, chopsticks flew into the air. Children fled in every direction. By the time the train was still twenty-five yards away, not a single child remained on the platform. The wooden carriages clattered to a halt. The engine subsided into heavy, steamy breathing, and Gladys tried to collect her charges.

The older boys and girls, already ashamed of their sudden panic, were rounding up the younger ones, plaintively protesting that they had only run away to catch the others. One batch of eight-year-olds were found to have raced all the way back to the refugee centre. Children were retrieved from under boxes and bales, from every conceivable hiding-place within 200 yards of the station. Group by group, she assembled them once more on the platform. Fortunately, the train seemed to be in no hurry to go anywhere at all. The carriages were simply wooden boxes with roofs on. There were no seats. And there were many other refugee passengers with their bundles and basins.

She managed to pile all the children into one long carriage and when, an hour later, the train jogged slowly into motion, the children began to enjoy their experience. There was only one other moment of panic. About two hours later an elderly Chinese gentleman sitting a few yards from Gladys, and surrounded by children, carefully produced a stub of candle from his pocket. He placed it on the floor and tenderly lit it. At least three little boys immediately blew it out. At that moment the train plunged into a tunnel. The darkness was impenetrable; the wails and panic beyond description. The elderly gentleman, after a minute or two, succeeded in relighting the candle, and—the objective of his performance established—no little boy emitted even a zephyr breath in its direction this time.

For four days they stayed aboard the train as it rattled forward in slow, short stages. Occasionally it stopped for hours, and everyone got off and stretched their legs. At intervals along the line there were refugee feeding camps where they were given food and tea. Gladys dozed a great deal of the time. It wasn't that she felt ill; it was as if a general tiredness had settled into her bones. They had been almost three weeks on the road now, soaked by the rains and chilled by the winds. She had slept badly and gone without food for days on end; it was only to be expected, she told herself, that she didn't feel as well as normally.

At the small village of Tiensan the train stopped. It went no farther. An important bridge had been blown up, the lines destroyed. Here the undulating plain ended, and the mountains rose steeply ahead of them. They had to cross those mountains; the train lines continued on the other side. A thin stream of refugees moved up through the rocky passes; old men, young women, fathers, mothers, families laden with bundles, all fleeing westwards away from the malison of the Japanese. They begged food in the village, and Gladys looked at the high peaks ahead. They frightened her. She didn't want to go on; she just wanted to stop where she was and rest. But she knew it was impossible. Their only hope was Madame Chiang Kai-shek's organization in Sian. Even though the city was still many days' journey away, somehow she had to summon up sufficient reserves of strength to get there. But those mountains! They looked so high and cruel. The sun sank behind them, and every valley and peak was suffused with its crimson glow. At any other time she would have admired the scene: now she thought the world was bathed in blood. Next day they started on their journey again.

At first the trail ran upwards. They were all practically barefooted and the sharp flints cut their feet. Looking back from the first ridges, they could see the dust rising slowly from the plain below; with the red ball of the sun glaring like a demon eye through the haze. For four hours they toiled upwards, the youngsters scrambling ahead, Gladys and the older girls coming up more slowly. From a high shoulder of the mountains they had their last glimpse of the plain; then, as they dropped down following the winding path, the peaks closed them in.

Late in the afternoon Liang and Teh, the inevitable scouts, came back to report a village ahead hidden in a turn of the valley. When Gladys reached it the children were already drinking basins of *mentang*, the water left after the millet has been cooked, and the villagers were sharing amongst them rice cakes and other odd fragments of food. She drank some tea and felt better. The people were kindly. It would take them two more days to cross the mountains and reach Tung Kwan, they told her. There were other villages on the track where they might get food. Slowly she struggled to her feet. Another high ridge stood up against the skyline in front of them. She reckoned that if they could cross that, they could spend the night in the valley beyond. Another hour's climbing and the five-year-olds were already hanging round her coat tails as usual. Four of the fourteen-year-old boys took it in turns to carry them. Gladys carried one also, the big girls being much too tired and weak to help. It was all they could do to stagger along.

The progress of the entire party was very slow now. The sun was sinking before they reached the ridge, and Gladys realized that they would not cross it before dark. The only thing was to find some sheltered spot and spend the night. As upon the previous night, the sun went down in the same stupefying welter of crimson, and darkness came swiftly up out of the valleys to wrap them in. In the overhang of a cliff they found a little shelter and huddled together, seeking warmth. The younger ones were so tired that they were asleep as soon as they were wrapped in their quilted bedding. It quickly got cold, and she could feel the chill striking through to her bones. She wedged herself between two rocks and fell into a deep, troubled sleep.

As soon as it was light, they wrapped up their bedding and set off again, the youngsters tearing off ahead. They crossed the ridge as the sun came up. All round were bare peaks running away in all directions, intimidating and desolate. A chill little thought settled in her mind. If ever they lost the track, they could wander until they died amid such desolation. All that day they filed painfully onwards. It was in the afternoon, seated on a rock for one of their frequent rests, that the break suddenly came.

Her face streaked with lines where the sweat had coursed down the white mountain dust, she stared round at the children. The eight- and nine-year-olds were still ahead, but two dozen of the little ones with mournful faces, the fives and sixes and sevens, were gathered round her, almost too dumb to plead to be carried or be given food or drink. The girls were slumped on the rocks in attitudes of utter dejection. Even Liang and Teh sat glumly, their chins in their hands, worn out by carrying the small ones for hour after hour.

It was then that Gladys felt something wet flowing down her cheek. She tried to flick the tears away, but they only came faster, faster and faster, and soon she was sobbing aloud, abandoning herself to grief, sobbing because she had no strength to stay her tears, sobbing from sheer weakness and exhaustion, sobbing for all the children, for all China, and all the world, so deep was her misery. At that moment she had no heart to go on any farther. She was convinced that they were all finished; that they would all die in the mountains. She was convinced that she had brought them all to this plight, that she had betrayed them, and she sobbed because of her guilt. The children sobbed with her, and the little boys coming back down the trail stood open-mouthed and then, also influenced by the contagion of grief, they too began to wail. For many minutes the sound of their distress echoed in the valley. When it was over Gladys wiped her face with her coat sleeve, and sniffed. The tears had cleansed her soul, washed away the bleak desperation, washed away even a little of the aching tiredness which weakened her will and her determination. She smiled wanly at Sualan, who crouched against her.

"A good cry is always good for you!" she said stoutly. "Now that's enough, all of you! We'll sing a hymn, and while we're singing it, we shall march down the track to that big buttress of rock. So stand up, everybody, and no more crying. Let's see who can sing the loudest, shall we? One . . . two . . . three. . . ."

The mountains in their long years of sun and wind and rain must have seen many strange sights, but it is doubtful if they had seen anything more unusual, or more gallant, than this column of children led by a small woman with a tear-stained face, carolling with such shrill determination as she led her band onward towards the promised land.

232

Just before sunset they came upon another village, and the kindly people ransacked their houses for food. The Village Elder wagged his thin goatee beard at Gladys and said simply, "You have many mouths to feed, but who can resist you!" They camped that night in a cave at the edge of the village, and the children, with a little food in their bellies, slept as soundly as ever. The third day was a repetition of the others, except that they found no more villages and ate no more food; and that night, as they crouched on the mountainside, the mist was very heavy. The younger ones were asleep, but Gladys and the boys went round arranging basins to catch drips from the rocks so that at least there would be a few drops to drink when they woke up.

Next day they came down through the mountains and on to the plain. It was still many miles to Tung Kwan, but they got there just before dark. Most of the houses were in ruins, for the town had been badly bombed, but a woman directed them to a courtyard where a refugee organization was to be found. Two women were in charge of the steaming pots, and the children clamoured around them. A few— the inevitable few who were always losing their basins and chopsticks—clung to Gladys, mewing their dire distress to the world, and wearily she sorted things out and saw that they all had enough to eat. As usual, when all the children had fed, there was only the pot scrapings for her. Not that she minded; she felt too tired for food.

She discovered from the women that the railway line ran from Tung Kwan to Hwa Chow, but no trains ran along it. The line passed close to the river and the Japanese occupied the opposite bank. They would have to go on walking. The news irritated her almost beyond reason, and to be irritated was so unlike her; she took most things in her stride. When two men came into the courtyard a little later and began to ask questions, "Where had she come from?" and "Where was she making for?" she answered them abruptly. When they pressed her, she snapped at them, "Oh, leave me alone, I'm tired!"

"We wish to help you," they said. "The women here have told us about you."

"How can you help me?"

"Every now and then a train *does* go through to Hwa Chow, which is on the way to Sian. It carries no passengers, only coal. It starts in the middle of the night, and it is still dark when it passes the Japanese positions on the other side of the river. Sometimes, however, they fire at it."

"You mean we might be able to go on it?" she said eagerly, her heart lifting at the news. "When does it leave?"

"Tonight, in a few hours."

She looked round at the rows of small bodies wrapped up like cocoons and fast asleep. Not even an earthquake would wake them up. Her hopes receded.

"How far away is the station?"

"Round the corner, not more than seventy yards from here."

Her hopes lifted again. "If we could carry the children to the trucks and put them in, would that be all right?"

Yes, they would help as best they could. Excitedly, Gladys called the bigger children together: Liang, Teh, Sualan, Ninepence, Timothy and Less. She explained what she intended to do. They were all to go to sleep at once and she would wake them when the time came. They would form a human chain down to the station: about five yards between each of them, and pass the young children down from person to person like fire buckets. Yes, just like they had done over the steep parts of the mountains.

The men smiled as she explained her plan. They would return when the train was ready, and tell her. She lay down and tried to sleep, watching the stars prick out one by one. She heard the soft breathing of the children all around her, such a soft, sighing rustle, and she fell asleep. The next thing she knew someone was shaking her shoulder. The men had returned; the train would soon be starting; they must not waste time. She went round waking the older children. Everyone spoke in whispers, but even in the darkness she could sense their excitement. They spaced themselves out at intervals; the two men went down to the train to superintend the arrangement of the small, inert bodies on the coal-trucks. As she lifted the first child, little San, a boy of five, she felt how light and yet how warm he was. He murmured in his sleep as she passed him to Sualan, and Sualan passed him on to Liang. She knew from experience that these children slept like hibernating squirrels and even if, inadvertently, they were dropped they would curl up again on the ground and sleep on. One by one they were passed down to the train; then Gladys rolled up the bedding into bundles and that, too, was passed along the line.

She went down to the train. She could hear the engine wheezing quietly somewhere up in the darkness, and she could see by the heaped-up silhouettes of the trucks that they were, indeed, seriously laden with coal. Each truck was piled above its sides, and the children had been placed between lumps of coal high in the air, and the men had wedged more lumps around them to prevent them falling off. She allotted two older children to each truck so that they could watch the young ones when they woke up.

She climbed up herself. She grazed her knee on an iron stanchion, then felt the gritty surface under her hands. There were six small ones wedged on her truck; they all seemed fairly safe. One of the men called out to her from below that he was going to tell the engine driver they were all aboard. A few minutes later the buffers began to clank and the train began to move forward in a series of jerks.

"Goodbye, woman! Good luck!" the second man called from the darkness below.

"Goodbye, friend," she called in reply. "Thank you for your help. And God bless you!"

The train picked up speed. The wind was cool on her face. Not cold like the mountain air; softer and warmer. The stars slid past, a moving canopy of light. She lay back, her head against a lump of coal. It was useless to think of dirt, but who would have thought that this black mineral buried a million years ago, mined from the deep earth, would prove such a good ally, if such a hard bed? She put out her hand and touched the smooth lumps of coal. The wheels rattled and rumbled beneath her. There was exhilaration in her heart. What was the year? 1940? April

1940; and here she was, rattling across China on an old coal train. She did not know that the Germans had broken through at Sedan and were pressing her countrymen back towards the defeat and glory of Dunkirk. She did not know that at that moment ships on every ocean were being blasted to matchwood. She did not know of the howling sirens that screamed round the blacked-out mansions in Belgrave Square like hungry wolves. She did not know that in America, in all the world without dictators, the great urge towards freedom was gathering strength, massing its forces, driven by the inner compulsion that caused the ancient Mencius to observe three hundred years before Christ, 'All men are naturally virtuous, just as water naturally flows downwards.'

None of this she knew. Only that she was content to lie on her coal-truck rattling along under the stars towards her distant goal of Sian. And presently she slept.

When she woke, dawn was breaking. The children were waking also, and she could hear their delighted screams all along the trucks. Little San, five years old, waking two feet away from Gladys, stared at Lufa rubbing his eyes, and screamed with laughter. "Lufu, you've gone black in the night!" And Lufu screamed back at him in happy and concerted agreement. "And you've gone black in the night, too. Ai-weh-deh's black! We've all gone black. Isn't it funny?" It was a concurrence of opinion which rattled every truck with happy laughter, and Gladys laughed with them.

The Japanese had not fired at the train, or if they had, she had not heard them. She felt refreshed, but weaker. They had left the yellow dust of northern Honan, and the river; now they were passing across pretty undulating country with orchards in full blossom and glimpses of pagoda roofs through heavy green trees, and the children exclaimed and pointed as each vista swung into view. They had seen nothing like this before in their lives. In the early afternoon they came to Hwa Chow, one of the holy mountain shrines of China, bombed, but still very beautiful. The mountainside was studded with temples, each roof a soft curving arabesque against the trees; there were trickling streams and bridges; pilgrims who bought yellow incense sticks or candles of bright scarlet to burn at the hundred holy places. Soft bells tolled at all hours of the day, and many prayers were said for Buddha.

It was in one of the numerous temples that the refugee organization of the Nationalists had been set up. Gladys and the children were given food, and she could sleep at last. Everything was a little dreamlike. So much soft, near-tropical beauty was alien to her. She was a mountain woman; she longed for the keen airs, the snows and the winds of Shansi. Without protest she drank the medicine the children brought to her. Liang and Ninepence insisted that she drink it. She asked them where they had got it from, and they told her from the Buddhist priests. They had told the priests that Ai-weh-deh was ill and demanded medicine from them; the priests provided herbs of various kinds which they had to boil in water, and give the liquid to Ai-weh-deh when it was cool. It had a bitter taste, but was not unpalatable.

She did not really remember how many days they spent in Hwa Chow. She only knew that it had been March when they set out and now it was late in April. Except for the daily quota of cuts, and bruises, and bumps, and narrow escapes from awful disaster, which are the normal hazards of childhood, they were all healthy. The trains ran spasmodically to Sian, and the woman who looked after the refugee centre, a keen young Chinese girl imbued with the spirit of the 'New Life' group which under Madame Chiang Kai-shek's patronage was sweeping China, told her that she must not worry; they would see she got aboard a train for Sian when the time came.

One morning they helped her steer the children down to the station and into the carriages. They gave them food to carry with them because the journey would take at least three or four days. Chinese trains at that time possessed vagaries beyond the comprehension of the European mind. They travelled or stopped as the whim took them. Gladys did not remember if the journey took three or four or even five days. The children gambolled, screamed and shouted, as always; the countryside, lovely in the April sunshine, passed slowly before them. They stopped sometimes for hours on end; then they jogged on again through the days and nights. And at last one noontime she was aware of a communal excitement among all the refugees. She struggled up, and could see the walls and pagodas beyond the station and a jumble of low buildings. The children were already piling out on to the platform and she realized that she must follow them. Outside the station she assembled them into the familiar crocodile. "As we march through the gates of Sian we shall sing a hymn," she announced. An old Chinese lifted his head as she spoke. He looked at her through shadowed, rheumy eyes. "Woman," he said, "you will never get into Sian. The gates are closed. No more refugees are allowed into the city!"

She did not believe him. She could not believe him. The mute faces of the children were turned up towards her. All these long weeks she had sustained them with the mirage of Sian.

"Where shall we go, then?" she said desperately. "Where shall we go?"

The old man pointed. "There is a refugee camp near the walls yonder. They will feed you."

It was true. It was terribly, blatantly, ironically true. Gladys led the children to the camp and, while the welfare helpers there were feeding them, she marched by herself along the road to the city. As she got closer she could see that the walls were high and buttressed. It was bigger by far than Yangcheng. She could see the high, green-tiled roofs of the pagodas above the walls. The massive wooden gates were barred and shut. A watcher from the walls above shouted: "Woman! Go away! The city is packed with refugees. No one comes into the city. Woman, go away!" She leant her face against the hard surface of the door and wept a little. So long a journey! And for this! For this!

CHAPTER SEVENTEEN

SHE WALKED slowly back to rejoin the children, not knowing what to tell them. But they had news for her instead. Representatives of the 'New Life' movement had discovered them. They reaffirmed that it was impossible for them to stay at Sian; for the time being the city was closed to refugees. It would probably reopen in a few days' time, but in any case arrangements had been made to care for the children at Fufeng, a nearby city. An orphanage and a school were operating there. All the children Tsin Pen Kuang had brought from Tsehchow were already in residence.

"But how do we get there?" asked Gladys. "We've been travelling for a month already."

"By train," they said. "Tomorrow, we'll put you on a train to Fufeng. It won't take many days to get there."

"Days!" she echoed weakly. "Many days!"

"Perhaps two, that's all, if the train hurries."

"All right," she said.

Too many things had happened for her to protest. She hardly remembered the train journey to Fufeng, only that there were pleasant young women on the platform with food, to meet them; girls with armbands of the 'New Life' movement who smiled at her, marshalled the children, and said, "Now, we shall all be happy!"

They marched in through the gates of the ancient Chinese city of Fufeng. Like Yangcheng, it belonged to the old China. The streets were narrow and choked with shops and shoppers, with beggars, mules and carts. But it was hot, humid and filthy, and stank in the April sun. Gladys yearned desperately for the high, windy keenness of Yangcheng. A huge disused temple housed the orphans of 'New Life'. As there are at least 1,500 temples built in honour of the master, Confucius, throughout China, a disused one was not hard to come by. The children were put through a rehabilitating process that equipped them with new clothes and shoes, which fed them and allotted them places to sleep. The food did not appeal to them very much, for in this part of Shensi they ate bread, and not millet. Gladys was given a little room in the temple, and the children were backwards and forwards through it, coming in all the time to show off their new clothes or receive comfort for a new bruise or just to tell 'Mother' the latest news. It was all rather hazy to her. Outside the city the country was very pretty, and she remembered going to the banks of the river one day and bathing there and washing her clothes, trying to kill the lice, and then sitting in the sun waiting for them to dry.

She did not know quite what she was going to do. The children were delivered; they would be taken care of; her own world had collapsed. She had to earn her living, somehow or other. Then she met the two Chinese women who ran a small Christian mission in Fufeng, who said they would be glad of her help; they were, in fact, going out to a nearby village that very afternoon. Would she care to accompany them; it was a Christian household they were visiting; she could perhaps preach a short sermon?

Nothing, said Gladys, would give her more pleasure. As she walked with them along the sunbaked road with the green wheat fields stretching away on either side, she remembered having trouble with her feet. They did not seem to want to go down in the right places. And when they reached the household she was given a basin of food and chopsticks and sat on a little stool to eat it. But the food wouldn't go into her mouth; somehow she could not control her hands even to perform such a simple act. It really was most annoying. She wanted the food, yet could not eat it. She noticed the others looking at her rather strangely. Had she a headache? Yes, she had a headache. Would she like to lie down for a little while before she gave her sermon? Yes, she would like to lie down. It must be the heat which made her feel a little odd.

It was nothing, the women said, as they helped her to a small room off the courtyard; she had had a very hard time over the past few weeks and she must be very tired. She must rest for a little while, and in an hour or two she could deliver her sermon.

She stretched out wearily on the hard bed, her Bible by her side. Now, I shall preach from John, she thought. She remembered thinking: 'Now from John, what shall I take for the sermon?' From the woman of Samaria: *Whosoever drinketh of this water shall thirst again. But whosoever drinketh of the water that I shall give him shall never thirst; but the water that I shall give him shall be in him a well of water springing up into everlasting life. . . .*

The retina of her eyeballs was shot with a great whirring blaze of colour; scarlets and purples and yellows. She felt hot. She tried to raise her hand to her forehead but it would not lift. No matter . . . the Gospel according to St John . . .

Woman, where are those thine accusers? Hath no man condemned thee? . . .

There was a rusty dryness in her throat. If only she could have a little drink . . . the Gospel according . . .

In the beginning was the Word, and the Word was with God, and the Word was God. The same was in the beginning with God. All things were made by Him. In Him was life; and the life was the light of man. And the Light shineth in the darkness; and the darkness comprehended it not . . .

The great lights faded from the back of her eyes and from her brain and she fell downwards, downwards into darkness. When they came to fetch her an hour later, she was raving in delirium.

.   .   .   .   .

It is fairly certain that the Christian women must have prevailed upon the Chinese peasants to put the sick woman in their ox-cart and take her the comparatively long journey to the Scandinavian–American Mission at Hsing P'ing, and so into the hands of the senior physician. After the bombing of Sian, the senior physician, who now practises at Croydon in Surrey, induced a friend to take her out in the back of his car to his house in the country outside Sian. There is no doubt whatsoever that she owes her life to him and to the staff of the English Baptist Jenkins Robertson

Hospital at Sian; and although one may say it was a doctor's duty, the efforts of this doctor went far beyond those narrow boundaries.

Later, because the bombing continued, and she was progressing favourably, they moved her back to the Mission at Hsing P'ing, and then Mr and Mrs Fisher of the China Inland Mission at Mei Hsien, near the foot of the holy T'ai-Pei Mountain, helped to nurse her back to some state of health. Even after she left the good-hearted Fishers, she was still not really well; she had blackouts and spells of mental derangement. But she did not want to exist on charity any longer; she knew that she had to work for her living, and provide for the five children she had adopted.

They joined her from Fufeng, and went to school in Sian, and sometimes the children would miss Gladys and go round the city, searching, and find her sitting on the pavement somewhere, not knowing who she was, or where she lived, and they would take her gently by the arm and lead her home again. But slowly she improved.

She made friends in Sian, and she earned a little money. A few pounds reached her from her parents in England. She worked for the 'New Life' movement; she taught English to two policemen and two yamen officials; and when two Christian men from Shansi arrived, she started a church for refugees, in a disused factory under the city walls. They took tiny collections and eked out a living.

Linnan came down to visit Sian, and she was glad to see him. He implored her to marry him, and go with him to Chungking, where he was now posted, but somehow, away from the mountain country, here in Sian, their relationship had altered. That day-to-day exhilaration of living had departed; and now all the practical obstructions to a mixed marriage were increasingly obvious. There were many Europeans in Sian with whom she could discuss her problem. "Children?" they said. "Children! If you marry, you will have children. Who will they belong to, China or England? Or to neither country?"

But it was not only that; something had happened to her feelings. She did not know what it was, only that things were different. She knew that if the war had not driven her out of Shansi, she would have married Linnan, and her life would have taken quite another course. "Wait," she had said then; "we cannot get married while this terrible war is on, or while we are here fighting." He had waited, and it was too late. Now, instead of that inner exaltation, the rounded delight of knowing that she loved and was loved in return, there was this nagging anxiety to do the right thing by her God, her children and the man she loved.

Somewhere in the mountains between Yangcheng and the Yellow River, somewhere on the plains between the Yellow River and the old capital of Sian, somewhere in the deep drifts of delirium and the fevers of her illness, certainty had been replaced by anxiety. All this, in tears, she tried to tell Linnan; all this in the despair of his love he tried to brush aside, saying that it would be better when she was well. In Chungking, he said, he would have high rank; they could make a home there and be happy; the children could go to school there. But it was no use; the coloured bird had flown away. Perhaps it could not live in the forest of deep despair that grew all over China. There was so much work to be done for the Lord, and she, the small woman, the small disciple, had her part to play in that work.

She said goodbye to him at the station outside Sian, and walked back through the narrow streets with an overwhelming ache of loneliness in her heart, aware that she would never know completely if she had acted wisely or not; only that through all her waking days she would remember Linnan as the one man she had loved. The war swept him away, and she never saw him again.

·   ·   ·   ·   ·

The Japanese came closer to Sian; there seemed a great possibility that they would eventually attack the city, so with her five children Gladys journeyed even farther westwards. The enemy never did capture Sian, but Gladys settled with the children in Baochi, in the westerly province of Chengtu. It became one of the great resistance centres of the Chinese Nationalists; they moved their colleges and factories and co-operative organizations out to the west.

The children went away to school, Ninepence got married, and Gladys was left alone. She heard that an American Methodist Mission in western Szechuan, almost on the borders of Tibet, was working with thousands of refugees from the north, and they wanted an evangelist who spoke the Shansi dialects. Gladys applied for the job in a letter written in Chinese. She never forgot the look of utter astonishment on the face of the American missionary, Dr Olin Stockwell, when she met him; he had expected a *Chinese* evangelist. She did all sorts of work, and became great friends with Esther and Olin Stockwell.

Dr Stockwell was eventually arrested when the Communists swept down into Chengtu, and was kept in prison for two years. In a book entitled *Meditations from a Prison Cell*,[1] he wrote:

> I remember a little pint-sized missionary lady from England who had been with us out in West China for a year or so. She went into a leper colony to minister to lepers' needs. She found a Christian man there who worked with her. She preached and served with such enthusiasm that she brought new hope to that whole group of lepers. Before she came, the lepers had been quarrelsome and jealous, fighting among themselves. Many of them felt that life was hopeless. She came to tell them of a God who loved them. The tone of that colony changed. Christmas became a meaningful and happy day. On the Friday evening before Easter, the local Chinese pastor and I visited the leprosarium to join in a Passion Week service. At the close of the service, we administered the Sacrament of the Lord's Supper. We served bread and wine to men whose bodies were so twisted with disease that they could not kneel at the altar, and whose hands were so deformed that they could hardly receive the elements. But their eyes were alight with new joy and hope. God had used this little missionary as his Barnabas to them.

She also made lonely trips into the mountain country, but other missionaries had been there before her; she was only carrying on work which others had started. But it was

[1] Published by the Upper Room, 1908 Grand Avenue, Nashville, 5, Tennessee, USA.

important. She and the other Christians, like the Stockwells, knew that the Communists would soon sweep down over this territory; they wanted to leave behind a strong root of Christianity before they were forced to leave.

She was still ill. When the Japanese had beaten her up in the courtyard, they had inflicted severe internal injuries which grew more serious as the years passed. The European doctors she consulted told her that her only chance was to return to England and be operated upon there. But she had no money, so that was quite impossible; her chief hope was that one day she could return to her beloved Yangcheng.

Some time later she went up to Tsechung to hand over one of the Methodist Missions to a group of Americans who had been driven out of northern Shansi, and had come round to the west to continue their work. She was chatting to one of them as they walked along the road to the Mission, when they passed a refugee woman from Shansi whom Gladys knew slightly. The woman hailed her in the Shansi dialect, and Gladys replied in the same idiom. The American looked down at her with interest.

"You've been in that part of China?" he asked.

"Yes," said Gladys, "I was up in Shansi."

"I suppose," he said, "you didn't happen to hear about that woman missionary called Ai-weh-deh, who ran around behind the Japanese lines years ago? Never met her, did you? She must have been quite a gal. Certainly left some stories behind her."

"Yes, I knew her," said Gladys quietly. "That was me."

The American's eyebrows contracted in astonishment. "Well, I'll be darned," he said. "No kidding? Mam, I'm honoured!"

They talked for a long time, and he asked when she had last been home. She didn't quite understand what he meant.

"Back to England?" he said.

She smiled. "What chance have I of going back to England when I don't even know where tomorrow's dinner's coming from?"

His eyes opened. "How long have you been here?"

"Seventeen years!"

"Gosh!" he said. "But you'd like to go home, wouldn't you?"

"It would be nice to see them all again, I suppose," she said wistfully, "but it's quite impossible."

The conversation changed. She forgot all about it, even if the American did not. A few weeks later he rejoined his wife in Shanghai. She had been administering a fund raised in the USA to repatriate German Protestant missionaries and orphans back to Germany. Many of them—good, stout-hearted people—had been close to starvation, but now all the repatriations were completed, and a few hundred dollars still remained in the fund. The wife of the American told Gladys how it happened when they met in Shanghai. He had approached her very seriously.

"Listen, honey," he had said. "I've something very useful for you to do with all those dollars you've got left."

"Well?" she said.

"This is not for an orphan, and not for a German. This is for a little woman, a little limey called Gladys Aylward. I think it would be kinda nice if you used that money to send her home for a trip. She's in bad health. I've got that much from her friends. Now, let me tell you a little about her. . . ."

The first that Gladys Aylward knew about this typical act of American generosity was when one of the Chinese elders, a cheerful, friendly old man, came up to the village in the mountains where she was staying. He jogged down the village street and, seeing her standing at the Mission door, waved a letter at her and shouted: "I've been sent to find you. You're going back to England."

She looked at him in a bemused fashion. "What are you talking about?" she said.

His face was one wide grin. "All you have to do is to go to Shanghai and your fare will be paid to England. You're going home. Now what are you crying about, woman? Isn't that news good enough for you?"

I LOOKED across at Gladys. Nearly twenty years had passed since we first met, more than ten years since our last meeting. There were a few more lines around the eyes, a little more grey in the hair. Nothing else. No, she had hardly changed at all. Except that more people knew about her. And lots of schoolgirls did homework about what she had done with her life. That thought would have made her chuckle twenty years ago.

She was back in London for the first time for ten years. Naturally when she came to lunch near the BBC she brought one of her children with her.

Gordon stood on his small Chinese head and regarded the world with black, impassive, almond eyes. Gladys smiled up at the slightly disconcerted waiter who had just arrived at the table and explained gently, "Oh, yes, he'd eat all his meals like this if he could. Now Gordon, if you want your ice-cream you'll have to eat it right way up."

For a few inscrutable moments Gordon reflected gravely about the offer, and then, deciding that the delights of ice-cream outweighed the joy of standing on his head in his chair in a crowded restaurant, squirmed back down again and seized his spoon.

Gordon was five years old. He wore a high-collared, Chinese silk, mandarin coat and baggy trousers. His shining black hair was cut in a fringe across the pale lemon skin of his forehead, and his eyes darted around like little fishes leaping with joy at being five, at eating ice-cream and having the ability to stand on his head. The sight of him speeding around being a small Chinese express train delighted everyone within twenty yards and put the fear of destruction into Spanish waiters bearing trays around the restaurant.

From the moment she bought Ninepence from the child dealer in the streets of Yangcheng she has never been parted from successive generations of tiny Chinese children who have filled her life and her heart. Gordon was an almost exact reproduction of a couple of dozen other little orphan boys of the same age who had crossed the Shansi mountains with her all those years ago. They, too, had stood on their heads and looked at the world with upside-down eyes. They may not have been so well dressed or so well fed, but they had bubbled with the same excitement and the same curiosity.

When the publishers of this book asked me to add a postscript to the last chapter and bring it up to date the difficulties were greater than I had at first imagined. It is very hard to go back to a piece of work which was conceived as an idea more than twenty years ago, which has been in print for over ten years, which in its cadet edition has been read by many children and used in numerous schools throughout the world and which has become a film known to many millions of people as *The Inn of the Sixth Happiness*. Nevertheless, I suppose it may be of some interest to know how the book, which started in such a modest way, came to be written in the first place, particularly as this has some bearing on the life and times of Gladys herself, and certainly to discover what Gladys has done in the meantime.

A request to her to fill in some of the details of the past few years proved decisively that she still retained the ability for succinctness which had characterized her reports as the Mandarin of Yancheng's Foot Inspector. "Gladys Aylward has been to Chowtsun. Gladys Aylward has come back from Chowtsun."

But over the years Gladys has been sending letters to her many friends, and from these it is possible to find out what has happened. She even wrote in 1968 a potted version of her life: I quote from it here because it explains quite simply what she did, and it tells in her own words of the faith which supported her.

"I went to China thirty-eight years ago in 1930, because I know God told me to, and if I had my time all over again I would do just the same, even knowing all the heartaches,

248

tears and hard work, for God makes up to us in love and care all we suffer for Him.

"I went to Silver Street School, Upper Edmonton, London, N18. I had one sister and one brother, Violet and Laurence, both much younger than me. I left school at fourteen never, as far as I can find out, having passed one exam.

"My childhood was very happy, we were a close-knit family finding out joy in the church and in each other, my father at this time was a postman and my mother a very energetic woman, away ahead of her time in many ways in thought and ideas and a great speaker for temperance, having known as a child the evils of drink.

"I praise God for my parents in that although they did not understand why I wanted to go to China they were willing to let me go, believing God was in it. They did not help me, but they certainly did not hinder.

"My first job was in Marks and Spencer's, which was then a penny bazaar, but later, because there was no future in this, I trained as a parlourmaid and went into service. I had good jobs—I was not considered clever, but I was quick, so when dressed in a smart black dress and a pretty apron with a bow on my hair, I could open the door properly and politely to anyone and was soon conversant with many notable people of that time. I enjoyed the freedom and the fact that all the money I got was my own to use as I liked, for I got all my food and a good living. I met many interesting people and learnt much that was to stand me in good stead later on in China.

"Despite refusal of missionary societies to accept me for training, I, knowing it was God's will I should go to China, read the Bible and found that through faith one could do anything. He kept His promises and it just needed me to take Him at His word and all would be well. I got the money to go by doing all sorts of things working night and day, selling all my personal belongings (in those days girls had 'Bottom Drawers') and together with my savings I bought a third-class ticket on the Trans-Siberian railway across Europe, Poland and Russia to China, believing that as God had worked for the men and women in the Bible so He could work for me.

"Conditions in China were very bad, the people were poor and worked very hard. There were no schools or shops as we know them, no roads, the only way to travel where I lived was to walk or ride an animal, a camel, mule or donkey—there was nothing on wheels, as there were only mountain tracks.

"The standard of living was of course low. The people had to eat what was grown right there, it was not possible to carry far afield. We lived on millet, buck-wheat and maize, there was no wheat or rice and very few vegetables other than hard pears, apricots, peaches and wild dates.

"Clothes were made for each person from cloth woven in the homes by the women and girls. It was very coarse and rough, but wore well and was always blue, this being the only dye that could be got from a root grown there. Our shoes were made of cloth, too, and one had twelve or more pairs made all at once, for if one was walking a great deal one could wear out a pair of shoes in two weeks. They were made to fit the feet, the sole being made from the bark of a tree.

"There were no hospitals, so if you were ill you died, the doctors were herbalists or witch doctors, and the death rate among babies was very high. No one wanted little girls, they all wanted boys who would work on the land for them and not have to go and be the wife of someone else.

"In order to spread the gospel we opened an Inn where traders stayed overnight and heard the gospel and then went on their way over the mountains to tell others. It is not hard to talk about someone you love, so telling them of Jesus Christ was not hard or difficult, especially as the Chinese are a very intelligent and receptive people.

"The Inn was my home for many years. From here I worked as inspector of feet for the Chinese National Government to stop the old custom of binding little girl's feet, and afterwards took in the children who became my family. My wages from the Government provided only for one person, and as I was not nor never have been connected or belonged to anything like a church organization or fellowship I received gifts from my mother and friends to be able to keep going—there was never very much, but always enough, and this is what God promised.

"For seventeen years I moved around, coming out of Shansi, which had been my home with the children, crossing the mountains and the Yellow River into Shensi, then down to Szechuan in the West, where we met up with the Reds. We managed to keep together as a family, although many of the older ones had joined the forces or medical units, but now when the final break came there were not many of us left. . . ."

It was these years in Szechuan which nearly broke her heart. China was still at war. The Japanese held the ports, the towns, the centres of communication, the railway lines. The Nationalists fought them on the plains and in the mountains. The Reds fought the Nationalists and the Japanese indiscriminately. It was a time of hunger and cruelty and oppression.

The China Gladys had known and loved in the past had been hungry and poor, but at least there had been friendship and freedom of religious belief. Gladys preached about Christ, of the joy and happiness to be gained here and now, on this earth, from faith and purity of heart, as well as beyond the earthly state. The Communists believed none of this. She, and people like her, were enemies. Christians were enemies. She saw her fellow missionaries maltreated and persecuted and forced to leave China. She saw the faith of her friends and converts outlawed and attacked by every moral and physical means imaginable, by a godless philosophy with its lunatic assertion that "the ends justify the means". And this drove her close to despair. "I watched my boys and girls die, be taken away to concentration camps, or to prison. Less was to die, shot by the Reds when, as a student, he refused to do something which was contrary to his Christian beliefs. . . ."

She never wanted to talk about her years under the Reds: the memories were too painful, the agonies too close. When she arrived in England she was still in a state of great anxiety about those she had left behind. In her newsletter she wrote: "Much has happened since I left the land of my adoption where those I love, together with thousands of others of the household of faith, were going through terrible suffering, hardship and persecution. . . ."

It was during this early period of her return that I first met Gladys. In 1949 I was writing and producing a series of BBC dramatized radio programmes, mainly concerned with war heroes, called "The Undefeated", when I noticed a small newspaper cutting which reported briefly that a woman missionary had just returned to England after twenty years in China.

I rang up the newspaper, obtained her address and, because she was not on the telephone, caught a bus to North London, and found my way to Cheddington Road, Edmonton: twin rows of terraced houses, neat and respectable. I knocked at the front door, and it was opened by a small woman who barely came up to my shoulder. She had dark hair parted in the middle and coiled in a braid at the back, she wore horn-rimmed spectacles and a high-collared Chinese gown.

I introduced myself and said I was from the BBC. Gladys seemed terribly impressed by this, but then, of course, one of Gladys' most endearing characteristics is the way she is impressed by the rest of humanity, no matter how poor or undistinguished they are, and her reactions would have been equally stimulating if I had been selling hair tonic.

Standing on the doorstep, I told her about my series, and she smiled delightedly. "Oh," she said, "but I've done nothing at all that the BBC might be interested in."

And the complete truth of the matter was that Gladys sincerely believed that in her past twenty years she had done nothing that was unusual or very exciting. It was not mock modesty: the stories she had been telling came from the Bible. They thundered of the beginning of the world, the creation of man and his corruption by sin; they trumpeted the great victories, the floods and famines, the pomp and passions of homo sapiens; they told of the coming of the young carpenter from Nazareth who brought love, mercy, compassion and hope into a despairing world. What had Gladys to offer compared with this? She had crossed Russia by train and worked as a missionary in China; that wasn't very extraordinary.

"But do come in and have a cup of tea," she said with the matter-of-fact spontaneity of warmth which is also so typical. In the front parlour she produced China tea and explained the mysteries of the Chinese tea basket. We talked for perhaps half an hour, and at the end of that time I began to feel that perhaps, after all, Miss Aylward had passed twenty uneventful years in China. The Japanese? Oh, they were very nice people, many Japanese soldiers used to come to the mission at Tsehchow for the Christian services.

In some desperation I pressed this point. Within the past few months I had produced several programmes dramatizing the stories of several men and women who had experience of the Japanese Army in wartime. And these were not pleasant. I pointed this out to her. After all, the Chinese were at war with the Japanese at the time?

Gladys thought about this and then confessed that she had "once taken some children across the mountains".

The rest of the conversation is a verbatim memory I have never forgotten:

"Across the mountains? Where was this?"

"In Shansi in North China; we travelled from Yangcheng across the mountains to Sian."

"I see. How long did it take you?"

"Oh, about a month."

"Did you have any money?"

"Oh, no, we didn't have any money."

"I see. What about food? How did you get that?"

"The Mandarin gave us two basketfuls of grain, but we soon ate that up."

"I see. How many children did you say there were?"

"Nearly a hundred. A 'bei' in Chinese."

From that conversation stemmed the hour-long radio dramatized documentary in which Gladys' part was played by that famous English actress Celia Johnson.

The production was memorable to me for two things. The first was that Peter Fleming, author and traveller, who is married to Celia Johnson and is, in his own right, an explorer and adventurer of some standing, came to one of the rehearsals, chatted to Gladys and afterwards stared with some bewilderment at the small figure sitting demurely behind the glass panel in the studio. The second was that her father, grey haired, dignified and very friendly, confided to Ella Milne, one of the actresses in the cast, that he liked to bring Gladys down to the Piccadilly studio during the rehearsals because the traffic was so heavy around Piccadilly Circus and he did not like to think of Gladys crossing the road by herself! Mr Aylward was a gentleman of the old school, and his small daughter was very dear to him.

When Stanley Jackson, at that time Literary Editor of Evans, asked me to write a book about Gladys I approached her with the idea. I said that I didn't think a book about a missionary in China would be much of a success, but what did she think.

Gladys was more interested than I thought she would be. She was an evangelist. She preached the word of God. A book could bring this work to the attention of many more people, especially those who were not committed to Christ; therefore she was in favour of it. She also thought that far too many books had been written about missionaries which were so overlaid with piety and dogma that the simple message they were intended to convey became so blurred and confused that the audience they were intended to reach were repelled rather than attracted. She would like a book written from a layman's point of view.

Gladys had now been five years in Britain. She had travelled around the country, lecturing and preaching at churches and schools and mission halls. She mothered scores of students from Singapore and Hong Kong. She helped to set up a hostel in Liverpool for Chinese nationals and Chinese seamen. She collected clothes for refugees in Kowloon.

I researched those parts of Gladys' story about which she knew very little because she had either been unconscious

—the story of the Japanese attack on the women's quarters in the mission at Tsehchow came directly from David Davies in Cardiff—or too ill to comprehend what was going on. I recall going to Croydon to visit the Senior Physician, Dr Hanley Stockley, who lived in retirement there. Dr Stockley provided the material for all the incidents at the beginning of this book. At the end of his account I said, "But Doctor—relapsing fever, typhus, a patch of pneumonia, malnutrition, exhaustion—how do you think, as a doctor, that she managed to stay alive?" And Dr Stockley said quietly, "I can only presume that God had other work for her to do."

On 15th March 1957 just before the book was published Gladys wrote in her newsletter: "God has again done wonders and my heart is full of praise, for I sail on 4th April for Hong Kong, Singapore and Formosa. . . . I have sought to do what I believe God sent me to England for, to preach the gospel and call forth prayer for China and her peoples. . . . From Ninepence there has been no word for two years, and the others I only know are dead or alive."

She added, just in case anyone was thinking that she was more than the smallest and humblest follower: "I shall think many times of the things that happened when I stayed with you. To all my nephews and nieces love and prayers, and I shall expect to hear one day of you called not to follow Auntie Gladys but Jesus Christ."

The Gladys Aylward who left England for the second time in 1957 was a very different person from the young and hopeful Gladys who had left Liverpool Street station twenty-seven years earlier. Those years had taught her much about a world echoing with violence. She had a little more money—not that money ever meant very much—the currencies of human need, affection, love and gentleness had always been much more important to her. Her faith, if anything, was stronger than ever; all the hardships and heartbreaks, the cruelties and cynicisms had tempered the blade of her belief rather than dulled it.

But there was a little sadness at the heart of her enthusiasm. She had to go back to the East; her bones and blood and the cells of her mind demanded it. She loved England, but there was more need for her elsewhere. But where could she go? China was hostile and closed to her. Many of her "children" were still there. Ninepence was married when Gladys left Red China; she had to choose between accompanying Gladys or abandoning her husband, who could not get a pass to leave. Perhaps she might find a home somewhere on the periphery of that enormous land; perhaps a new country on the way out to China might offer a solution.

"I had no idea that I was going to do anything with children; in fact, I had given up that idea, because I believe that God made mothers young, and I was no longer young. Therefore He must have something for me to do other than work with children. When I left England, therefore, I expected I would find some place where I could have a mission or preach, or join with somebody in some sort of church work."

She enjoyed the journey by boat and the stops at South Africa, Ceylon, Singapore and Malaya. "At each place I visited I asked myself the question: 'Should I remain here?' Every time there was no evidence, no conviction that I should do so and I travelled on."

Hong Kong was, as always, beautiful, bewildering and exciting. The high green mountain and the mainland of Kowloon encircled the sun-glazed water of the harbour crowded with junks and sampans, tugs and ferries and liners; the narrow streets were hung with brilliantly painted signs and bubbling with people; the sun was hot and strong in this artificial island city perched like a gay, green parrot on the shoulder of the ancient continent.

At Hong Kong she took her luggage off the boat. She did not know what she was going to do, but she sensed that she was closer to home, and although they spoke Cantonese in Hong Kong and Gladys' main language was Mandarin, she could make herself understood. She found a place to live. She looked up at the blue sky and around at the hordes of refugees already in the territory and wondered what she could do to help.

How that help started was in the true Aylward tradition. She was walking along the Nathan Road when she literally bumped into a young man. Their recognition was instantaneous. It was Michael, one of her "sons", who had crossed the mountains with her, and who she thought was still in Red China. They fell into each others' arms in great happiness.

They quickly realized that to a certain degree they were both refugees. Michael was now a Minister doing what he could to help, and Gladys brought her practical mind to bear. If they were refugees, then they were in a position to assist others; they would open some sort of mission—make it grow out of the needs of refugees. They would open refugee schools and kindergartens; they would teach refugee youths and children. If they could not preach to the people *in* China, then they would do it to those who came out.

With Michael and his wife Maureen she began to make plans at once. And, although it was nearly two years before their dream actually came to fruition and the Hope Mission was in being, it all began through that seemingly accidental meeting in Nathan Road.

She would undoubtedly have stayed in Hong Kong much longer but for one important reason: "When I had been in Hong Kong for four months and was more or less expecting to settle down the authorities wouldn't give me a resident visa. Now I am a naturalized Chinese and I held a Chinese Nationalist Passport. The Hong Kong Government had nothing against me—they were very nice to me—but they wouldn't give me permission to stay. I didn't really mind, because I felt in my heart that this must be God—they couldn't do it simply because God was stopping them and not because of any British law or anything."

Formosa was the seat of the Chinese Nationalist Government. She knew that she would find at least two of her "children" there: two boys, Jarvis and Francis. She decided to pay them a visit.

"I left Hong Kong very tearfully. It was hard to tear myself away from those who in the four short months had

257

come to mean so much to me, and as I looked down from the ship I thanked God for everyone and hoped to see them again before long. Michael was really sick, and I was most concerned, but he would come, and as he stood there in the boiling sun I tried hard to persuade him to go back, but no, everyone watched until the ship sailed out.

"It was a very rough passage, but they say it always is. I have never been on a ship which rolled so, and I could only keep to my bunk. The Captain, a very jolly man at whose table I was put, was a good talker, and so from that point of view we were well. There were several missionaries on board, so there was fellowship."

She was immediately captivated by Formosa: "a dear little island that needs God so much and is ready and open for his love". And she hadn't been in the island a week when she learned why she had been directed by God to go there; "The Chinese Government had issued a directive—I wouldn't say that it was a law—which they were trying to enforce as kindly as possible, that everyone spoke one language. They said that much of the trouble on the mainland was that half of the people didn't understand what the other half said." Indeed, Gladys could remember during her early days in Yangcheng when five different interpreters facing in five different directions explained her words to people from five neighbouring villages.

"They had made a rule that all churches, schools, banks and public services had to use this one language—Mandarin Chinese—the very language that I spoke. I found that there were dear godly men who couldn't preach in their own church unless they had somebody there who could speak Mandarin, and so my services as a preacher in Mandarin Chinese, or as an interpreter were much in demand. I travelled all over the island, I hardly ate and I travelled when I should have been sleeping because I wanted to do all I could to help during this interim period until enough people learnt the official language. I had a most glorious time. I was able to speak in the colleges, in the schools, in churches, to all kinds of people—old, young and even to those in prison."

She was tremendously stimulated in her work by a meeting with Madame Chiang Kai-shek. It was to her "War Orphans Association" that Gladys handed over her "bei" of children in Shensi all those years ago. The friendship, graciousness, dignity and naturalness of this famous woman moved Gladys deeply. "I, who have never hero-worshipped in my life, collapsed before the charm and definiteness of purpose . . ." she wrote. "Her beauty outshines crowns and things because it comes from a heart at peace with God and therefore full of love for people, and I am proud to belong to this people for Him and to own this lady as my leader, and I will serve her and my country with all my heart."

There were other things also to bring her joy. She stayed with Jarvis and his family, and . . . "On the second day after I arrived a most wonderful thing happened. Someone came to me saying, 'Here is your girl!' I had not heard anything about any of my girls getting out of Red China. I went along slowly wondering, to be swept off my feet, hugged, laughed, cried over all at once, so it seemed, until I wondered I had any breath left. It was one of my own girls Yu Hwa (Pauline). What a reunion. Sitting with our arms around each other with tears flowing, we compared notes of our escapes and news. What of the others? Dear Ninepence, Yu Hwa's constant companion and playmate and the boys who were marched off by the Reds. Where are they all? Are we ever going to see them again? There is no news of them."

She was also happy in the knowledge that Jarvis and Francis were doing very well, that she hadn't brought them over the mountains just to endure and survive, but that they were playing a useful part in society: "Francis is not married and is very clever; he studied medicine in China and has gone in for psychiatry and is in charge of a mental hospital here. He is doing a good piece of work, for this needs a Christian and he is quiet and good and I am very proud of him." And then the voice of the mother breaking through: "Later on I would like him to have a home, so that we could all be together sometimes, and when he gets tired he could come and have a rest, for he works very hard. How good God is to give me these to make up for all the lonely years."

And of course Gladys had forgotten one thing. Although God made mothers young, he also gave children a need for aunties and grandmas. Small, unwanted babies gravitated towards Gladys with the inevitability of small glass marbles rolling down an incline into a waiting bowl; but her "glass marbles" opened their mouths and wailed. One was wailing, abandoned and unhappy, when she came back to her room one day. "I went home to the room which was my head-quarters, and I found that someone had got in and left a baby there. This brought it home to me that, although I felt I was too old to look after babies, it was evidently God's plan for me to go back to doing that work, and I accepted it as a sign."

Now Gladys was in the middle of her travels and preaching. She had no baby clothes, baby food or baby time, but she accepted the fact that the baby was her responsibility. Nearby was a woman who looked after several babies, and Gladys went to see her. Would she look after the baby for a while, and Gladys would pay her to do so? The woman agreed, and they discussed the whole idea. If any more babies turned up the woman would look after their day-to-day needs, and Gladys would find the money for the food and clothes and the dozen and one essentials to baby life.

And of course the babies and small children turned up. Within weeks there were dozens; children whose mothers were sick or couldn't look after them, children whose fathers were dead, children of all ages and shapes and sizes, lost or strayed or mislaid, desperately needing the "lady with the heart of pity". It was no use Gladys saying she would just look after the finances. She was committed. An orphanage grew up around her in the same way that kitchen gardens grow up around other people. She parted from the woman, rented an old hotel and started the "Gladys Aylward Orphanage". She soon found she had a hundred children, the same number that had crossed the mountains of Shansi with her.

For six years she did this work, and she had to face the fact that she was getting older and finding the work much harder. "I couldn't run round and play ball with them for instance." Even though by now she had been joined by Kathleen Langton Smith, a young woman from Nottingham who proved a wonderful help, it was all getting too much for her, and besides the need for an orphanage was not nearly so acute. The lease of the old hotel expired, and they had to either give it up or find a larger place.

"It was just at this time that the Lord began to do some very wonderful things. We were finding it very difficult looking after the big boys and girls now. I came down one night after much prayer and decided that not only had God made mothers young but he had created two people to look after children—a mother and a father—and that was how it should be. Here I was seeking to break through that natural law—two old maids were trying to bring up these children contrary to God's plan.

"I was very definite about this. People have thought that I gave up the orphanage because of lack of money, but this was not true. It was just this fact that I did not feel I could be both mother and father to these big children. The time had come to make changes in the running of our Home. How should we go about it?

"Well, so we prayed. We contacted the parents or relatives of the children who had people belonging to them, and told them that our lease was running out. Could they come and see us and discuss the future of their child? This bore instant results, and the Lord removed these children in a most amazing and wonderful way."

For example one morning very early, a little man trotted up the hill and saw Kathleen and the girl who interprets for her. He was managing a barber's shop. He would like to extract his son from the orphanage and apprentice him to his trade. Was this possible?

Was it possible? Gladys and Kathleen said several hallelujahs of joy. His son was the naughtiest boy in the whole orphanage. They patted him on the head and said goodbye to him without a twinge of conscience.

For the next two weeks parents and relatives arrived to collect more children, but at the end of that time they still had all the real orphans and, of course, all the tiny unwanted babies. These they knew they would keep and bring up as their own. But the older orphans were still a problem.

Then a Mr Graber of the Christian Children's Fund Orphanage called to see them. He had been thinking of coming to see her for some time. They had just opened a new orphanage and were looking for real orphans. Gladys almost fell over. Yes, she could satisfy all his requirements.

With three days of the lease still remaining they searched desperately for a house where they could start up their new home with the twenty babies they had left. And again God was good to them. A woman calling quite casually about some other business mentioned a fine new house down the Hangchow South Road. It had been empty for a long time as far as she knew.

Gladys flew down to see it. It was brand new, just the right size, just the right number of rooms. Of course there was a catch. A whole family had been murdered next door, and no one wanted to live in the new house because of the proximity of the spirits of the murdered people. Gladys remembering that the "Inn of Eight Happinesses" was also supposed to be haunted had no such qualms. But the landlord wanted a year's rent in advance.

They could raise the money all right, but was it a wise investment? Should they wait for a sign from God? Within hours a government official whom Gladys knew slightly called to see them. Slowly and formally he told them why he had come. A business acquaintance of his who had just become a Christian had made a lot of money selling ice-cream. Apparently the quality of the ice-cream had been a little dubious, and the man, now wealthy, wished to make a donation to charity. Possibly thinking of the children he had fleeced, what better place to offer his alms but a children's home. The official smiled and bowed politely and placed in Gladys' hand a cheque practically equivalent to a year's rent.

It was, of course, during these years that the film *The Inn of the Sixth Happiness,* based upon this book, was made.

Advance publicity about the film released in England filtered back to her, and she heard that Linnan was going to be played by a German actor Curt Jurgens. It was not really Curt Jurgens' fault that, equipped with black contact lenses to conceal his blue eyes, he was cast as a half-Chinese, half-European intelligence officer. But in Chinese eyes the suggestion that Linnan was half-caste was an insult. Linnan had been slender and dark, of impeccable Mandarin culture and manners; the militant panzer soldier played by Jurgens did not match Gladys' memory at all.

Ingrid Bergman also, even though she was an actress of world stature and immense talent, was a choice which both puzzled and concerned her. The fact that cinema-going audiences everywhere thought the film marvellous, and that Christian bodies and churches in every English-speaking country in the world praised it extravagantly, did not console her. In the United States the League of Decency and the National Council of the Churches of Christ all thought it excellent. Bishop Kennedy of the Methodist Church, after seeing the film, was moved to write to each of the four hundred ministers under his jurisdiction asking them to see the film and preach about it.

I myself, who played a tiny part in recording Gladys' story, thought it very good, and Ingrid Bergman's portrayal of Gladys' spiritual belief and certainty of purpose a moving, and evocative masterpiece of cinema art. Certainly it made Gladys Aylward an international figure, possibly one that will pass into history. But Gladys has never seen the picture. When we last talked she revealed this fact and I could understand her feelings. That part of her life is now past. It is a personal and precious past, magical in memory. Coloured images flickering on the screen are for other people not for her.

The film, too, is in the past now. And there is still work to be done.

Today in Great Britain the Gladys Aylward Charitable Trust is administered by friends of hers and helps to collect funds for the thirty-six babies she and Kathleen look after in Formosa. Gladys still dries tears, wipes noses, sings songs, coaxes food down small throats and tells stories of such marvels that dark eyes grow round in wonder and astonishment. She is happy now and relaxed, travelling around the islands occasionally and preaching, and sometimes visiting Hong Kong, where she is still deeply concerned with the Hope Mission; working hard in fact at what she does wonderfully well, and what she likes doing more than anything else in the world. Her philosophy has never changed: "I read the Bible and found that through faith in Jesus Christ one could do anything. He kept His promises and it just needed me to take Him at his word and all would be well."

Today the children in this book are scattered all round the world. There are many many grandchildren. Every Christmas they send tiny presents to Grandma Gladys. Perhaps they will comprehend dimly in the years to come that agonizing spring of 1940 when the world was a madhouse of war. Certainly they will hear the story of how their mothers and fathers were gathered up by a little missionary girl from Edmonton who was filled with the spirit of the Lord, and how she brought them to safety over the high mountains, across the Yellow River and then for three hundred miles to Shensi west of Shansi.

Gladys Aylward is one of the most remarkable women of our generation, and although one can never enter completely into the heart and mind of a fellow human being, it is clear that she possesses that inner exaltation, that determination to go on, unto death, which adversity, torture, brainwashing and hardship cannot eradicate from the human soul, and which is the natural corollary of a tenacity of faith so unusual in an age with little faith.

I thank Miss Gladys Aylward for telling me her story, and for allowing me to set it down. I can only hope that I have done this small woman justice.

GAVIN MAXWELL

The House of Elrig   illus. 6/-

The story of the author's childhood and adolescence,
this book shows the vivid impact of the countryside on
a sensitive child.
'Sensitive, brilliantly evocative, with implications far
beyond its matter, this is a book to read, re-read and
keep' Spectator

Ring of Bright Water   illus. 5/-

Now an enchanting film starring
Bill Travers and Virginia McKenna.

Camusfeàrna, a remote home in the Scottish Highlands,
a pet otter as intelligent and affectionate as a dog, this
is both a moving and a fascinating account of the
author's homelife.

'A masterpiece. . . will delight and fascinate even those
most indifferent to animals' The Listener

The Rocks Remain   illus. 5/-

A sequel to 'Ring of Bright Water', this book is packed
with adventure, humour and suspense. And there are
two new otters to join Maxwell, but not quite such
well-behaved ones as Mijbil, the first otter who lived
at Camusfeàrna.

'As beautifully written, as vivid, and as moving as its
predecessor' Guardian

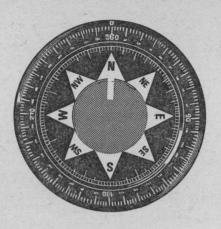

Godfrey Winn

'Shakes hands with people's hearts'—
Lord Beaverbrook.

'A phenomenon'—*The People.*

'A great reporter reporting on himself with as
much detachment as if he were a fire or a royal
wedding'—*Dame Rebecca West.*

THE INFIRM GLORY

Volume One : **THE GREEN YEARS**

Volume Two : **THE GROWING YEARS**
Illustrated. 5/- each.

Uninhibited recollections that turn the author's
own spotlight on the very private life and thoughts
of a much-loved public figure. A fascinating
story that shows a man of many roles—
schoolboy, junior tennis champion, actor, author
and ends in 1939 after Godfrey Winn has begun
his meteoric rise in the field of personality
journalism, meeting the known and the unknown,
the famous and the infamous . . .

'Packed with just that right kind of detail which
has ever distinguished this author's work'—
The Times.

Two superb novels by one of the most
stimulating and informed writers of today

REBECCA WEST

THE BIRDS FALL DOWN 7/6

A powerful and engrossing novel of the
events that led up to the Russian Revolution
. . . seen through the eighteen-year-old eyes
of Laura, daughter of an English MP and
grandchild of an exiled Russian royalist.

'One of the greatest works of fiction
written in English since the war'
Robert Pitman, Sunday Express

'A long, gripping story of betrayal and
double-agents'
Arthur Pottersman, Sun

THE THINKING REED 8/-

'A brilliant study of the heart and mind of a
woman'
The New Yorker

'Among the best novels in the short
memory of modern man'
Time Magazine

'There's more to bird-watching than watching.
Reading **The Bird Table Book** by Tony Soper you
soon realize it's not enough just to sit back and
expect the birds to come to you . . .'
DAILY TELEGRAPH

THE BIRD TABLE BOOK 5/-

Tony Soper

How much do you know about the birds which
hop about outside your window or perch on the
sill? How can you help them to survive when they
are short of food or shelter?

If you or your friends are interested in birds, this
book by the well-known television naturalist is a
unique guide to feeding, encouraging and enjoying
wild birds.

Where are the best nesting sites, what makes
suitable nesting boxes? Who are the birds' natural
enemies, how can you protect them?

Although primarily a work of reference, it is also a
book to be read for sheer enjoyment—enhanced by
photographs, and illustrations by Robert Gillmor.

'Packed with fascinating information.'
WOMAN'S REALM

'It is a work that goes far beyond the indication of
its title . . . the book combines charm and
usefulness in an unusual degree.'
ANIMALS

'A splendid present for any young ornithologist'.
THE BOOKSELLER

A SELECTION OF POPULAR READING IN PAN

Fiction

☐	BATH TANGLE	Georgette Heyer	5/—
☐	THE TOLL-GATE	„ „	5/—
☐	COTILLION	„ „	5/—
☐	THE QUIET GENTLEMAN	„ „	5/—
☐	BLACK SHEEP	„ „	5/—

Non-fiction

☐ **THE BATTLE OF BRITAIN (illus.)**
Leonard Mosley   5/—

☐ **GIPSY MOTH CIRCLES THE WORLD (illus.)**   Francis Chichester   6/—

☐ **QUEENS OF THE PHARAOHS (illus.)**
Leonard Cottrell   6/—

☐ **RING OF BRIGHT WATER (illus.)**
Gavin Maxwell   5/—

☐ **THE HOUSE OF ELRIG (illus.)**
„   „   6/—

☐ **THE DAM BUSTERS (illus.)**
Paul Brickhill   5/—

☐ **THE INFIRM GLORY, VOL. I (illus.)**
Godfrey Winn   5/—

☐ **THE INFIRM GLORY, VOL. II (illus.)**
„   „   5/—

☐ **LIFE OF CHRIST**   Fulton J. Sheen   7/6

☐ **THE BIRD TABLE BOOK (illus.)**
Tony Soper   5/—

☐ **BEYOND BELIEF**   Emlyn Williams   7/6

Obtainable from all booksellers and newsagents. If you have any difficulty, please send purchase price plus 9d. postage to P.O. Box 11, Falmouth, Cornwall.

I enclose a cheque/postal order for selected titles ticked above plus 9d. per book to cover packing and postage.

NAME...

ADDRESS...

....